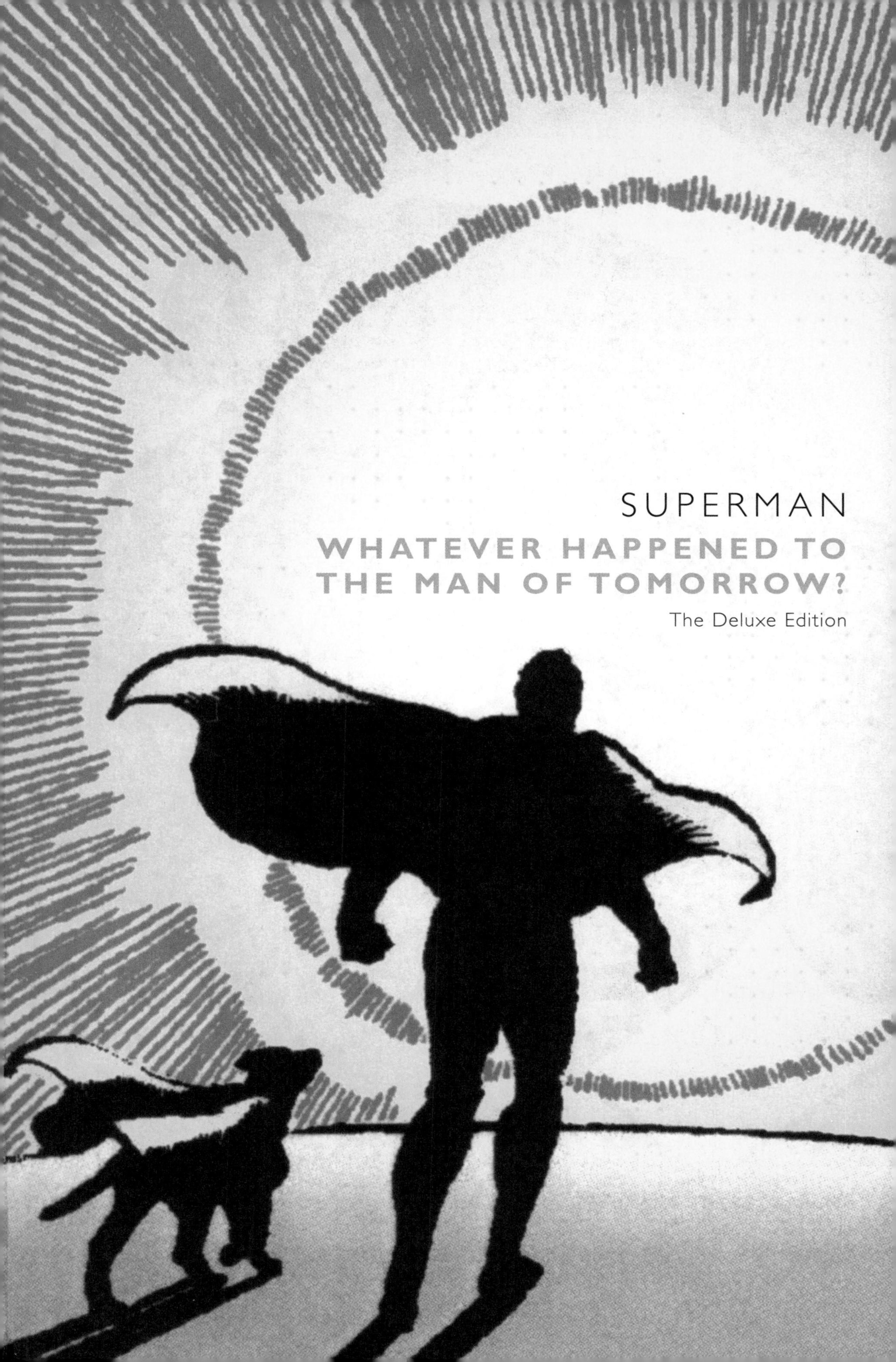

SUPERMAN

WHATEVER HAPPENED TO THE MAN OF TOMORROW?

The Deluxe Edition

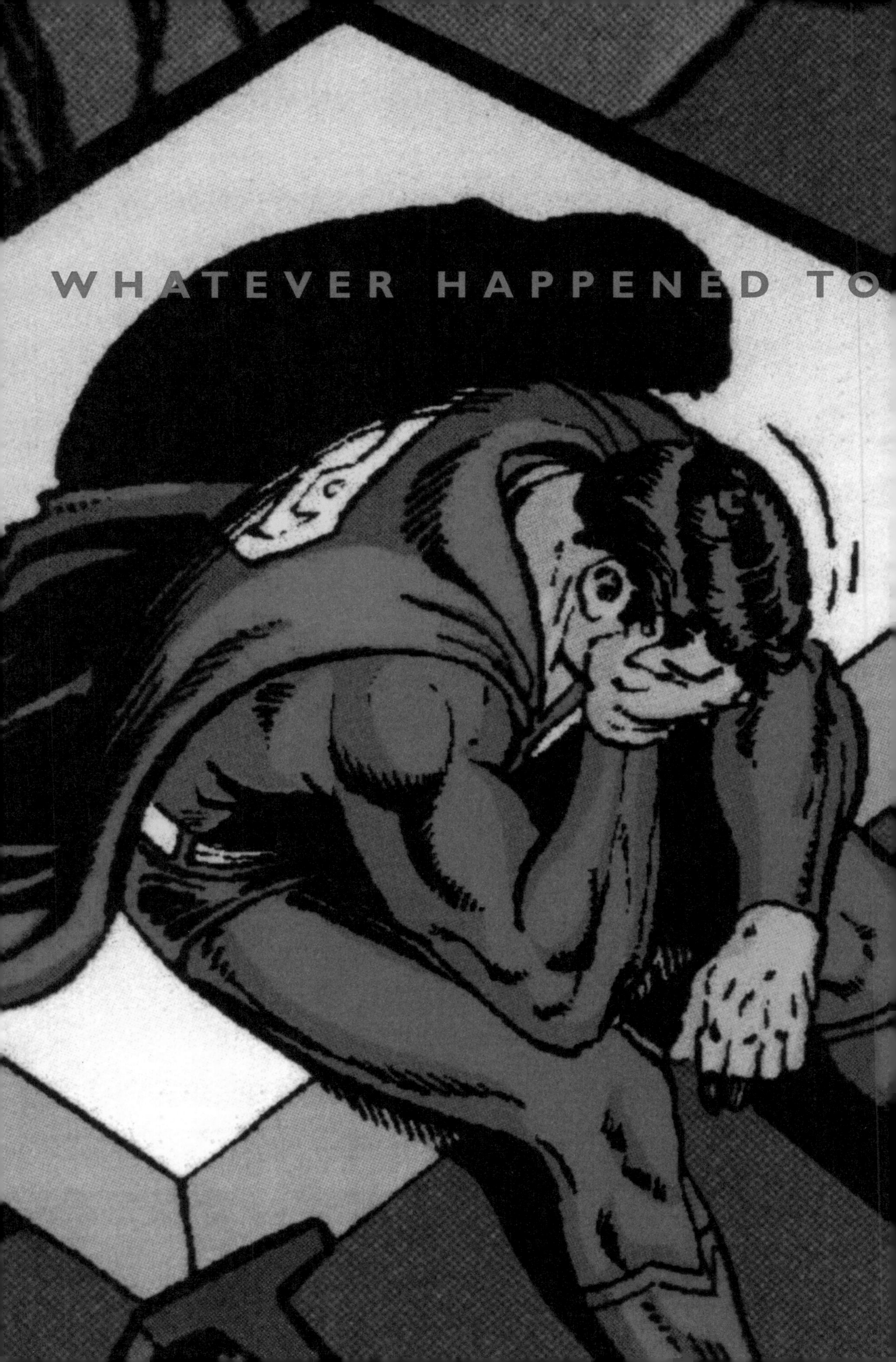
WHATEVER HAPPENED TO

written by
Alan MOORE
SUPERMAN
THE MAN OF TOMORROW?
The Deluxe Edition

art by
Curt SWAN
Dave GIBBONS
Rick VEITCH
George PÉREZ
Kurt SCHAFFENBERGER
Al WILLIAMSON

colored by
Gene D'ANGELO
Tom ZIUKO
Tatjana WOOD

lettered by
Todd KLEIN
Dave GIBBONS
John COSTANZA

original series cover art by
Curt SWAN
Murphy ANDERSON
Dave GIBBONS
Rick VEITCH

Superman created by **JERRY SIEGEL** and **JOE SHUSTER**
Batman created by **BOB KANE**
Wonder Woman created by **WILLIAM MOULTON MARSTON**
Swamp Thing created by **LEN WEIN**
and **BERNIE WRIGHTSON**

DAN DIDIO Senior VP-Executive Editor JULIUS SCHWARTZ Editor-original series
SCOTT NYBAKKEN Editor-collected edition ROBBIN BROSTERMAN Senior Art Director
PAUL LEVITZ President & Publisher GEORG BREWER VP-Design & DC Direct Creative
RICHARD BRUNING Senior VP-Creative Director PATRICK CALDON Executive VP-Finance & Operations
CHRIS CARAMALIS VP-Finance JOHN CUNNINGHAM VP-Marketing
TERRI CUNNINGHAM VP-Managing Editor AMY GENKINS Senior VP-Business & Legal Affairs
ALISON GILL VP-Manufacturing DAVID HYDE VP-Publicity
HANK KANALZ VP-General Manager, WildStorm JIM LEE Editorial Director-WildStorm
GREGORY NOVECK Senior VP-Creative Affairs SUE POHJA VP-Book Trade Sales
STEVE ROTTERDAM Senior VP-Sales & Marketing
CHERYL RUBIN Senior VP-Brand Management
ALYSSE SOLL VP-Advertising & Custom Publishing
JEFF TROJAN VP-Business Development, DC Direct
BOB WAYNE VP-Sales

Cover art by BRIAN BOLLAND, after CURT SWAN and MURPHY ANDERSON.
Color reconstruction on SUPERMAN 423 and
ACTION COMICS 583 by TOM McCRAW and DIGIKORE.
Color reconstruction on DC COMICS PRESENTS 85 by JAMISON.
Color reconstruction on SUPERMAN ANNUAL 11 by DIGIKORE.
Publication design by ROBBIE BIEDERMAN.

SUPERMAN:
WHATEVER HAPPENED TO THE MAN OF TOMORROW?
THE DELUXE EDITION

DC Comics 1700 Broadway, New York, NY 10019
A Warner Bros. Entertainment Company. Printed in the USA. First Printing.
ISBN: 978-1-4012-2347-2

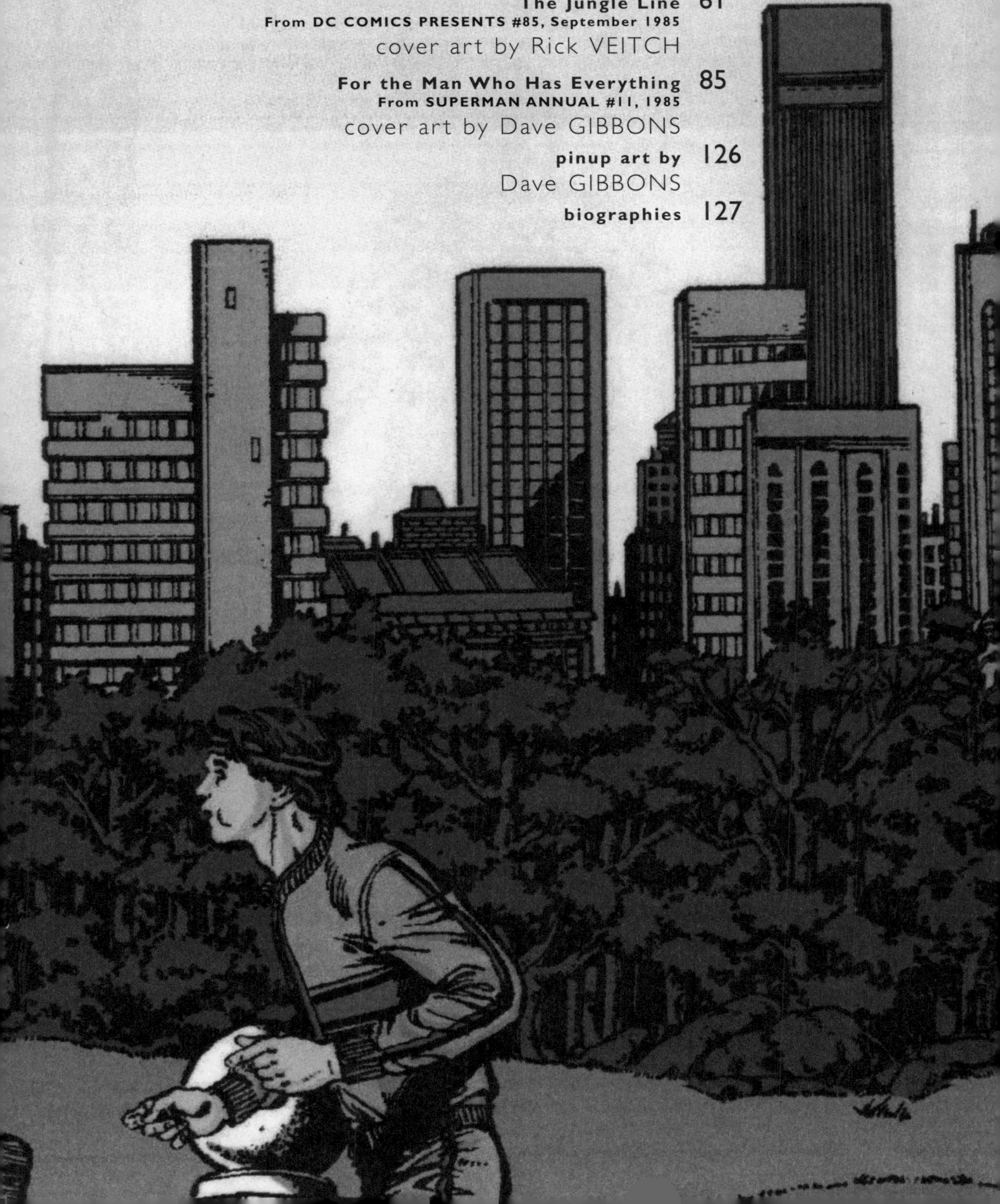

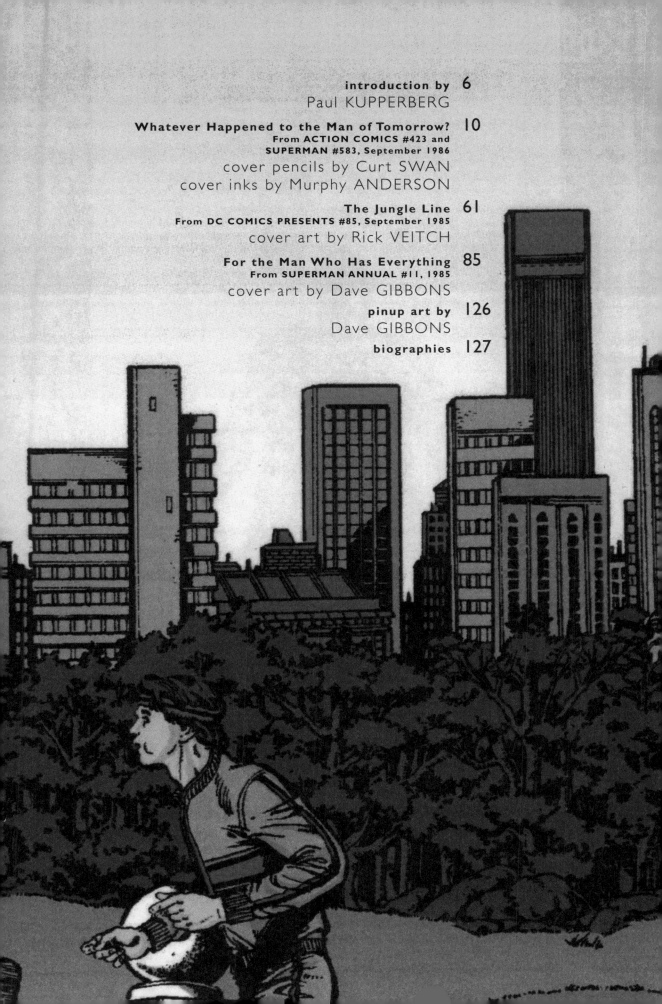

This introduction originally ran in the first SUPERMAN: WHATEVER HAPPENED TO THE MAN OF TOMORROW? collected edition, released in 1997.

THE TIME HAS COME!

An Introduction by Paul KUPPERBERG

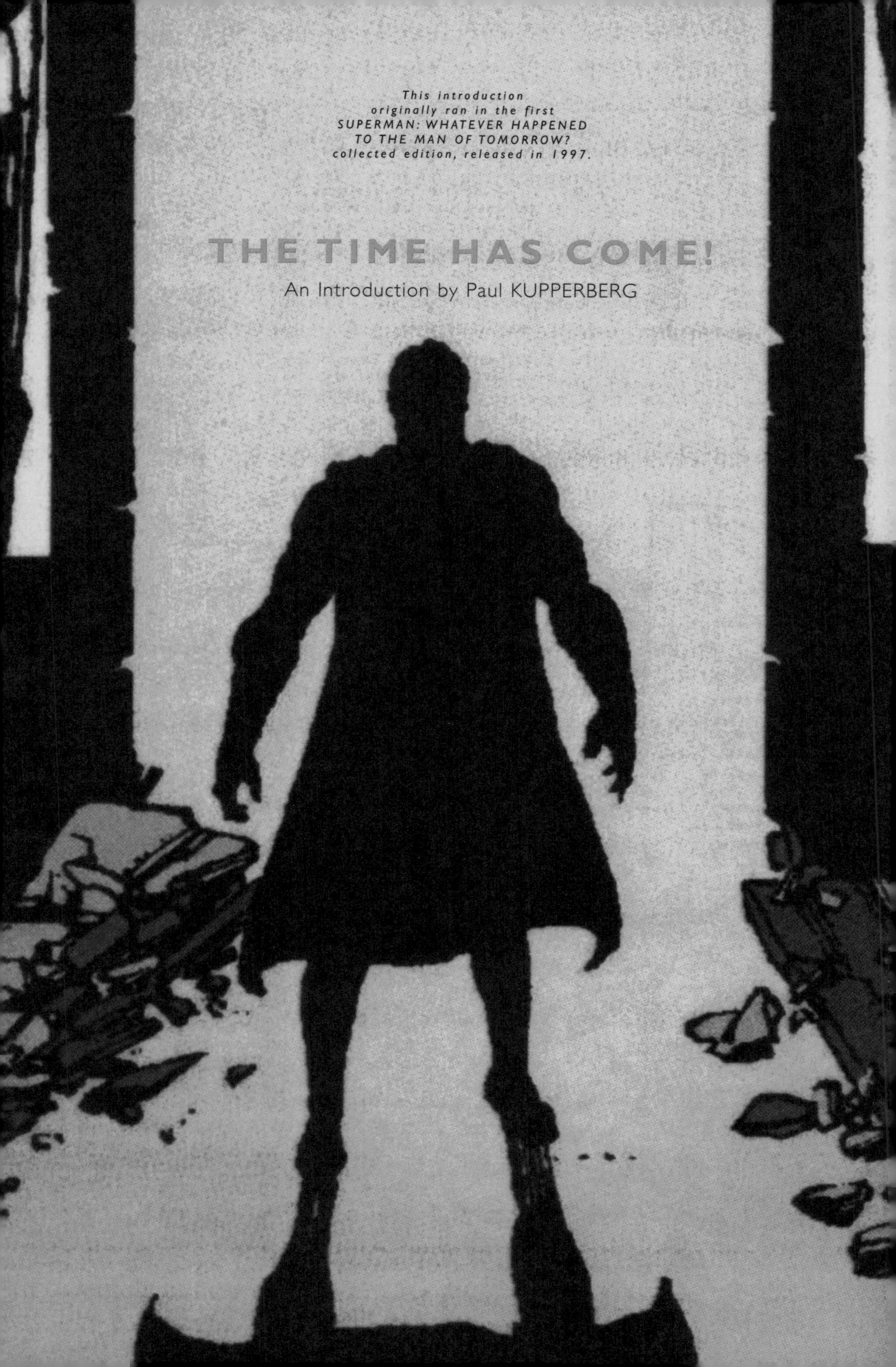

It was in June of 1938 that the first Superman story saw print in ACTION COMICS #1.

It was a little more than forty-eight years later, in ACTION #583, that DC published the "last" Superman story.

Of course, "Whatever Happened to the Man of Tomorrow?" wasn't actually the last Superman story. Obviously, the Man of Steel is still being published, but it was, in its own way, the final story of the Superman that generations of readers had grown up on. The end of an era... at least of that particular era.

A lot of things were changing in comics during the mid-1980s. The way things had been done for the previous fifty or so years had come under the scrutiny of a slew of creators who were finding new ways to do things. Frank Miller's BATMAN: THE DARK KNIGHT RETURNS and Alan Moore and Dave Gibbons's WATCHMEN were essentially redefining the conventions of the super-hero comic, while DC's year-long CRISIS ON INFINITE EARTHS was literally reshaping the DC Universe itself.

And it was CRISIS ON INFINITE EARTHS that was responsible for "Whatever Happened to the Man of Tomorrow?" because in CRISIS, the DC Universe was being streamlined, with decades' worth of multiple-universe continuities and redundant characters being eliminated. No longer was there to be many different Earths set in many different dimensions, each host to many different versions of Batman or Flash or Wonder Woman or Superman. No more would readers have to be conversant with fifty-plus years of characters and continuities in order to read a title. There was to be only one Earth, existing in one universe, featuring (for the most part) only one version of any given character.

As a result of this, it was decided that the post-CRISIS era — in which a character's back story was effectively a blank slate — offered the perfect opportunity to revamp or relaunch a host of DC's top-tier heroes, including Wonder Woman, Flash, Hawkman, the Justice League...

... and Superman.

John Byrne had signed on to write and pencil the relaunched Superman, beginning with THE MAN OF STEEL miniseries that went on sale in July of 1986. This left Superman editor Julius Schwartz with the opportunity to do a grand finale for his stewardship of SUPERMAN and ACTION COMICS. "I started to think, 'What am I going to put in my last two issues?' and in the middle of the night it came to me: I would make believe that *my* last issues of SUPERMAN and ACTION COMICS were *actually* going to be the last issues," Schwartz recalls. "Therefore it was incumbent upon me to clear up, to explain all the things that had been going on in the previous years. For example, did Lois Lane ever find out that Clark Kent was Superman? Did they ever get married? What happened to Jimmy Olsen, to Perry White, to all the villains? I had to clear it up."

With a clear story direction in mind, Julie set out to find a writer to handle the scripting. "I ask this at comic conventions: 'Who would you, sitting in my editorial chair, mid-1985, ask to write that story?'" he chuckles in recollection. The answer was, to Julie, obvious. "He wrote the first one, let him write the 'last' one — Jerry Siegel!" Schwartz happened to be going out to the annual comic book convention in San Diego that year, where one of his fellow guests was to be writer Jerry Siegel, the co-creator (with artist Joe Shuster) of Superman. "Jerry and I spent a lot of time together at the DC booth, and I finally asked him the critical question: Would he be willing to write the 'last' Superman story? Jerry's response was, 'Oh... boy, well, I have to think about that... no, no need to think about it. I would love to write it!' But it turned out there were legal problems that, because of the schedule, we didn't have time to resolve, so Jerry wasn't able to do it after all.

"The next morning, still wondering what to do about it, I happened to be having breakfast with Alan Moore. So I told him about my difficulties. At that point he literally rose out of his chair, put his hands around my neck, and said, 'If you let anybody but me write that story, I'll kill you.' Since I didn't want to be an accessory to my own murder, I agreed."

The fact that Alan Moore was recognized as one of the best writers to work in comics probably had more to do with Julie's decision than fear for his own mortality. Moore had already cemented his reputation as a postmodern master of comics with his work on the British strip *Marvelman* (published in America as *Miracleman*), and his work on DC's SWAMP THING and the aforementioned WATCHMEN was emerging — though both were still in progress — as being among those rare works that would redefine the medium for the future.

So, in a letter to Moore dated September 19, 1985, Julie proclaimed, "The time has come! Meaning — that I've just been informed that the September cover-dated issues of SUPERMAN and ACTION will be my last before John Byrne and Co. take over.

"What I'm getting at is: the time has come for you to type up the story your 'mouth' agreed to do — that is, an 'imaginary' Superman that would serve as the 'last' Superman story if the magazines were discontinued — what would happen to Superman, Clark Kent, Lois Lane, Lana Lang, Jimmy Olsen, Perry White, Luthor, Brainiac, Mr. Mxyzptlk, and all the et cetera you can deal with."

The matter of an artist for the 'last' Superman story was never in question. In the preceding thirty years or so, Curt Swan had become, in the minds of generations of readers, the definitive Superman artist, responsible for a staggering number of stories starring the Last Son of Krypton. Certainly if anyone deserved to do the honors on what was sure to become one of the most memorable Superman stories of all time, it was Curt. To this day, more than a decade later, Curt's contribution to the Superman legend stands undiminished even in light of the distinguished artists who have followed in his footsteps. This reprint of his last "official" Superman story is a fitting tribute both to Curt's memory and to his legacy on Superman.

To ink the last Superman stories under his editorial reign, Julie Schwartz called on THE NEW TEEN TITANS co-creator George Pérez for Part One. "George heard I was giving up Superman and had always wanted to ink a Curt Swan story," Julie recalls. Pérez agrees, "It was a dream come true for me to finally get to ink Curt Swan's pencils, especially on his last Superman story, and to work with Alan Moore. Like everyone else, I grew up reading Curt's Superman, so it was thrilling to be working with him on just that level alone. To work with him on this story, which was a bit of history in the making, made it even more special."

Julie chose longtime Superman Family artist Kurt Schaffenberger to ink the concluding chapter because, as he says, "Kurt had been working on Superman material for as long as I can remember, pencilling and/or inking stories with Superman, Lois Lane, Superboy, Supergirl. But it occurred to me that in all those years, Kurt, an excellent inker in his own right, had never inked a Superman story over Swan, so I thought this would be his last chance to do so."

For the covers, Schwartz assigned Murphy Anderson to the inking chores, reasoning that this was the last chance for the classic "Swanderson" (Swan and Anderson) team to strut their stuff on Superman. And, Schwartz points out, if you look closely at the cover of ACTION #583, you'll notice some interesting special appearances. "It shows Superman flying off from the roof of the Daily Planet and everyone waving good-bye. The three people standing in front in the middle are Jenette Kahn, flanked on the left by Curt Swan, and by me (the guy with the glasses) on the right. And in the background are all the super-heroes." And looking closer still, at Superman's face, you'll see tears in the eyes of the Man of Steel. Says Schwartz, "The tears in Superman's eyes are really Curt's tears."

The "last" Superman made quite an impression on most everyone who read it. John Byrne, who was to follow Moore, Swan, Pérez and Schaffenberger, saw "Whatever Happened to the Man of Tomorrow?" as a story that no other creators would ever have the chance to do again. "That was the capper, the story that wrapped up the run of the old series, saying good-bye to all the characters the way they had been done and paving the way for what was to come. It's the kind of story that you couldn't normally do, and with a character like Superman, who'll last forever, it's a story the likes of which we'll never see again."

Andrew Helfer, who took over as editor of the Superman line of comics from Julie Schwartz, agrees. "It was a unique moment in the history of Superman. In that one moment, we were closing the book on Superman. And in that moment, it really was the last Superman story. It was not an imaginary story. You could utilize all the 'real' things that had preceded it and really create a definitive conclusion for the story of Superman. That only existed as a real story for a moment, because right afterwards, the first issue of THE MAN OF STEEL basically defined all of the previous Superman stories as imaginary stories. Of course that doesn't mean they were any less valid or any less enjoyable, but they were no longer in continuity, so Alan's story just wonderfully wrapped up the continuity in the way that he seemed best equipped to do.

"Alan, as a master of putting all the little pieces together into a coherent finality, had the ultimate opportunity to take all those hundreds of elements that he had grown up with and wrap them all up in this precious little bundle. It was a moment in time and it will never be repeated."

As is his wont, Schwartz comes up with the last words on this topic. "In Part One," he says, "in the legend that precedes the story, Alan Moore wrote the truest thing ever said about comics: 'This is an imaginary story. Aren't they all?'"

But the question of imaginary is in the eye of the beholder, and to those reading comics in 1986 when "Whatever Happened to the Man of Tomorrow?" was originally published, this was indeed the "last" Superman story.

Fortunately, for those reading *beyond* 1986, there was a new era waiting beyond it, and, as it turned out, the "last" Superman story merely paved the way for all the great stories that followed.

Paul Kupperberg is a former editor at DC Comics and former executive editor of Weekly World News, *as well as a writer of hundreds of comic books, novels, short stories and miscellany. He is the creator of ARION, LORD OF ATLANTIS, CHECKMATE!, and TAKION. His latest book is* Jewjitsu: The Hebrew Hands of Fury, *published by Citadel Press.*

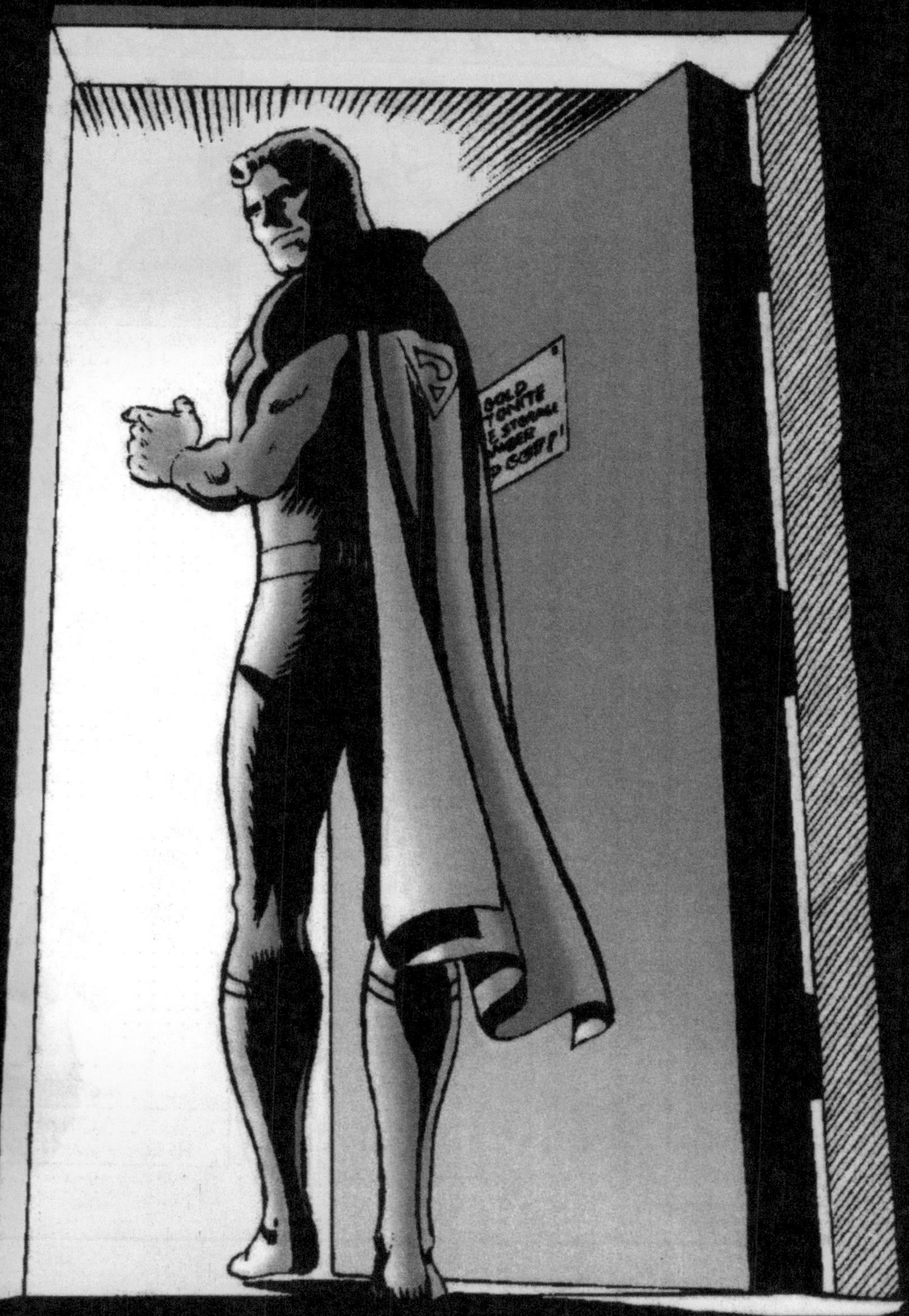

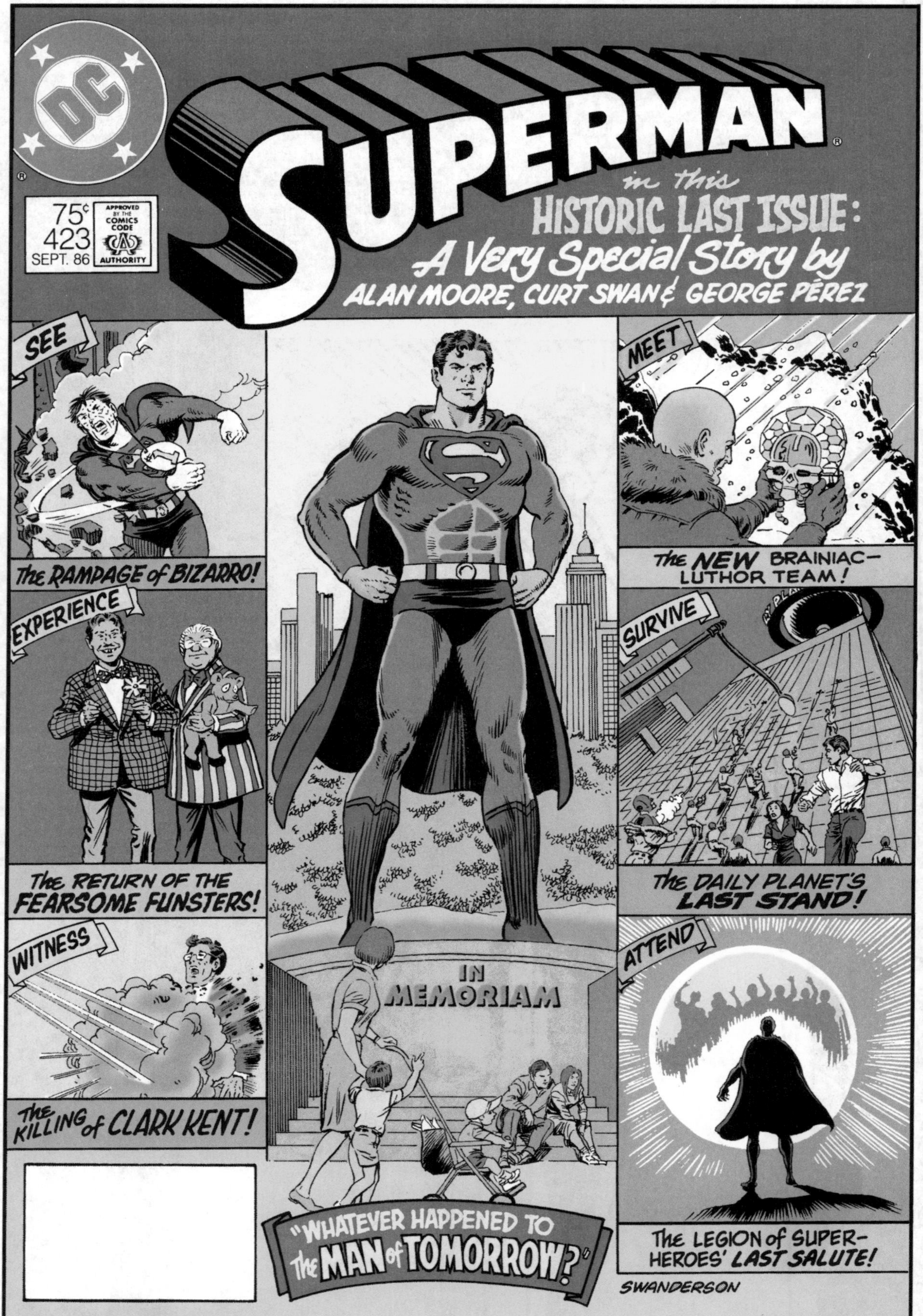

DC
SUPERMAN
75¢
423
SEPT. 86
APPROVED BY THE COMICS CODE AUTHORITY
in this
HISTORIC LAST ISSUE:
A Very Special Story by
ALAN MOORE, CURT SWAN & GEORGE PÉREZ
SEE
The RAMPAGE of BIZARRO!
EXPERIENCE
The RETURN OF THE FEARSOME FUNSTERS!
WITNESS
The KILLING of CLARK KENT!
IN MEMORIAM
"WHATEVER HAPPENED TO The MAN of TOMORROW?"
MEET
The NEW BRAINIAC-LUTHOR TEAM!
SURVIVE
The DAILY PLANET'S LAST STAND!
ATTEND
The LEGION of SUPER-HEROES' LAST SALUTE!
SWANDERSON

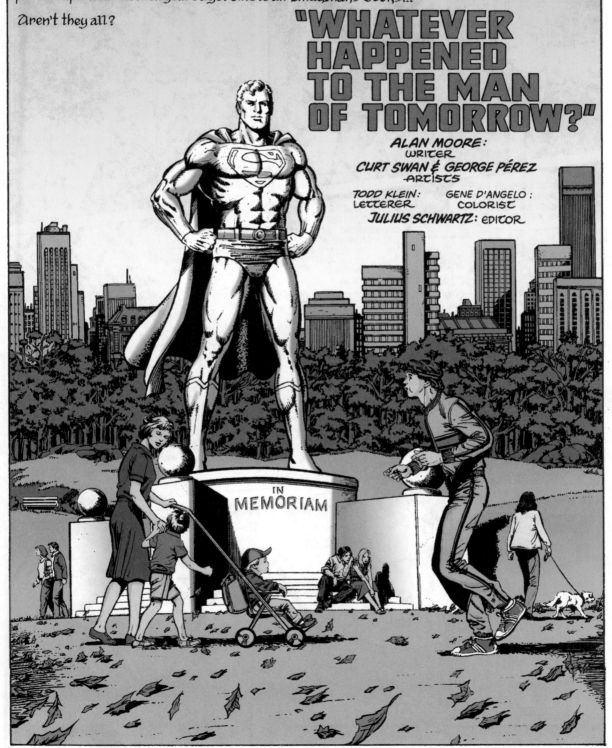

This is an IMAGINARY STORY (Which may never happen, but then again may) about a perfect man who came from the sky and did only good. It tells of his twilight, when the great battles were over and the great miracles long since performed; of how his enemies conspired against him and of that final war in the snowblind wastes beneath the Northern Lights; of the women he loved and of the choice he made between them; of how he broke his most sacred oath, and how finally all the things he had were taken from him save for one. It ends with a wink. It begins in a quiet midwestern town, one summer afternoon in the quiet midwestern future. Away in the big city, people still sometimes glance up hopefully from the sidewalks, glimpsing a distant speck in the sky... but no: it's only a bird, only a plane. Superman died ten years ago. This is an IMAGINARY STORY...

Aren't they all?

"WHATEVER HAPPENED TO THE MAN OF TOMORROW?"

ALAN MOORE:
WRITER

CURT SWAN & GEORGE PÉREZ
ARTISTS

TODD KLEIN:
LETTERER

GENE D'ANGELO:
COLORIST

JULIUS SCHWARTZ: EDITOR

IN
MEMORIAM

11

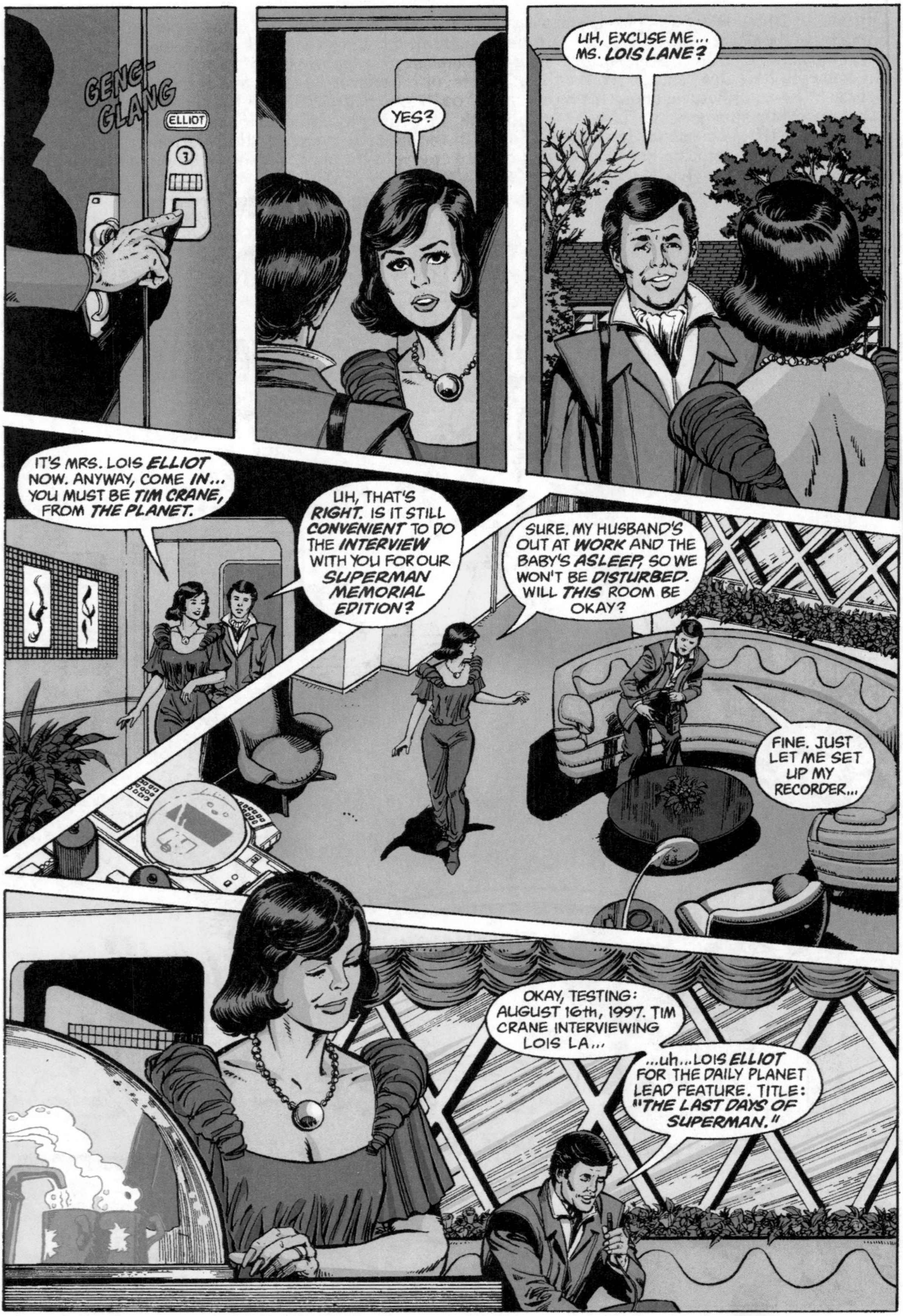
GENG-GLANG
ELLIOT
YES?
UH, EXCUSE ME... MS. LOIS LANE?
IT'S MRS. LOIS ELLIOT NOW. ANYWAY, COME IN... YOU MUST BE TIM CRANE, FROM THE PLANET.
UH, THAT'S RIGHT. IS IT STILL CONVENIENT TO DO THE INTERVIEW WITH YOU FOR OUR SUPERMAN MEMORIAL EDITION?
SURE. MY HUSBAND'S OUT AT WORK AND THE BABY'S ASLEEP, SO WE WON'T BE DISTURBED. WILL THIS ROOM BE OKAY?
FINE. JUST LET ME SET UP MY RECORDER...
OKAY, TESTING: AUGUST 16th, 1997. TIM CRANE INTERVIEWING LOIS LA...
...uh...LOIS ELLIOT FOR THE DAILY PLANET LEAD FEATURE. TITLE: "THE LAST DAYS OF SUPERMAN."

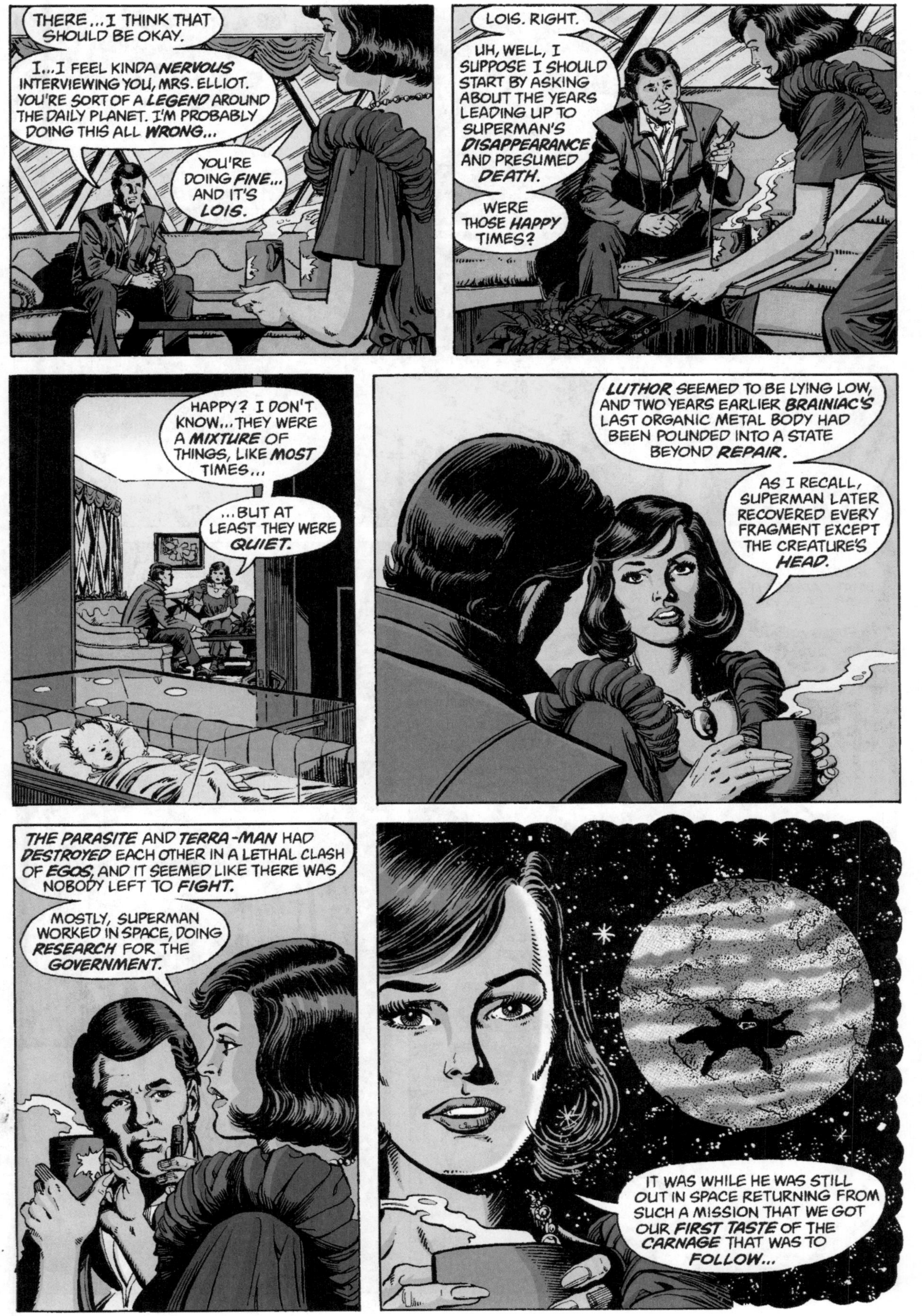
THERE...I THINK THAT SHOULD BE OKAY.
I...I FEEL KINDA NERVOUS INTERVIEWING YOU, MRS. ELLIOT. YOU'RE SORT OF A LEGEND AROUND THE DAILY PLANET. I'M PROBABLY DOING THIS ALL WRONG...
YOU'RE DOING FINE... AND IT'S LOIS.
LOIS. RIGHT.
UH, WELL, I SUPPOSE I SHOULD START BY ASKING ABOUT THE YEARS LEADING UP TO SUPERMAN'S DISAPPEARANCE AND PRESUMED DEATH.
WERE THOSE HAPPY TIMES?
HAPPY? I DON'T KNOW...THEY WERE A MIXTURE OF THINGS, LIKE MOST TIMES...
...BUT AT LEAST THEY WERE QUIET.
LUTHOR SEEMED TO BE LYING LOW, AND TWO YEARS EARLIER BRAINIAC'S LAST ORGANIC METAL BODY HAD BEEN POUNDED INTO A STATE BEYOND REPAIR.
AS I RECALL, SUPERMAN LATER RECOVERED EVERY FRAGMENT EXCEPT THE CREATURE'S HEAD.
THE PARASITE AND TERRA-MAN HAD DESTROYED EACH OTHER IN A LETHAL CLASH OF EGOS, AND IT SEEMED LIKE THERE WAS NOBODY LEFT TO FIGHT.
MOSTLY, SUPERMAN WORKED IN SPACE, DOING RESEARCH FOR THE GOVERNMENT.
IT WAS WHILE HE WAS STILL OUT IN SPACE RETURNING FROM SUCH A MISSION THAT WE GOT OUR FIRST TASTE OF THE CARNAGE THAT WAS TO FOLLOW...

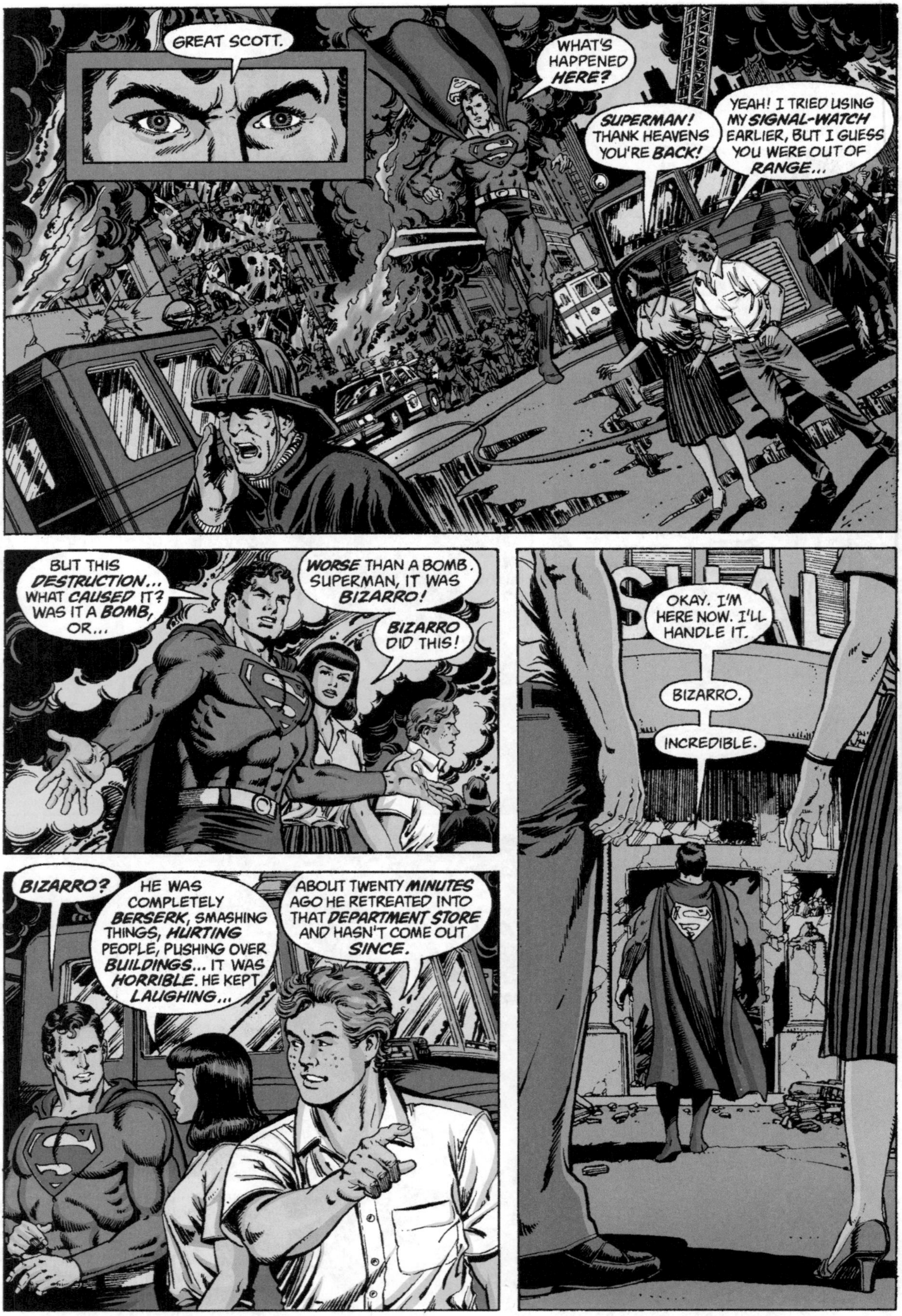
GREAT SCOTT.
WHAT'S HAPPENED HERE?
SUPERMAN! THANK HEAVENS YOU'RE BACK!
YEAH! I TRIED USING MY SIGNAL-WATCH EARLIER, BUT I GUESS YOU WERE OUT OF RANGE...
BUT THIS DESTRUCTION... WHAT CAUSED IT? WAS IT A BOMB, OR...
WORSE THAN A BOMB. SUPERMAN, IT WAS BIZARRO!
BIZARRO DID THIS!
BIZARRO?
HE WAS COMPLETELY BERSERK, SMASHING THINGS, HURTING PEOPLE, PUSHING OVER BUILDINGS... IT WAS HORRIBLE. HE KEPT LAUGHING...
ABOUT TWENTY MINUTES AGO HE RETREATED INTO THAT DEPARTMENT STORE AND HASN'T COME OUT SINCE.
OKAY. I'M HERE NOW. I'LL HANDLE IT.
BIZARRO.
INCREDIBLE.

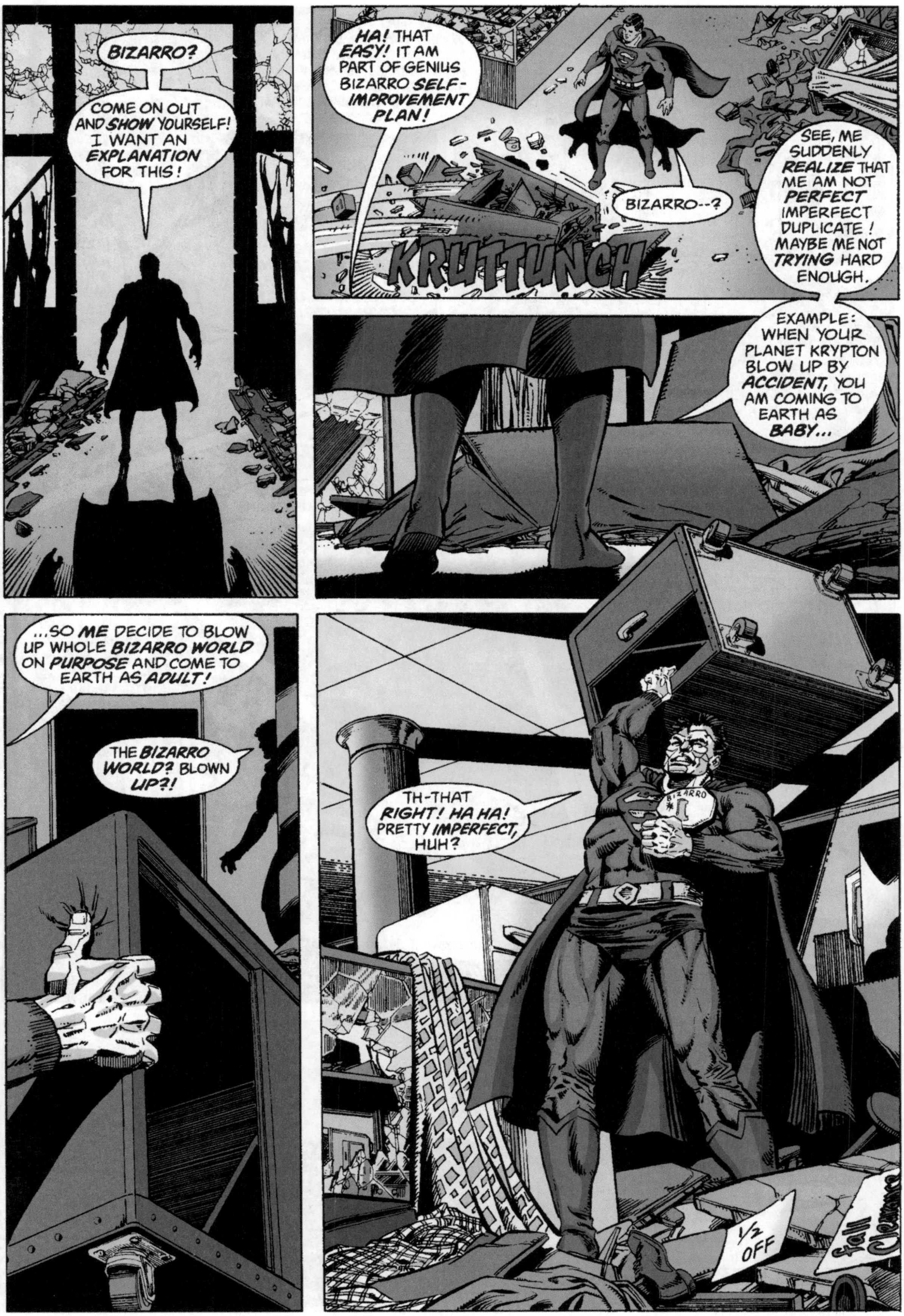
BIZARRO?
COME ON OUT AND SHOW YOURSELF! I WANT AN EXPLANATION FOR THIS!
HA! THAT EASY! IT AM PART OF GENIUS BIZARRO SELF-IMPROVEMENT PLAN!
KRUTTUNCH
BIZARRO--?
SEE, ME SUDDENLY REALIZE THAT ME AM NOT PERFECT IMPERFECT DUPLICATE! MAYBE ME NOT TRYING HARD ENOUGH.
EXAMPLE: WHEN YOUR PLANET KRYPTON BLOW UP BY ACCIDENT, YOU AM COMING TO EARTH AS BABY...
...SO ME DECIDE TO BLOW UP WHOLE BIZARRO WORLD ON PURPOSE AND COME TO EARTH AS ADULT!
THE BIZARRO WORLD? BLOWN UP?!
TH-THAT RIGHT! HA HA! PRETTY IMPERFECT, HUH?
BIZARRO #1
1/2 OFF
Fall Clearance

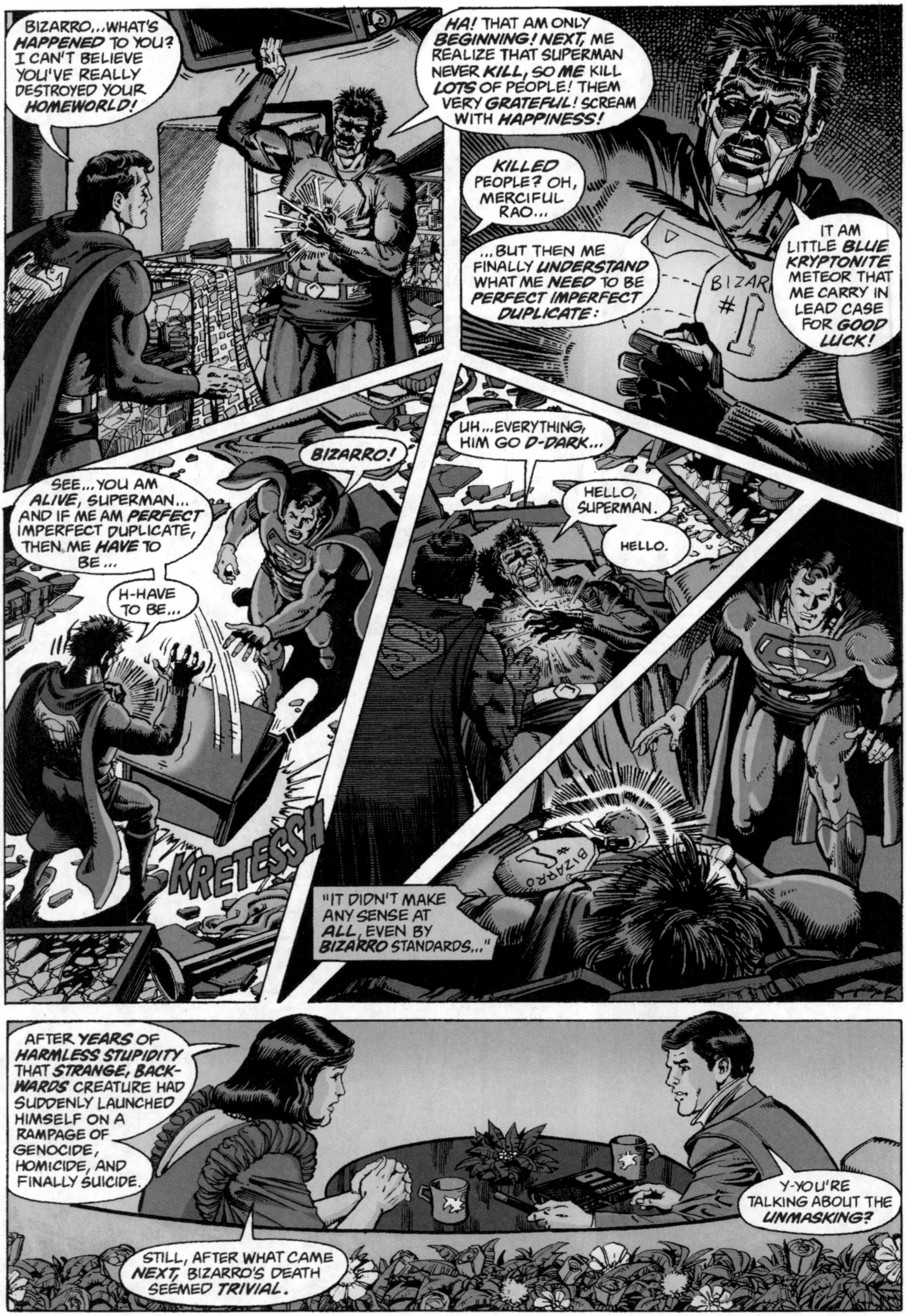
BIZARRO... WHAT'S HAPPENED TO YOU? I CAN'T BELIEVE YOU'VE REALLY DESTROYED YOUR HOMEWORLD!
HA! THAT AM ONLY BEGINNING! NEXT, ME REALIZE THAT SUPERMAN NEVER KILL, SO ME KILL LOTS OF PEOPLE! THEM VERY GRATEFUL! SCREAM WITH HAPPINESS!
KILLED PEOPLE? OH, MERCIFUL RAO...
...BUT THEN ME FINALLY UNDERSTAND WHAT ME NEED TO BE PERFECT IMPERFECT DUPLICATE:
IT AM LITTLE BLUE KRYPTONITE METEOR THAT ME CARRY IN LEAD CASE FOR GOOD LUCK!
BIZARRO!
SEE... YOU AM ALIVE, SUPERMAN... AND IF ME AM PERFECT IMPERFECT DUPLICATE, THEN ME HAVE TO BE...
H-HAVE TO BE...
KRETESSH
UH... EVERYTHING, HIM GO D-DARK...
HELLO, SUPERMAN.
HELLO.
"IT DIDN'T MAKE ANY SENSE AT ALL, EVEN BY BIZARRO STANDARDS..."
AFTER YEARS OF HARMLESS STUPIDITY THAT STRANGE, BACK-WARDS CREATURE HAD SUDDENLY LAUNCHED HIMSELF ON A RAMPAGE OF GENOCIDE, HOMICIDE, AND FINALLY SUICIDE.
STILL, AFTER WHAT CAME NEXT, BIZARRO'S DEATH SEEMED TRIVIAL.
Y-YOU'RE TALKING ABOUT THE UNMASKING?

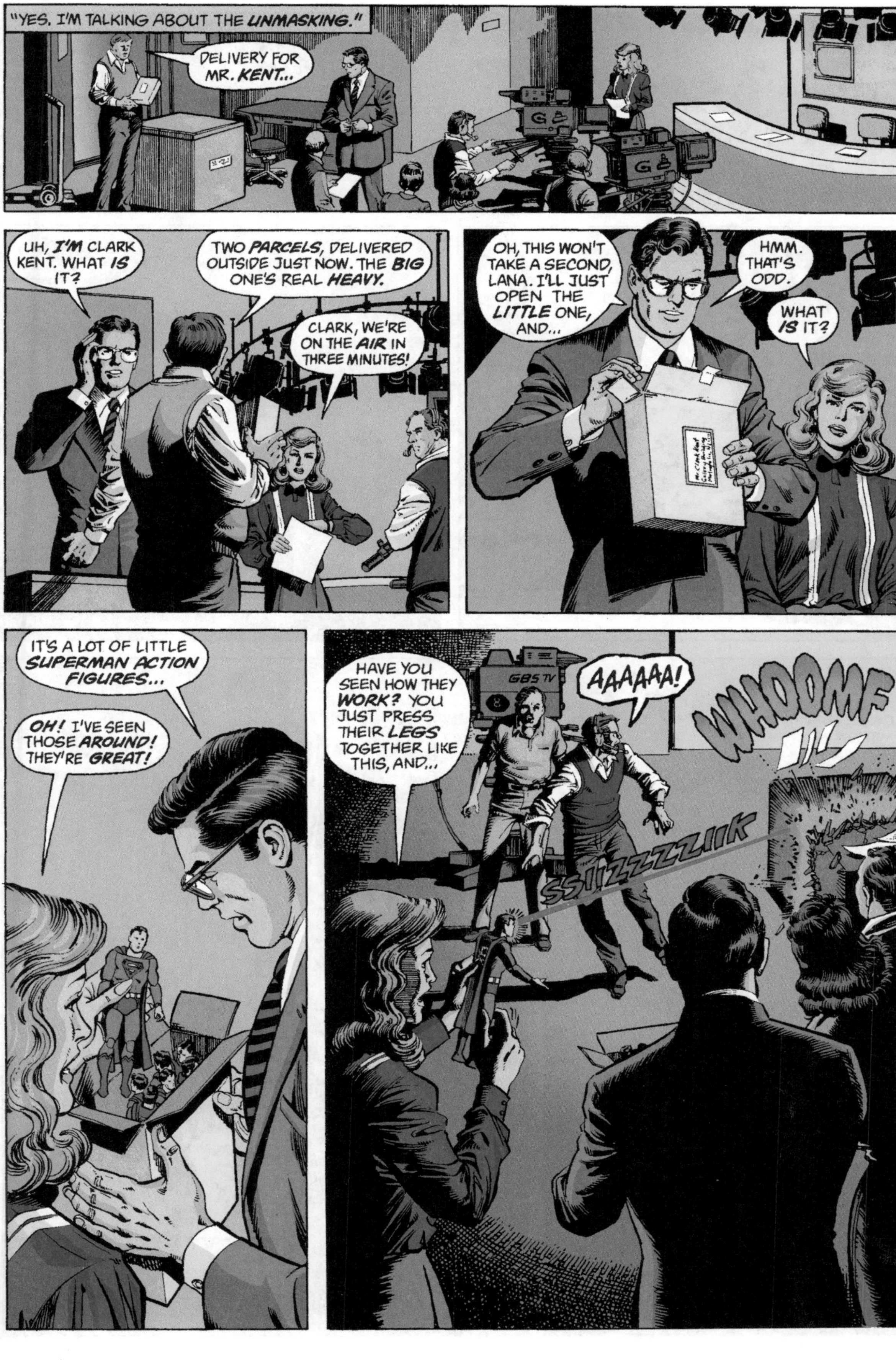
"YES. I'M TALKING ABOUT THE UNMASKING."
DELIVERY FOR MR. KENT...
UH, I'M CLARK KENT. WHAT IS IT?
TWO PARCELS, DELIVERED OUTSIDE JUST NOW. THE BIG ONE'S REAL HEAVY.
CLARK, WE'RE ON THE AIR IN THREE MINUTES!
OH, THIS WON'T TAKE A SECOND, LANA. I'LL JUST OPEN THE LITTLE ONE, AND...
HMM. THAT'S ODD.
WHAT IS IT?
IT'S A LOT OF LITTLE SUPERMAN ACTION FIGURES...
OH! I'VE SEEN THOSE AROUND! THEY'RE GREAT!
HAVE YOU SEEN HOW THEY WORK? YOU JUST PRESS THEIR LEGS TOGETHER LIKE THIS, AND...
GBS TV
AAAAAA!
WHOOMF
SSIIZZZZZIIIK

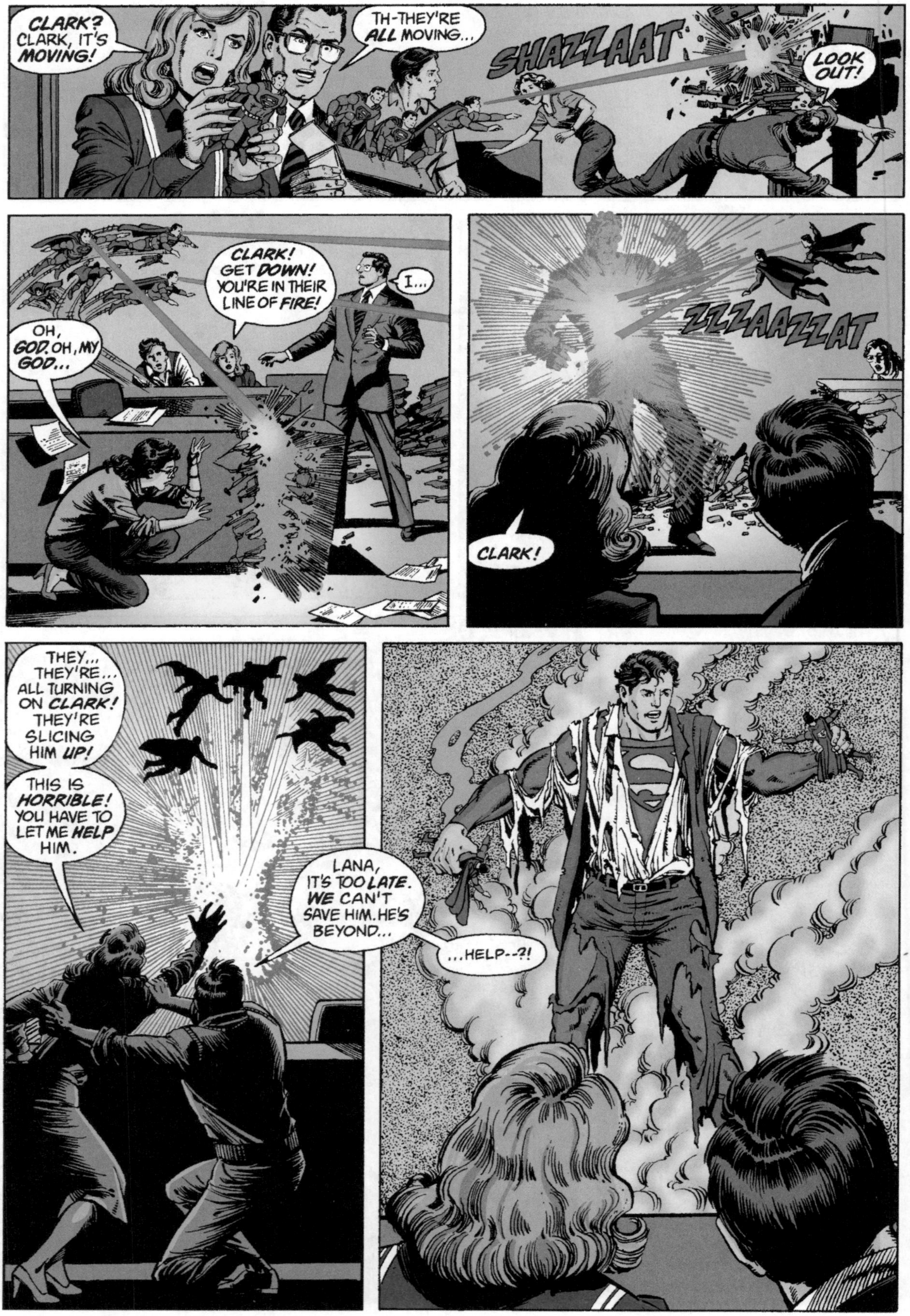
CLARK? CLARK, IT'S MOVING!
TH-THEY'RE ALL MOVING...
SHAZZAAT
LOOK OUT!
CLARK! GET DOWN! YOU'RE IN THEIR LINE OF FIRE!
I...
OH, GOD. OH, MY GOD...
ZZZAAZZAT
CLARK!
THEY... THEY'RE... ALL TURNING ON CLARK! THEY'RE SLICING HIM UP!
THIS IS HORRIBLE! YOU HAVE TO LET ME HELP HIM.
LANA, IT'S TOO LATE. WE CAN'T SAVE HIM. HE'S BEYOND...
...HELP--?!

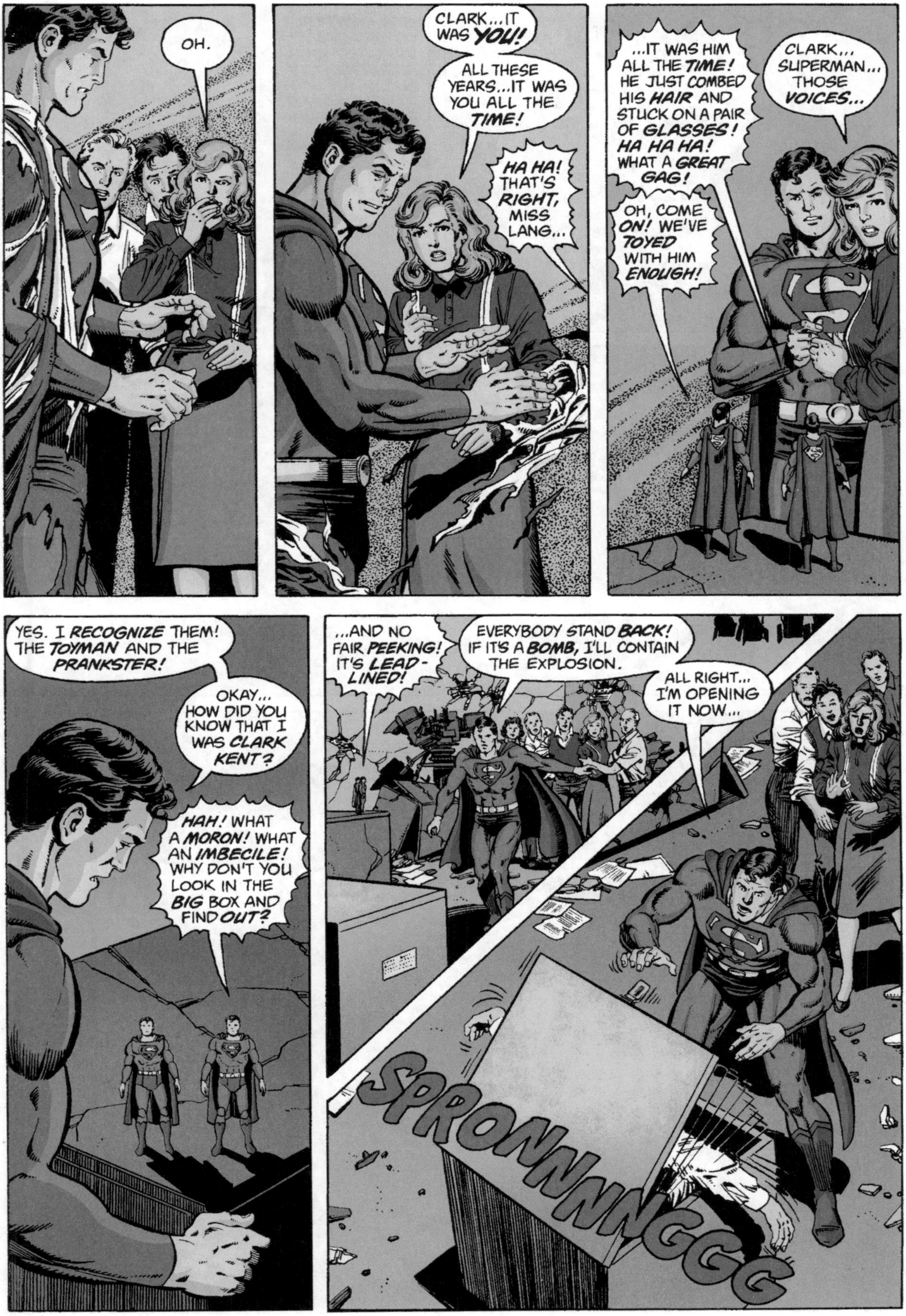
OH.
CLARK...IT WAS YOU!
ALL THESE YEARS...IT WAS YOU ALL THE TIME!
HA HA! THAT'S RIGHT, MISS LANG...
...IT WAS HIM ALL THE TIME! HE JUST COMBED HIS HAIR AND STUCK ON A PAIR OF GLASSES! HA HA HA! WHAT A GREAT GAG!
CLARK... SUPERMAN... THOSE VOICES...
OH, COME ON! WE'VE TOYED WITH HIM ENOUGH!
YES. I RECOGNIZE THEM! THE TOYMAN AND THE PRANKSTER!
OKAY... HOW DID YOU KNOW THAT I WAS CLARK KENT?
HAH! WHAT A MORON! WHAT AN IMBECILE! WHY DON'T YOU LOOK IN THE BIG BOX AND FIND OUT?
...AND NO FAIR PEEKING! IT'S LEAD-LINED!
EVERYBODY STAND BACK! IF IT'S A BOMB, I'LL CONTAIN THE EXPLOSION.
ALL RIGHT... I'M OPENING IT NOW...
SPRONNNNNGGG

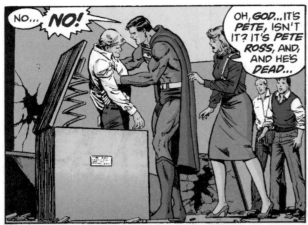

NO... **NO!**

OH, GOD... IT'S **PETE**, ISN'T IT? IT'S **PETE ROSS**, AND, AND HE'S **DEAD**...

RI-I-IGHT! BUT NOT BEFORE WE DRAGGED YOUR **SECRET IDENTITY** OUT OF HIM WITH A LITTLE **BOFFO BRAINWASHING!**

WE'D PLANNED TO WORK THROUGH YOUR **FRIENDS**, STARTING WITH THE FURTHEST **AWAY**, BUT WE HIT **PAYDIRT** FIRST **TIME!**

PRANKSTER... TOYMAN... LET ME ASK YOU ONE **QUESTION:**

DO YOU KNOW WHAT **RADIO WAVES** LOOK LIKE?

HUH? NO. WHY?

BECAUSE I **DO!**

YAAAGH!

20

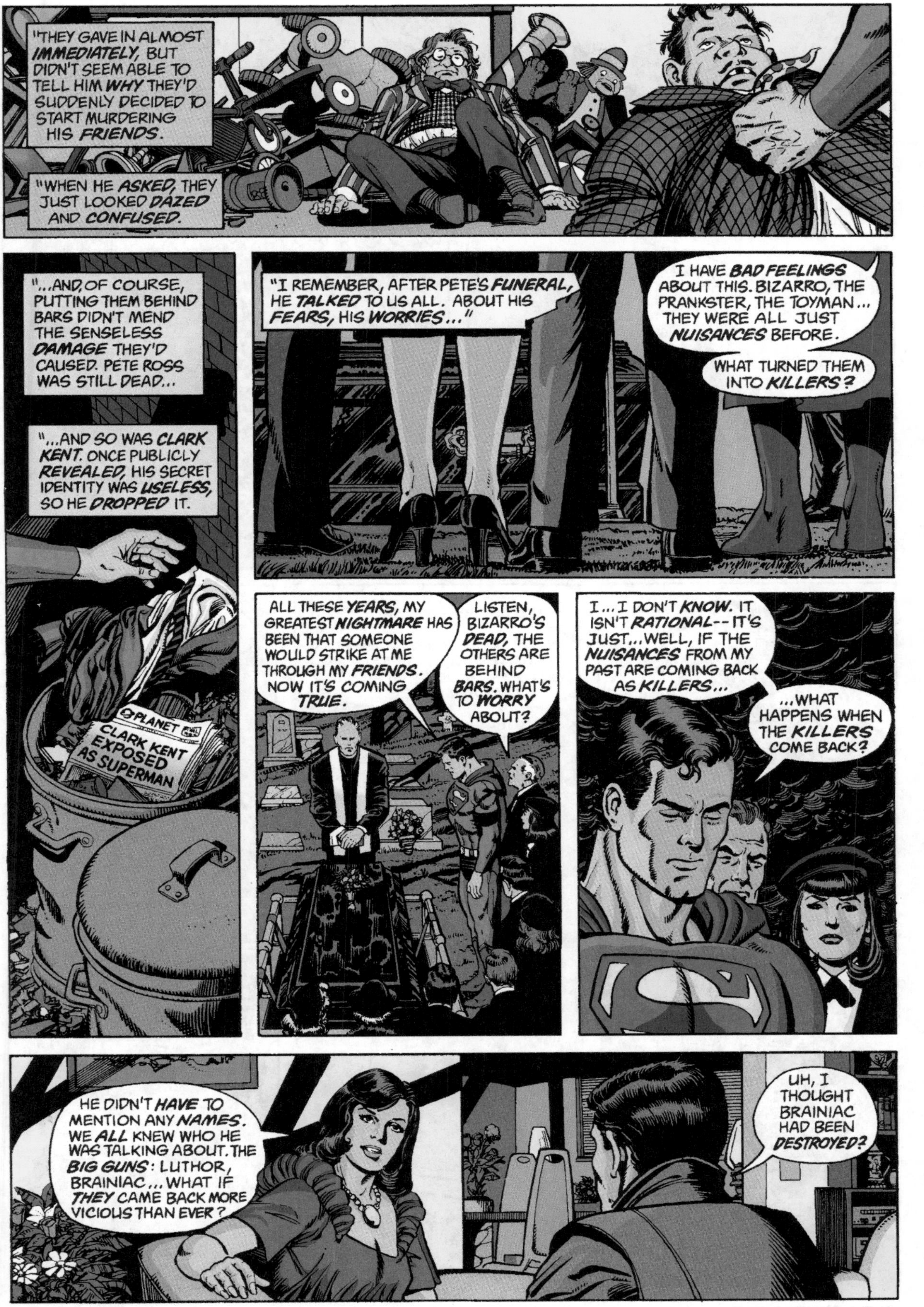
"THEY GAVE IN ALMOST IMMEDIATELY, BUT DIDN'T SEEM ABLE TO TELL HIM WHY THEY'D SUDDENLY DECIDED TO START MURDERING HIS FRIENDS.
"WHEN HE ASKED, THEY JUST LOOKED DAZED AND CONFUSED.
"...AND, OF COURSE, PUTTING THEM BEHIND BARS DIDN'T MEND THE SENSELESS DAMAGE THEY'D CAUSED. PETE ROSS WAS STILL DEAD...
"...AND SO WAS CLARK KENT. ONCE PUBLICLY REVEALED, HIS SECRET IDENTITY WAS USELESS, SO HE DROPPED IT.
PLANET
CLARK KENT EXPOSED AS SUPERMAN
"I REMEMBER, AFTER PETE'S FUNERAL, HE TALKED TO US ALL. ABOUT HIS FEARS, HIS WORRIES..."
I HAVE BAD FEELINGS ABOUT THIS. BIZARRO, THE PRANKSTER, THE TOYMAN... THEY WERE ALL JUST NUISANCES BEFORE.
WHAT TURNED THEM INTO KILLERS?
ALL THESE YEARS, MY GREATEST NIGHTMARE HAS BEEN THAT SOMEONE WOULD STRIKE AT ME THROUGH MY FRIENDS. NOW IT'S COMING TRUE.
LISTEN, BIZARRO'S DEAD, THE OTHERS ARE BEHIND BARS. WHAT'S TO WORRY ABOUT?
I... I DON'T KNOW. IT ISN'T RATIONAL-- IT'S JUST... WELL, IF THE NUISANCES FROM MY PAST ARE COMING BACK AS KILLERS...
...WHAT HAPPENS WHEN THE KILLERS COME BACK?
HE DIDN'T HAVE TO MENTION ANY NAMES. WE ALL KNEW WHO HE WAS TALKING ABOUT. THE BIG GUNS: LUTHOR, BRAINIAC... WHAT IF THEY CAME BACK MORE VICIOUS THAN EVER?
UH, I THOUGHT BRAINIAC HAD BEEN DESTROYED?

"SO DID WE...

DEET...
DEET...
DEET...

"...BUT AS WE FOUND OUT *LATER*, OTHER PEOPLE HADN'T GIVEN UP HOPE SO *EASILY*."

AHA!

DEET...DEET...
DEETDEET
DEET DEET
**DEETDEET
DEETDEET**

I *KNEW* IT! I *KNEW* YOU HAD TO BE UP HERE *SOMEPLACE*.

HA! I FEEL SOMETHING...JUST A *MOMENT*... UNGHH...

DEEDEET
DEEDEET
DEEDEET

THERE YOU ARE!

TO BE *FRANK*, I'VE SEEN YOU LOOKING *BETTER*.

NOT THAT I'M *COMPLAINING*. I'VE *ALWAYS* WANTED TO OPEN YOU UP AND STUDY THAT *ALIEN TECHNOLOGY*.

NOW THAT YOU'RE *DEAD*, I'M SAVED THE EMBARRASSMENT OF *ASKING*. AND *BESIDES*...

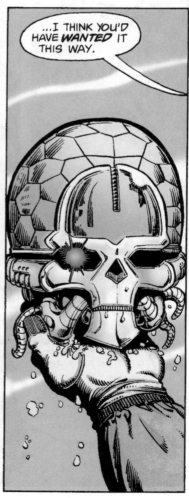

...I THINK YOU'D HAVE *WANTED* IT THIS WAY.

22

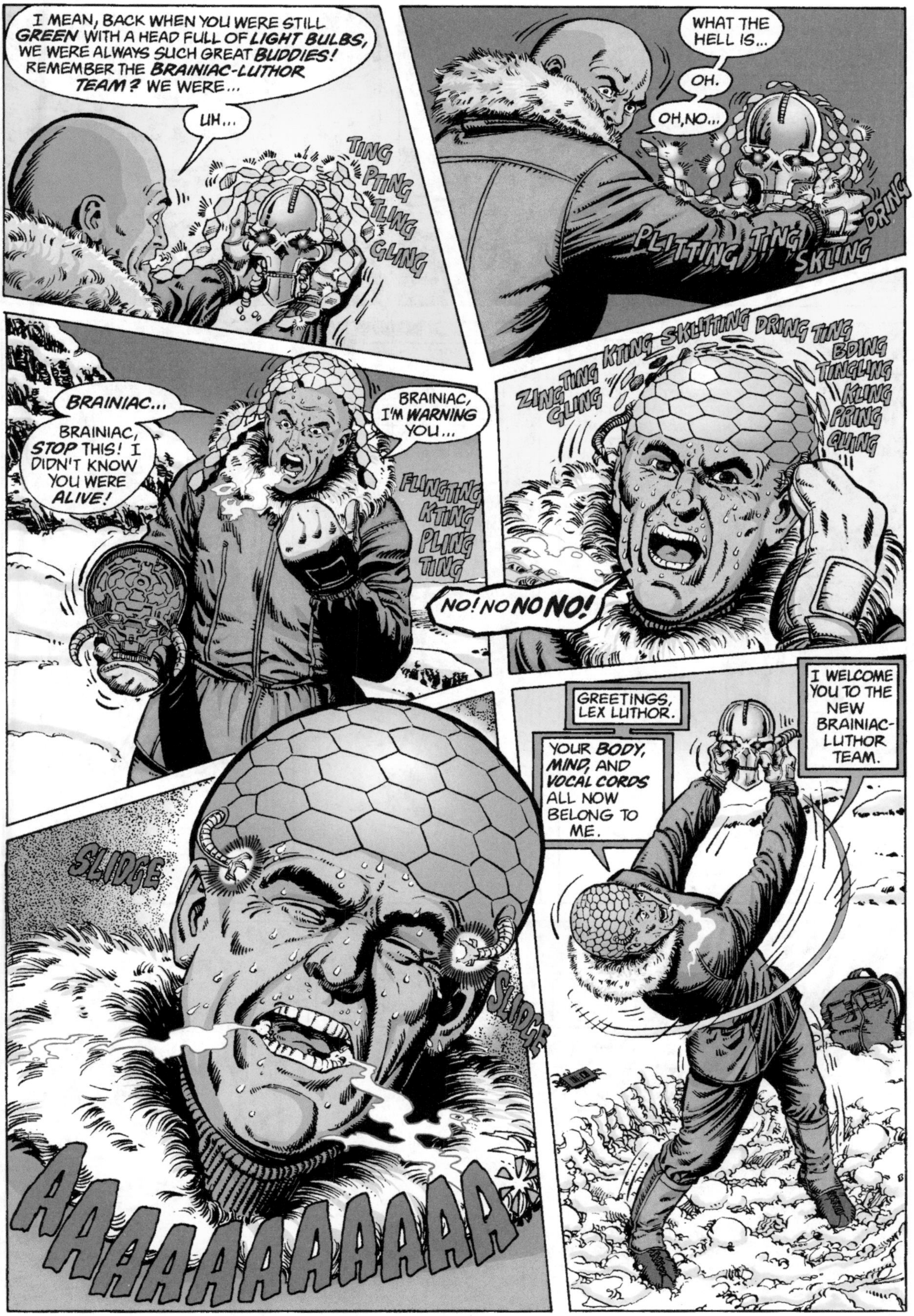
I MEAN, BACK WHEN YOU WERE STILL GREEN WITH A HEAD FULL OF LIGHT BULBS, WE WERE ALWAYS SUCH GREAT BUDDIES! REMEMBER THE BRAINIAC-LUTHOR TEAM? WE WERE...
UH...
TING PTING TLING GLING
WHAT THE HELL IS...
OH.
OH, NO...
PLITTING TING SKLING DRING
BRAINIAC...
BRAINIAC, STOP THIS! I DIDN'T KNOW YOU WERE ALIVE!
BRAINIAC, I'M WARNING YOU...
FLINGTING KTING PLING TING
ZING TING GLING KTING SKLITTING DRING TING BDING TINGLING KLING PRING QUING
NO! NO NO NO!
SLIDGE
SLIDGE
AAAAAAAAAAA
GREETINGS, LEX LUTHOR.
YOUR BODY, MIND, AND VOCAL CORDS ALL NOW BELONG TO ME.
I WELCOME YOU TO THE NEW BRAINIAC-LUTHOR TEAM.

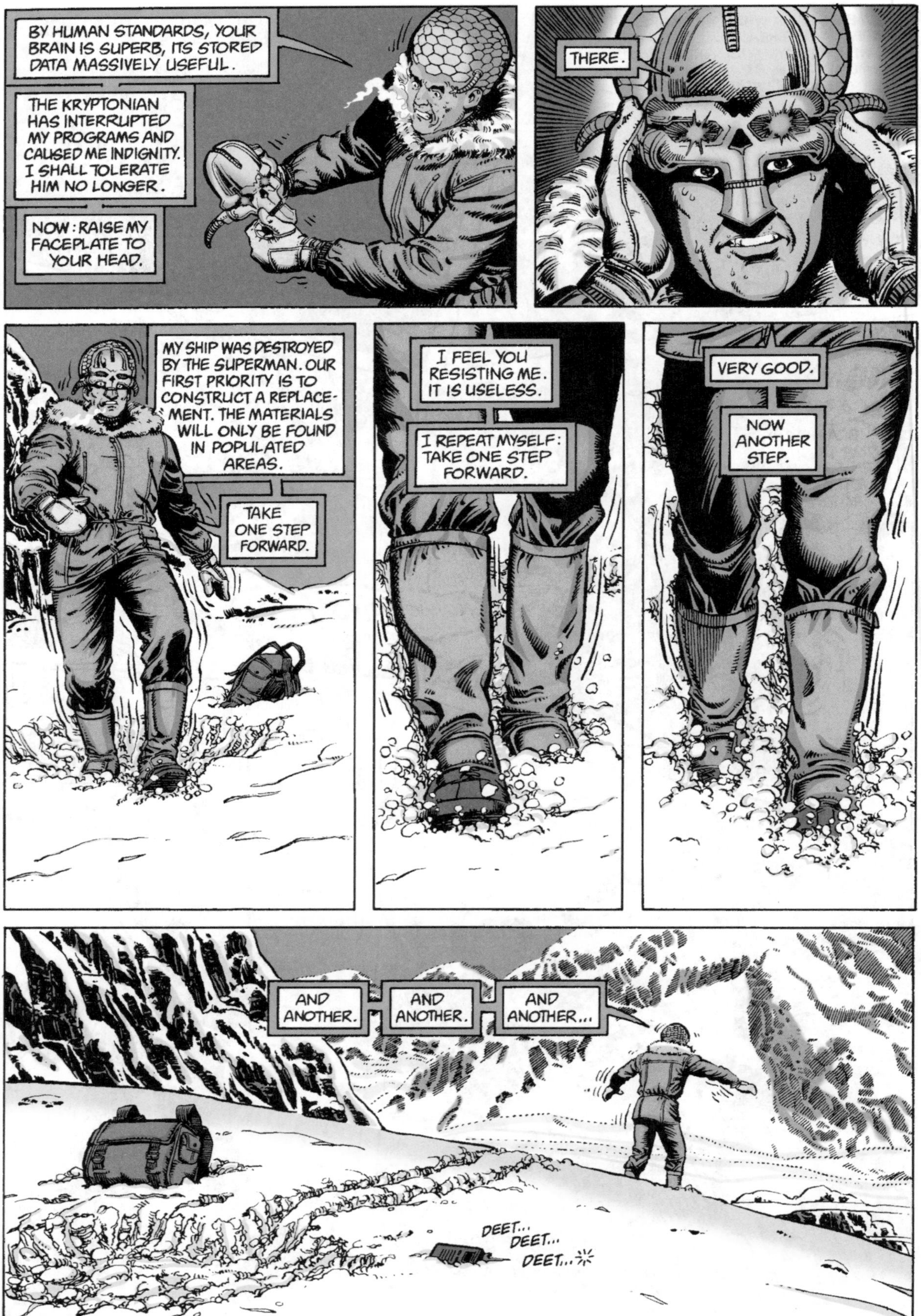
BY HUMAN STANDARDS, YOUR BRAIN IS SUPERB, ITS STORED DATA MASSIVELY USEFUL.
THE KRYPTONIAN HAS INTERRUPTED MY PROGRAMS AND CAUSED ME INDIGNITY. I SHALL TOLERATE HIM NO LONGER.
NOW: RAISE MY FACEPLATE TO YOUR HEAD.
THERE.
MY SHIP WAS DESTROYED BY THE SUPERMAN. OUR FIRST PRIORITY IS TO CONSTRUCT A REPLACE-MENT. THE MATERIALS WILL ONLY BE FOUND IN POPULATED AREAS.
TAKE ONE STEP FORWARD.
I FEEL YOU RESISTING ME. IT IS USELESS.
I REPEAT MYSELF: TAKE ONE STEP FORWARD.
VERY GOOD.
NOW ANOTHER STEP.
AND ANOTHER.
AND ANOTHER.
AND ANOTHER...
DEET... DEET... DEET...

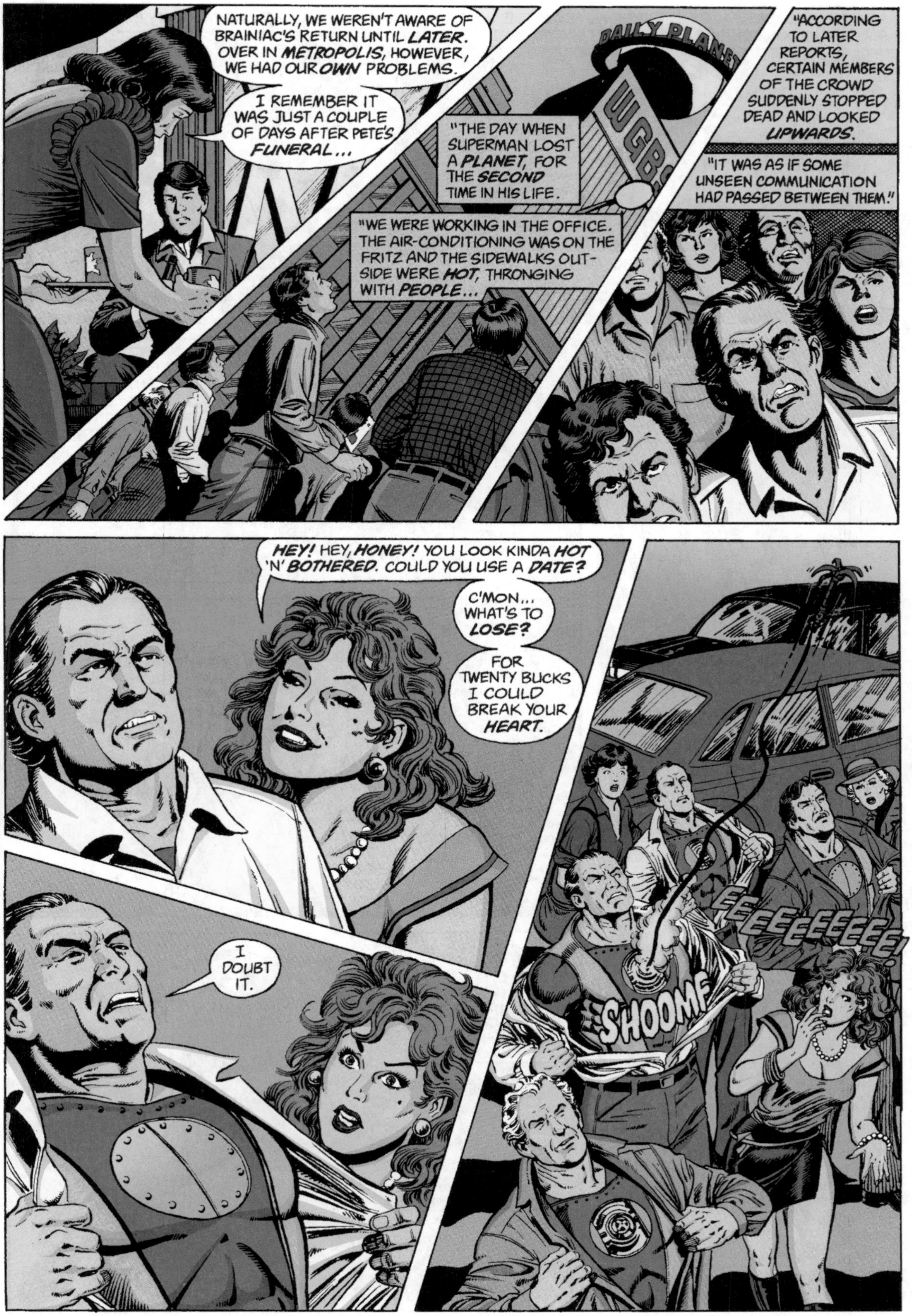
NATURALLY, WE WEREN'T AWARE OF BRAINIAC'S RETURN UNTIL LATER. OVER IN METROPOLIS, HOWEVER, WE HAD OUR OWN PROBLEMS.
I REMEMBER IT WAS JUST A COUPLE OF DAYS AFTER PETE'S FUNERAL...
DAILY PLANET
WGBS
"THE DAY WHEN SUPERMAN LOST A PLANET, FOR THE SECOND TIME IN HIS LIFE.
"WE WERE WORKING IN THE OFFICE. THE AIR-CONDITIONING WAS ON THE FRITZ AND THE SIDEWALKS OUTSIDE WERE HOT, THRONGING WITH PEOPLE...
"ACCORDING TO LATER REPORTS, CERTAIN MEMBERS OF THE CROWD SUDDENLY STOPPED DEAD AND LOOKED UPWARDS.
"IT WAS AS IF SOME UNSEEN COMMUNICATION HAD PASSED BETWEEN THEM."
HEY! HEY, HONEY! YOU LOOK KINDA HOT 'N' BOTHERED. COULD YOU USE A DATE?
C'MON... WHAT'S TO LOSE?
FOR TWENTY BUCKS I COULD BREAK YOUR HEART.
I DOUBT IT.
EEEEEEEEEE!
SHOOMF

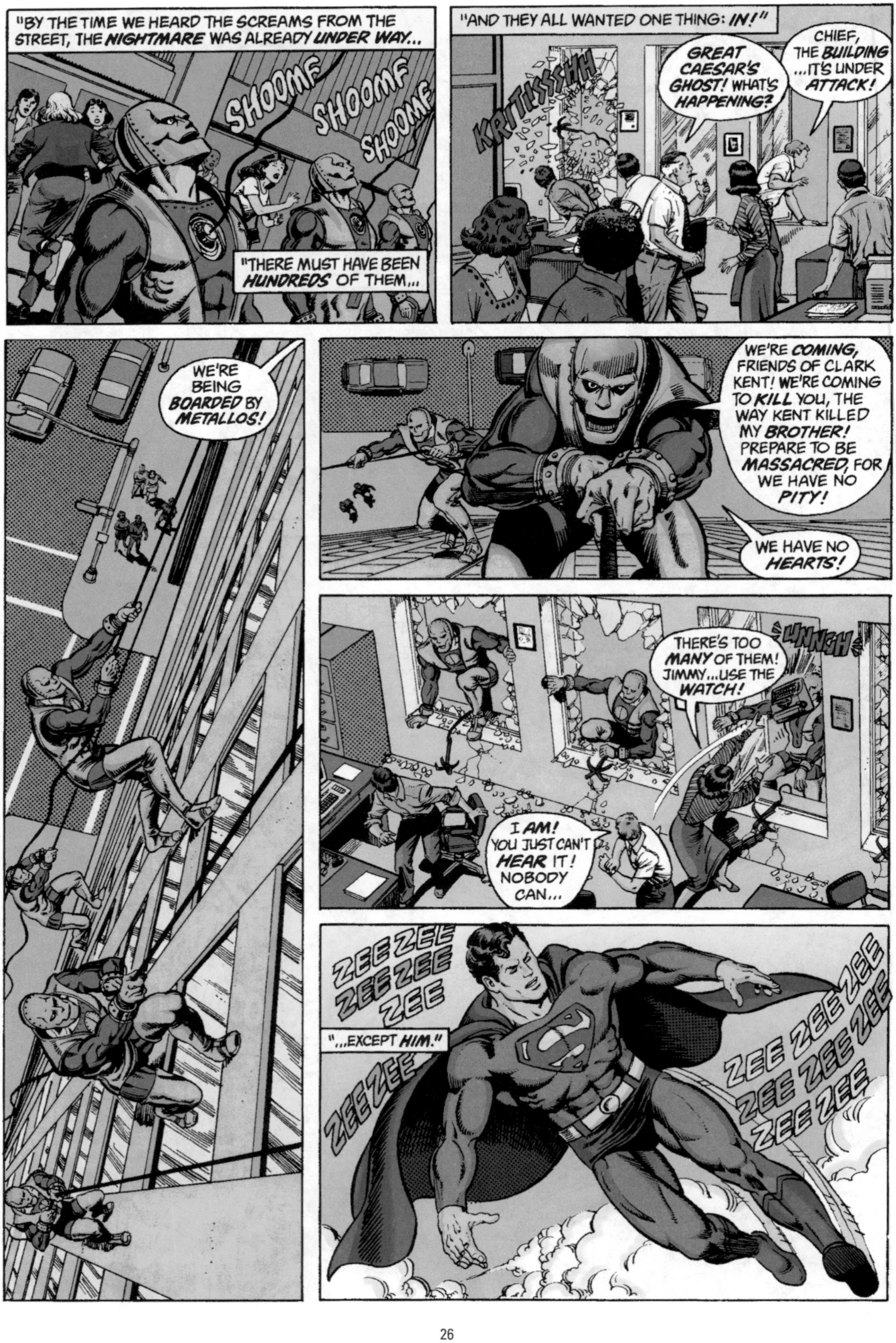
"BY THE TIME WE HEARD THE SCREAMS FROM THE STREET, THE NIGHTMARE WAS ALREADY UNDER WAY...
SHOOMF SHOOMF SHOOMF
"THERE MUST HAVE BEEN HUNDREDS OF THEM...
"AND THEY ALL WANTED ONE THING: IN!"
KRITSSSHH
GREAT CAESAR'S GHOST! WHAT'S HAPPENING?
CHIEF, THE BUILDING ...IT'S UNDER ATTACK!
WE'RE BEING BOARDED BY METALLOS!
WE'RE COMING, FRIENDS OF CLARK KENT! WE'RE COMING TO KILL YOU, THE WAY KENT KILLED MY BROTHER! PREPARE TO BE MASSACRED, FOR WE HAVE NO PITY!
WE HAVE NO HEARTS!
UNNGH
THERE'S TOO MANY OF THEM! JIMMY...USE THE WATCH!
I AM! YOU JUST CAN'T HEAR IT! NOBODY CAN...
ZEE ZEE ZEE ZEE ZEE
"...EXCEPT HIM."
ZEE ZEE
ZEE ZEE ZEE ZEE ZEE ZEE ZEE ZEE ZEE ZEE

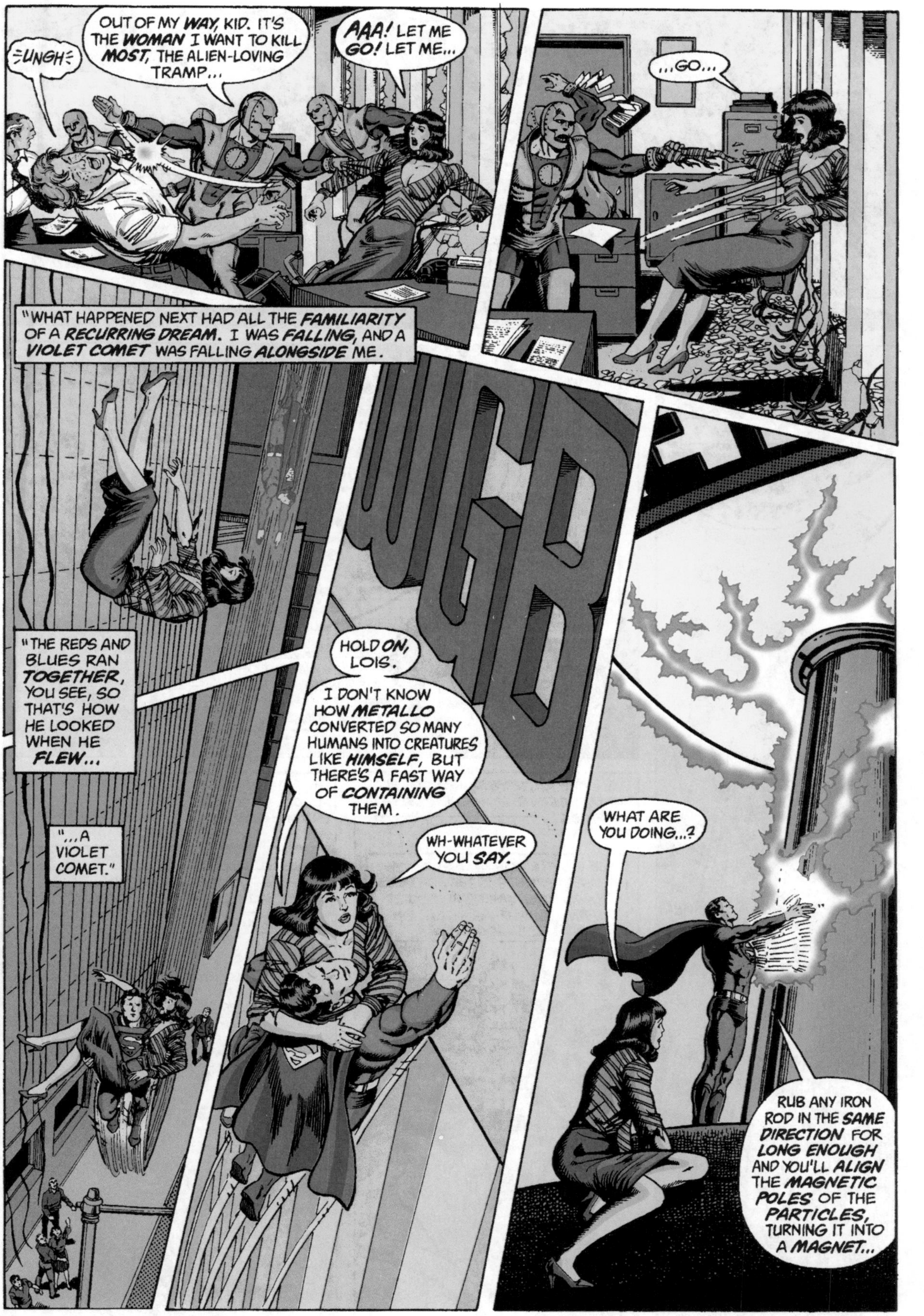

OUT OF MY WAY, KID. IT'S THE WOMAN I WANT TO KILL MOST, THE ALIEN-LOVING TRAMP...
UNGH
AAA! LET ME GO! LET ME...
...GO...
"WHAT HAPPENED NEXT HAD ALL THE FAMILIARITY OF A RECURRING DREAM. I WAS FALLING, AND A VIOLET COMET WAS FALLING ALONGSIDE ME.
"THE REDS AND BLUES RAN TOGETHER, YOU SEE, SO THAT'S HOW HE LOOKED WHEN HE FLEW...
"...A VIOLET COMET."
WGB
HOLD ON, LOIS.
I DON'T KNOW HOW METALLO CONVERTED SO MANY HUMANS INTO CREATURES LIKE HIMSELF, BUT THERE'S A FAST WAY OF CONTAINING THEM.
WH-WHATEVER YOU SAY.
WHAT ARE YOU DOING...?
RUB ANY IRON ROD IN THE SAME DIRECTION FOR LONG ENOUGH AND YOU'LL ALIGN THE MAGNETIC POLES OF THE PARTICLES, TURNING IT INTO A MAGNET...

...OR IN *THIS* CASE, A *SUPER-MAGNET*.

RRRENNCH

"HE LIFTED THE MAGNETIZED GLOBE INTO THE SKY ABOVE THE *GALAXY* BUILDING.

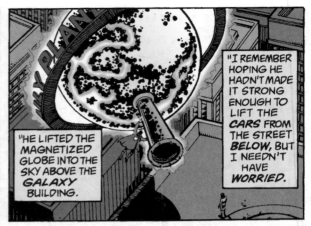

"I REMEMBER HOPING HE HADN'T MADE IT STRONG ENOUGH TO LIFT THE *CARS* FROM THE STREET *BELOW*, BUT I NEEDN'T HAVE *WORRIED*.

"HE GOT EVERYTHING JUST RIGHT.

"AS ALWAYS!"

"WHEN HE'D GATHERED UP ALL THE *METALLOS*... ALONG WITH MOST *OTHER* METAL FROM THE *PLANET* OFFICES...HE FLEW THE PARALYZED *CYBORGS* TO THE *ST. THERESA* PRISON COMPLEX.

"I GATHER MOST OF THEM WERE LATER SUCCESSFULLY *RE-HUMANIZED*.

"WHEN HE *RETURNED*, HE LOOKED AS *DEVASTATED* AS THE *PLANET* OFFICES.

"HE INSISTED ON TAKING ALL HIS CLOSEST FRIENDS TO THE *FORTRESS OF SOLITUDE*, WHERE HE COULD *DEFEND* THEM IF THE SITUATION CONTINUED TO *WORSEN*.

"HE FETCHED LANA, AND PERRY WHITE'S WIFE, *ALICE*. ALICE AND PERRY WERE NOT QUITE GETTING *ON*, AND SHE WAS VERY *CONFUSED* AND *SCARED*.

"I GUESS WE WERE *ALL* TENSE. EVERY-THING HAD SUCH AN AIR OF *FINALITY*...

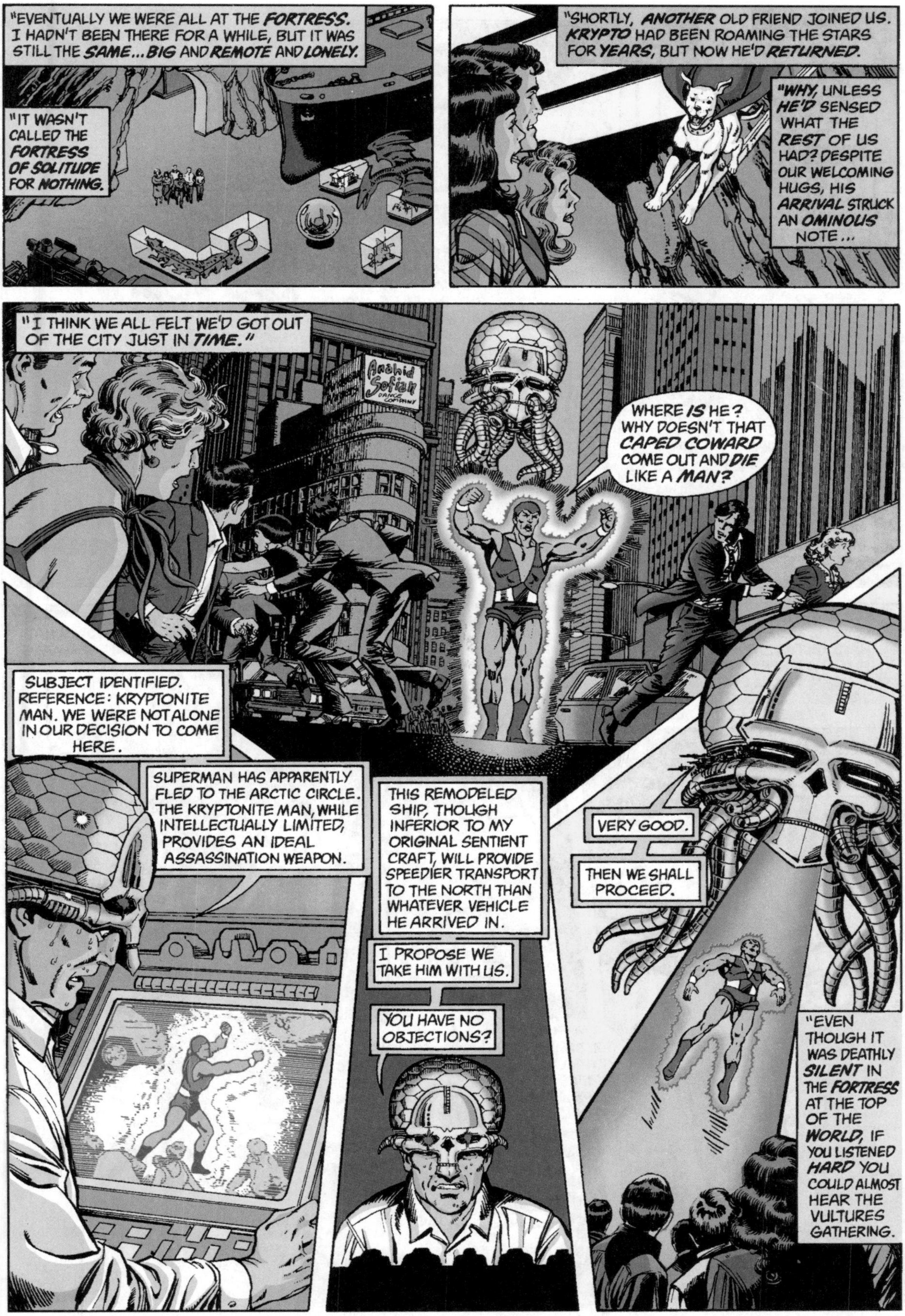
"EVENTUALLY WE WERE ALL AT THE FORTRESS. I HADN'T BEEN THERE FOR A WHILE, BUT IT WAS STILL THE SAME... BIG AND REMOTE AND LONELY.
"IT WASN'T CALLED THE FORTRESS OF SOLITUDE FOR NOTHING.
"SHORTLY, ANOTHER OLD FRIEND JOINED US. KRYPTO HAD BEEN ROAMING THE STARS FOR YEARS, BUT NOW HE'D RETURNED.
"WHY, UNLESS HE'D SENSED WHAT THE REST OF US HAD? DESPITE OUR WELCOMING HUGS, HIS ARRIVAL STRUCK AN OMINOUS NOTE...
"I THINK WE ALL FELT WE'D GOT OUT OF THE CITY JUST IN TIME."
WHERE IS HE? WHY DOESN'T THAT CAPED COWARD COME OUT AND DIE LIKE A MAN?
SUBJECT IDENTIFIED. REFERENCE: KRYPTONITE MAN. WE WERE NOT ALONE IN OUR DECISION TO COME HERE.
SUPERMAN HAS APPARENTLY FLED TO THE ARCTIC CIRCLE. THE KRYPTONITE MAN, WHILE INTELLECTUALLY LIMITED, PROVIDES AN IDEAL ASSASSINATION WEAPON.
THIS REMODELED SHIP, THOUGH INFERIOR TO MY ORIGINAL SENTIENT CRAFT, WILL PROVIDE SPEEDIER TRANSPORT TO THE NORTH THAN WHATEVER VEHICLE HE ARRIVED IN.
I PROPOSE WE TAKE HIM WITH US.
YOU HAVE NO OBJECTIONS?
VERY GOOD.
THEN WE SHALL PROCEED.
"EVEN THOUGH IT WAS DEATHLY SILENT IN THE FORTRESS AT THE TOP OF THE WORLD, IF YOU LISTENED HARD YOU COULD ALMOST HEAR THE VULTURES GATHERING.

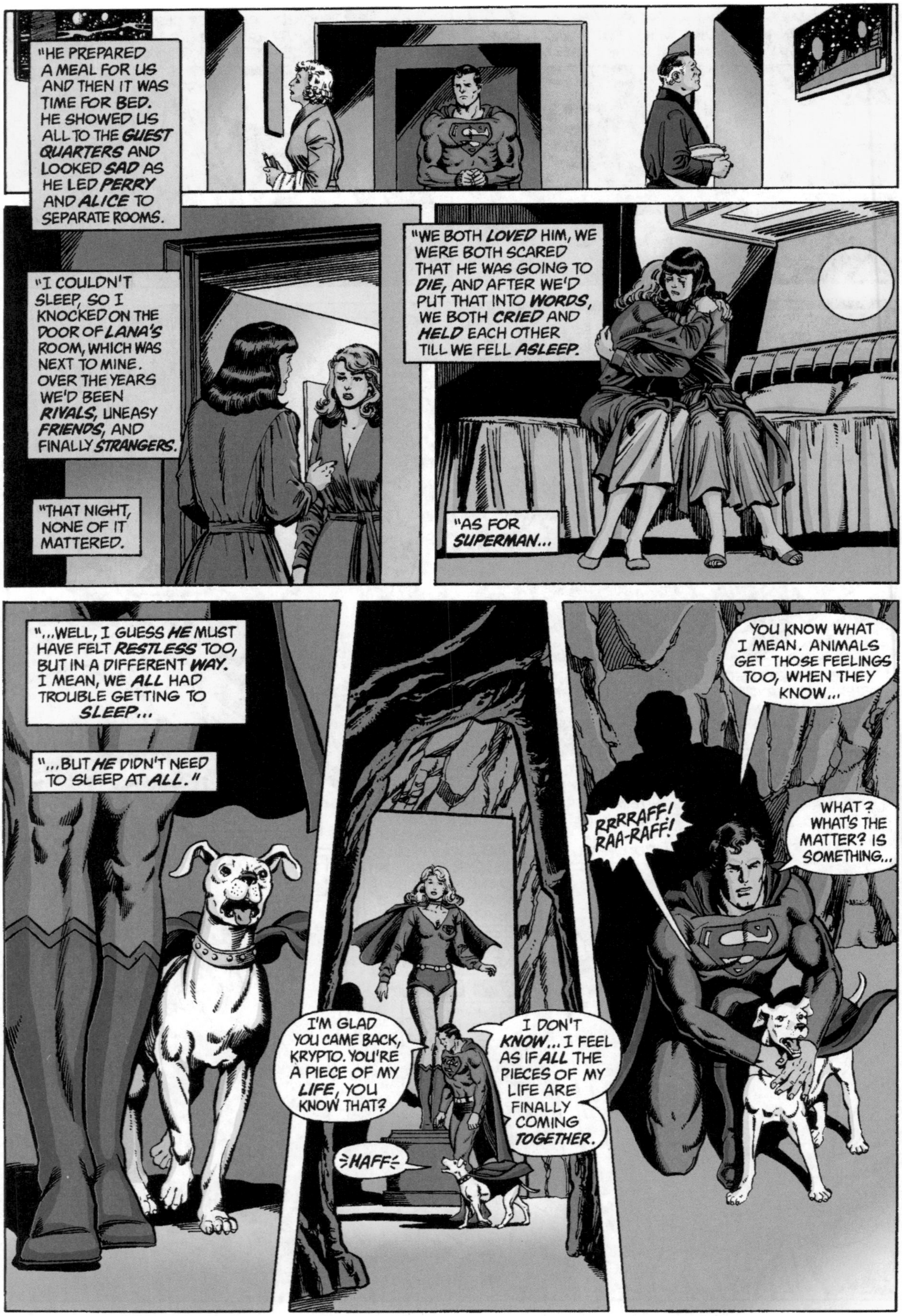
"HE PREPARED A MEAL FOR US AND THEN IT WAS TIME FOR BED. HE SHOWED US ALL TO THE GUEST QUARTERS AND LOOKED SAD AS HE LED PERRY AND ALICE TO SEPARATE ROOMS.
"I COULDN'T SLEEP, SO I KNOCKED ON THE DOOR OF LANA'S ROOM, WHICH WAS NEXT TO MINE. OVER THE YEARS WE'D BEEN RIVALS, UNEASY FRIENDS, AND FINALLY STRANGERS.
"THAT NIGHT, NONE OF IT MATTERED.
"WE BOTH LOVED HIM, WE WERE BOTH SCARED THAT HE WAS GOING TO DIE, AND AFTER WE'D PUT THAT INTO WORDS, WE BOTH CRIED AND HELD EACH OTHER TILL WE FELL ASLEEP.
"AS FOR SUPERMAN...
"...WELL, I GUESS HE MUST HAVE FELT RESTLESS TOO, BUT IN A DIFFERENT WAY. I MEAN, WE ALL HAD TROUBLE GETTING TO SLEEP...
"...BUT HE DIDN'T NEED TO SLEEP AT ALL."
I'M GLAD YOU CAME BACK, KRYPTO. YOU'RE A PIECE OF MY LIFE, YOU KNOW THAT?
HAFF
I DON'T KNOW... I FEEL AS IF ALL THE PIECES OF MY LIFE ARE FINALLY COMING TOGETHER.
YOU KNOW WHAT I MEAN. ANIMALS GET THOSE FEELINGS TOO, WHEN THEY KNOW...
RRRRAFF! RAA-RAFF!
WHAT? WHAT'S THE MATTER? IS SOMETHING...

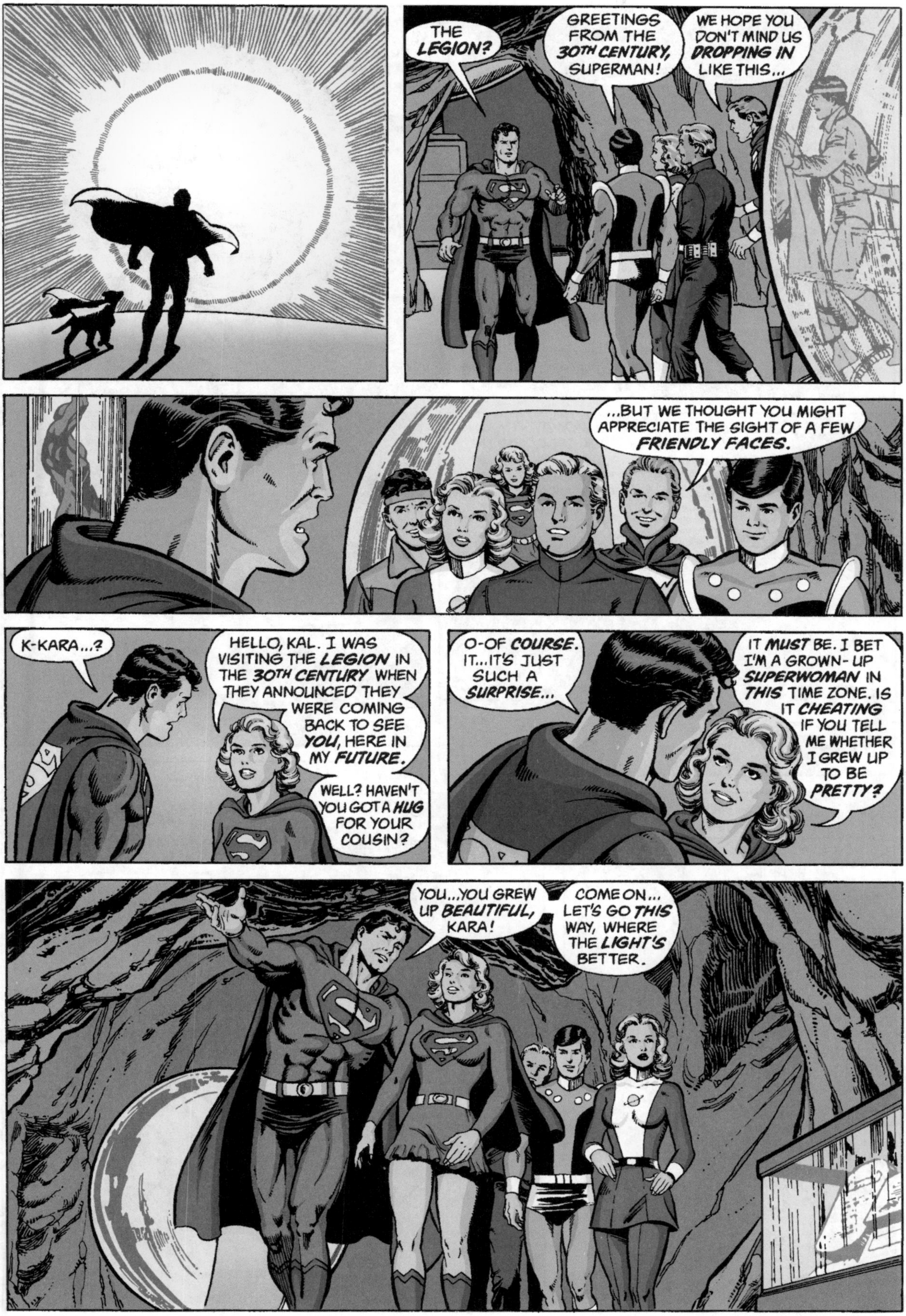

THE LEGION?
GREETINGS FROM THE 30TH CENTURY, SUPERMAN!
WE HOPE YOU DON'T MIND US DROPPING IN LIKE THIS...
...BUT WE THOUGHT YOU MIGHT APPRECIATE THE SIGHT OF A FEW FRIENDLY FACES.
K-KARA...?
HELLO, KAL. I WAS VISITING THE LEGION IN THE 30TH CENTURY WHEN THEY ANNOUNCED THEY WERE COMING BACK TO SEE YOU, HERE IN MY FUTURE.
WELL? HAVEN'T YOU GOT A HUG FOR YOUR COUSIN?
O-OF COURSE. IT...IT'S JUST SUCH A SURPRISE...
IT MUST BE. I BET I'M A GROWN-UP SUPERWOMAN IN THIS TIME ZONE. IS IT CHEATING IF YOU TELL ME WHETHER I GREW UP TO BE PRETTY?
YOU...YOU GREW UP BEAUTIFUL, KARA!
COME ON... LET'S GO THIS WAY, WHERE THE LIGHT'S BETTER.

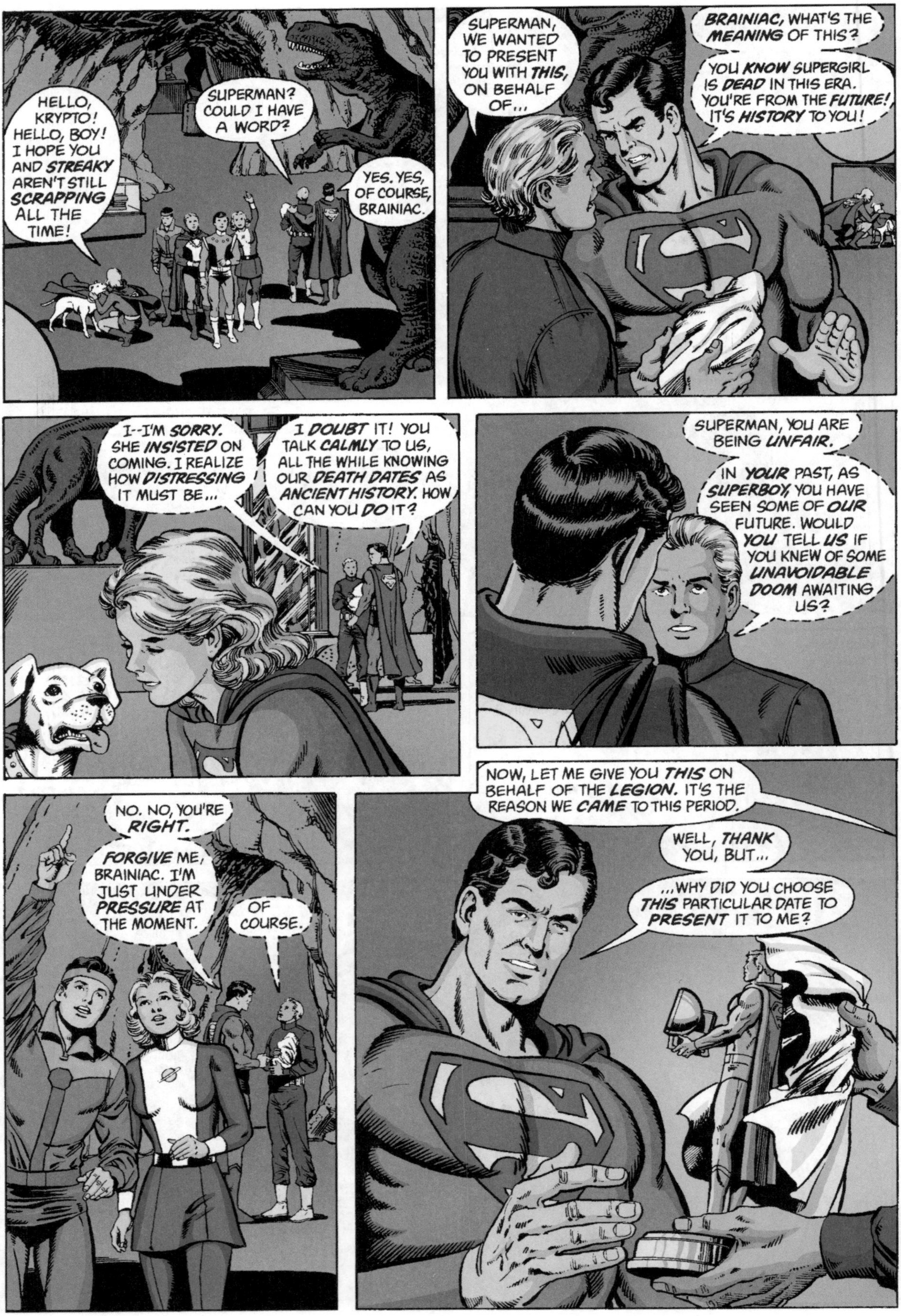
HELLO, KRYPTO! HELLO, BOY! I HOPE YOU AND STREAKY AREN'T STILL SCRAPPING ALL THE TIME!
SUPERMAN? COULD I HAVE A WORD?
YES. YES, OF COURSE, BRAINIAC.
SUPERMAN, WE WANTED TO PRESENT YOU WITH THIS, ON BEHALF OF...
BRAINIAC, WHAT'S THE MEANING OF THIS?
YOU KNOW SUPERGIRL IS DEAD IN THIS ERA. YOU'RE FROM THE FUTURE! IT'S HISTORY TO YOU!
I--I'M SORRY. SHE INSISTED ON COMING. I REALIZE HOW DISTRESSING IT MUST BE...
I DOUBT IT! YOU TALK CALMLY TO US, ALL THE WHILE KNOWING OUR DEATH DATES AS ANCIENT HISTORY. HOW CAN YOU DO IT?
SUPERMAN, YOU ARE BEING UNFAIR.
IN YOUR PAST, AS SUPERBOY, YOU HAVE SEEN SOME OF OUR FUTURE. WOULD YOU TELL US IF YOU KNEW OF SOME UNAVOIDABLE DOOM AWAITING US?
NO. NO, YOU'RE RIGHT.
FORGIVE ME, BRAINIAC. I'M JUST UNDER PRESSURE AT THE MOMENT.
OF COURSE.
NOW, LET ME GIVE YOU THIS ON BEHALF OF THE LEGION. IT'S THE REASON WE CAME TO THIS PERIOD.
WELL, THANK YOU, BUT...
...WHY DID YOU CHOOSE THIS PARTICULAR DATE TO PRESENT IT TO ME?

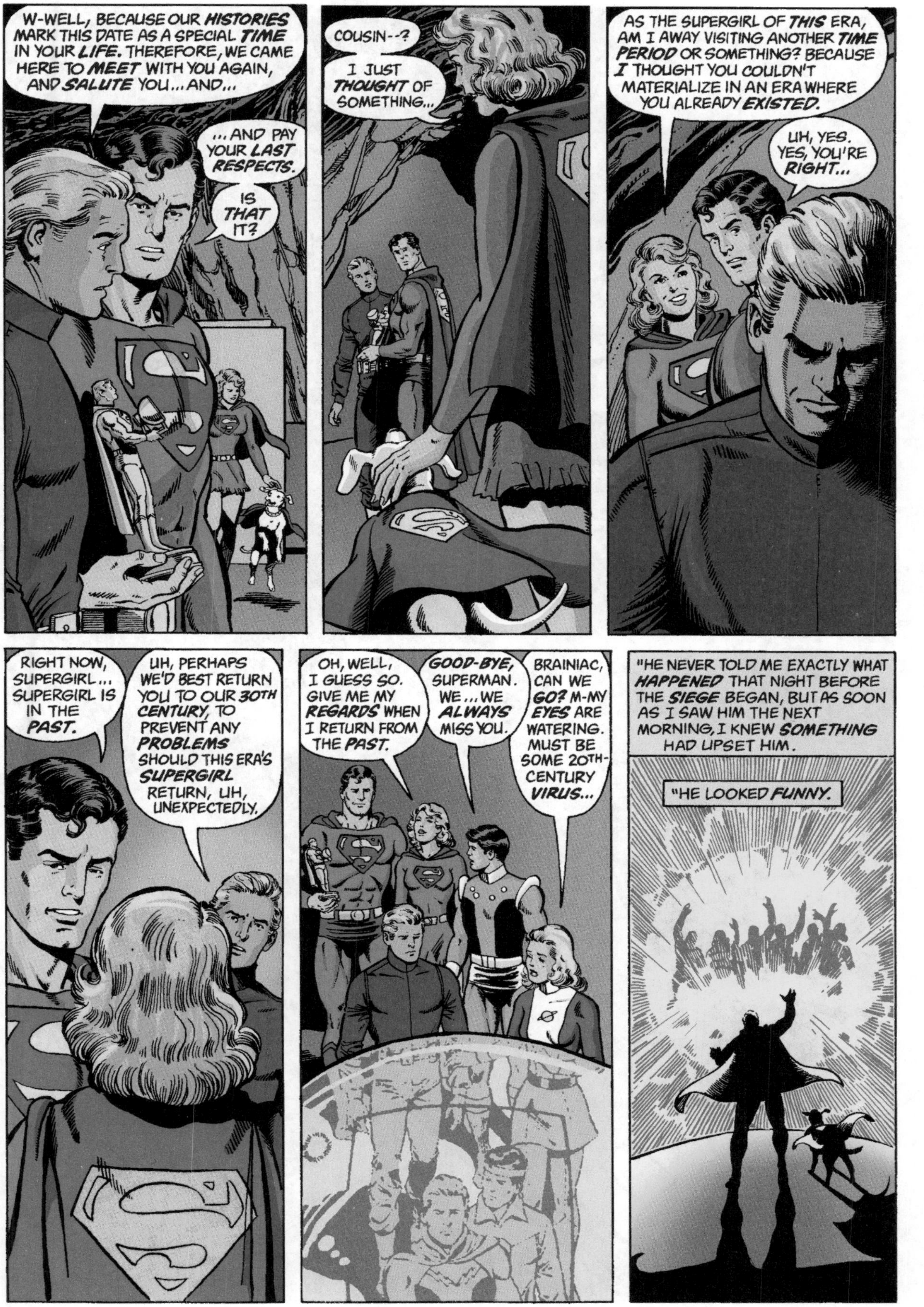

W-WELL, BECAUSE OUR HISTORIES MARK THIS DATE AS A SPECIAL TIME IN YOUR LIFE. THEREFORE, WE CAME HERE TO MEET WITH YOU AGAIN, AND SALUTE YOU... AND...
...AND PAY YOUR LAST RESPECTS.
IS THAT IT?
COUSIN--?
I JUST THOUGHT OF SOMETHING...
AS THE SUPERGIRL OF THIS ERA, AM I AWAY VISITING ANOTHER TIME PERIOD OR SOMETHING? BECAUSE I THOUGHT YOU COULDN'T MATERIALIZE IN AN ERA WHERE YOU ALREADY EXISTED.
UH, YES. YES, YOU'RE RIGHT...
RIGHT NOW, SUPERGIRL... SUPERGIRL IS IN THE PAST.
UH, PERHAPS WE'D BEST RETURN YOU TO OUR 30TH CENTURY, TO PREVENT ANY PROBLEMS SHOULD THIS ERA'S SUPERGIRL RETURN, UH, UNEXPECTEDLY.
OH, WELL, I GUESS SO. GIVE ME MY REGARDS WHEN I RETURN FROM THE PAST.
GOOD-BYE, SUPERMAN. WE... WE ALWAYS MISS YOU.
BRAINIAC, CAN WE GO? M-MY EYES ARE WATERING. MUST BE SOME 20TH-CENTURY VIRUS...
"HE NEVER TOLD ME EXACTLY WHAT HAPPENED THAT NIGHT BEFORE THE SIEGE BEGAN, BUT AS SOON AS I SAW HIM THE NEXT MORNING, I KNEW SOMETHING HAD UPSET HIM.
"HE LOOKED FUNNY.

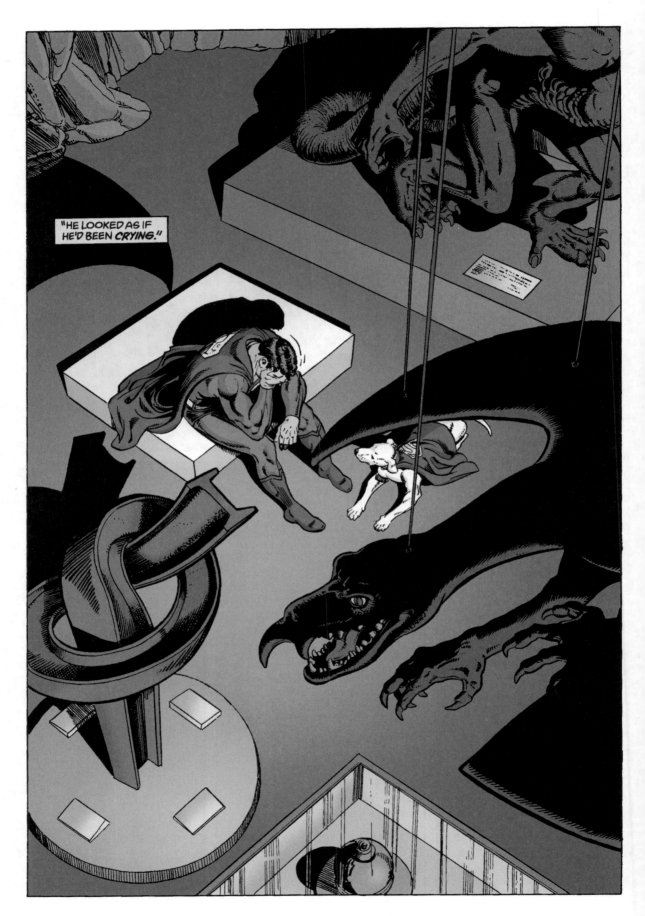

"HE LOOKED AS IF HE'D BEEN *CRYING*."

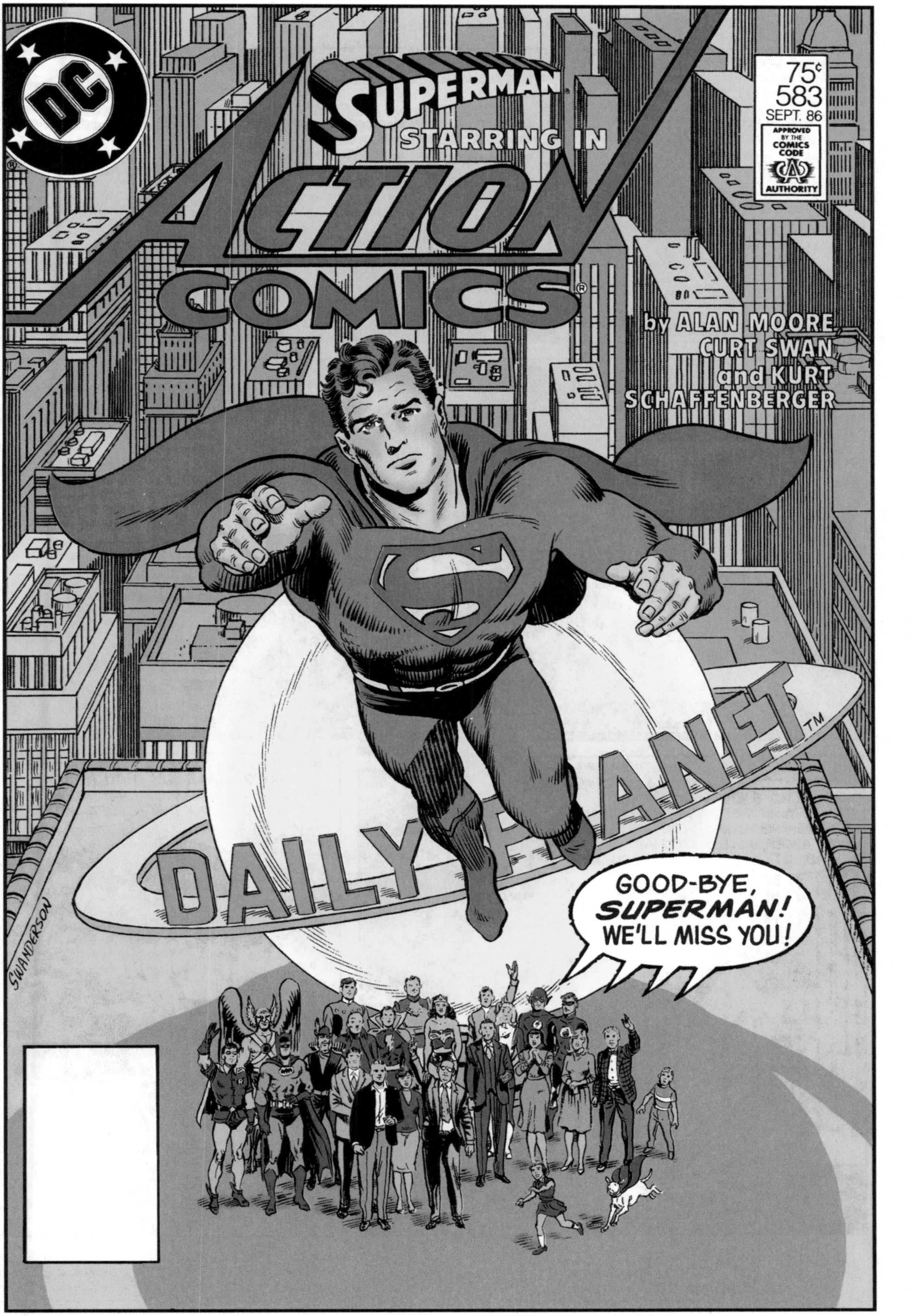
DC
SUPERMAN
STARRING IN
ACTION COMICS
75¢
583
SEPT. 86
APPROVED BY THE COMICS CODE AUTHORITY
by ALAN MOORE
CURT SWAN
and KURT
SCHAFFENBERGER
DAILY PLANET
GOOD-BYE, SUPERMAN! WE'LL MISS YOU!
SWANDERSON

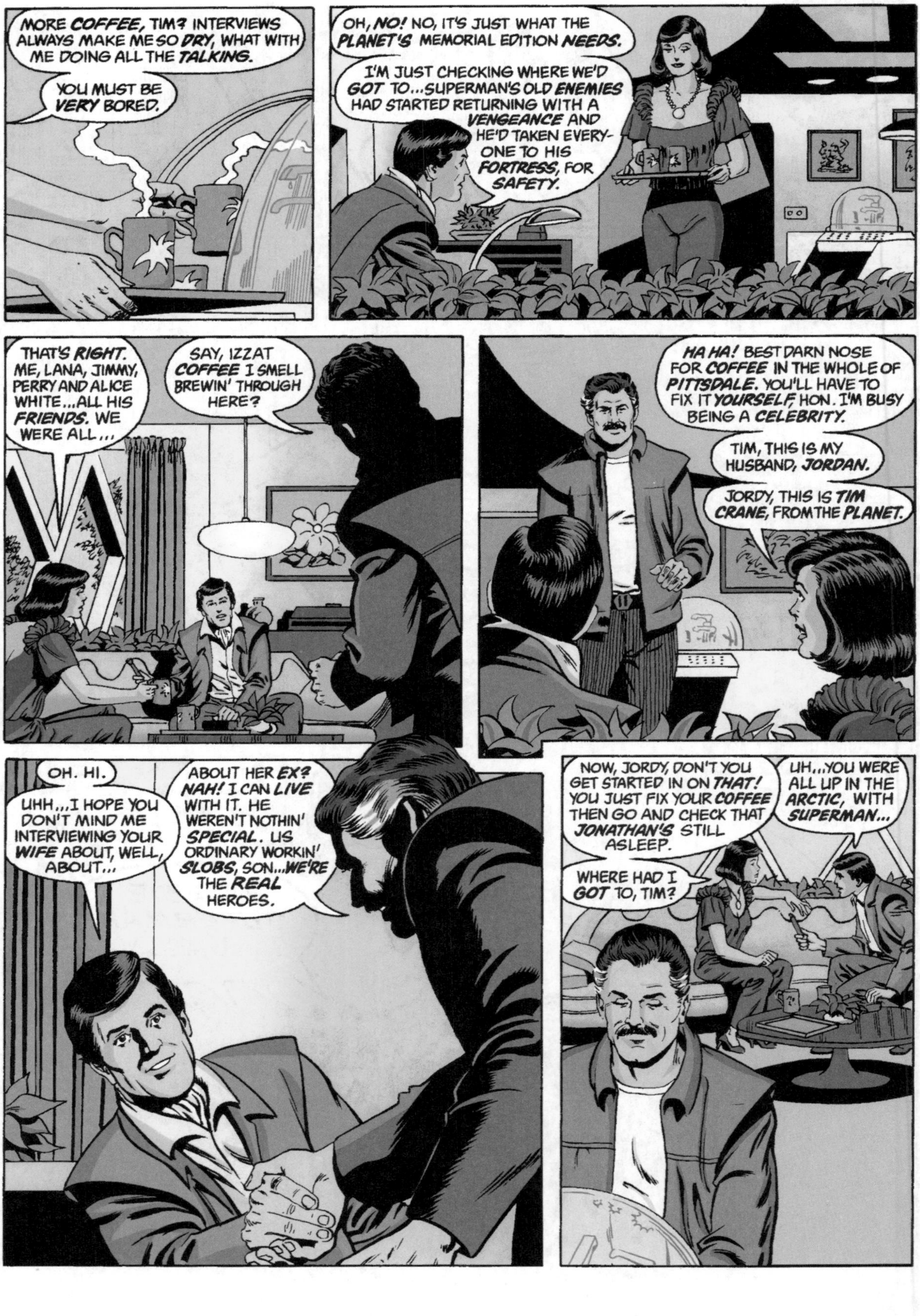

MORE COFFEE, TIM? INTERVIEWS ALWAYS MAKE ME SO DRY, WHAT WITH ME DOING ALL THE TALKING.
YOU MUST BE VERY BORED.
OH, NO! NO, IT'S JUST WHAT THE PLANET'S MEMORIAL EDITION NEEDS.
I'M JUST CHECKING WHERE WE'D GOT TO...SUPERMAN'S OLD ENEMIES HAD STARTED RETURNING WITH A VENGEANCE AND HE'D TAKEN EVERY-ONE TO HIS FORTRESS, FOR SAFETY.
THAT'S RIGHT. ME, LANA, JIMMY, PERRY AND ALICE WHITE...ALL HIS FRIENDS. WE WERE ALL...
SAY, IZZAT COFFEE I SMELL BREWIN' THROUGH HERE?
HA HA! BEST DARN NOSE FOR COFFEE IN THE WHOLE OF PITTSDALE. YOU'LL HAVE TO FIX IT YOURSELF, HON. I'M BUSY BEING A CELEBRITY.
TIM, THIS IS MY HUSBAND, JORDAN.
JORDY, THIS IS TIM CRANE, FROM THE PLANET.
OH. HI.
UHH...I HOPE YOU DON'T MIND ME INTERVIEWING YOUR WIFE ABOUT, WELL, ABOUT...
ABOUT HER EX? NAH! I CAN LIVE WITH IT. HE WEREN'T NOTHIN' SPECIAL. US ORDINARY WORKIN' SLOBS, SON...WE'RE THE REAL HEROES.
NOW, JORDY, DON'T YOU GET STARTED IN ON THAT! YOU JUST FIX YOUR COFFEE THEN GO AND CHECK THAT JONATHAN'S STILL ASLEEP.
WHERE HAD I GOT TO, TIM?
UH...YOU WERE ALL UP IN THE ARCTIC, WITH SUPERMAN...

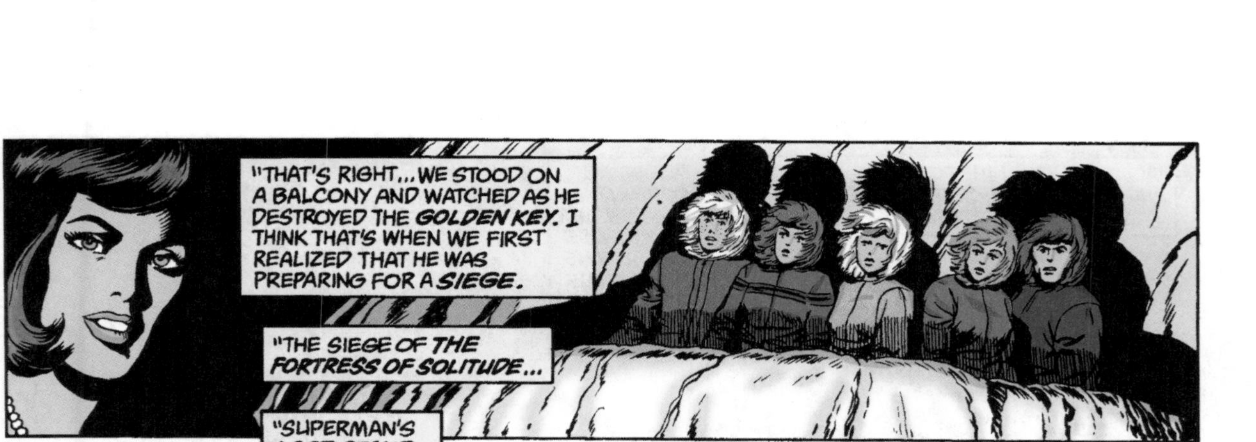
"THAT'S RIGHT... WE STOOD ON A BALCONY AND WATCHED AS HE DESTROYED THE GOLDEN KEY. I THINK THAT'S WHEN WE FIRST REALIZED THAT HE WAS PREPARING FOR A SIEGE.
"THE SIEGE OF THE FORTRESS OF SOLITUDE...
"SUPERMAN'S LAST STAND.

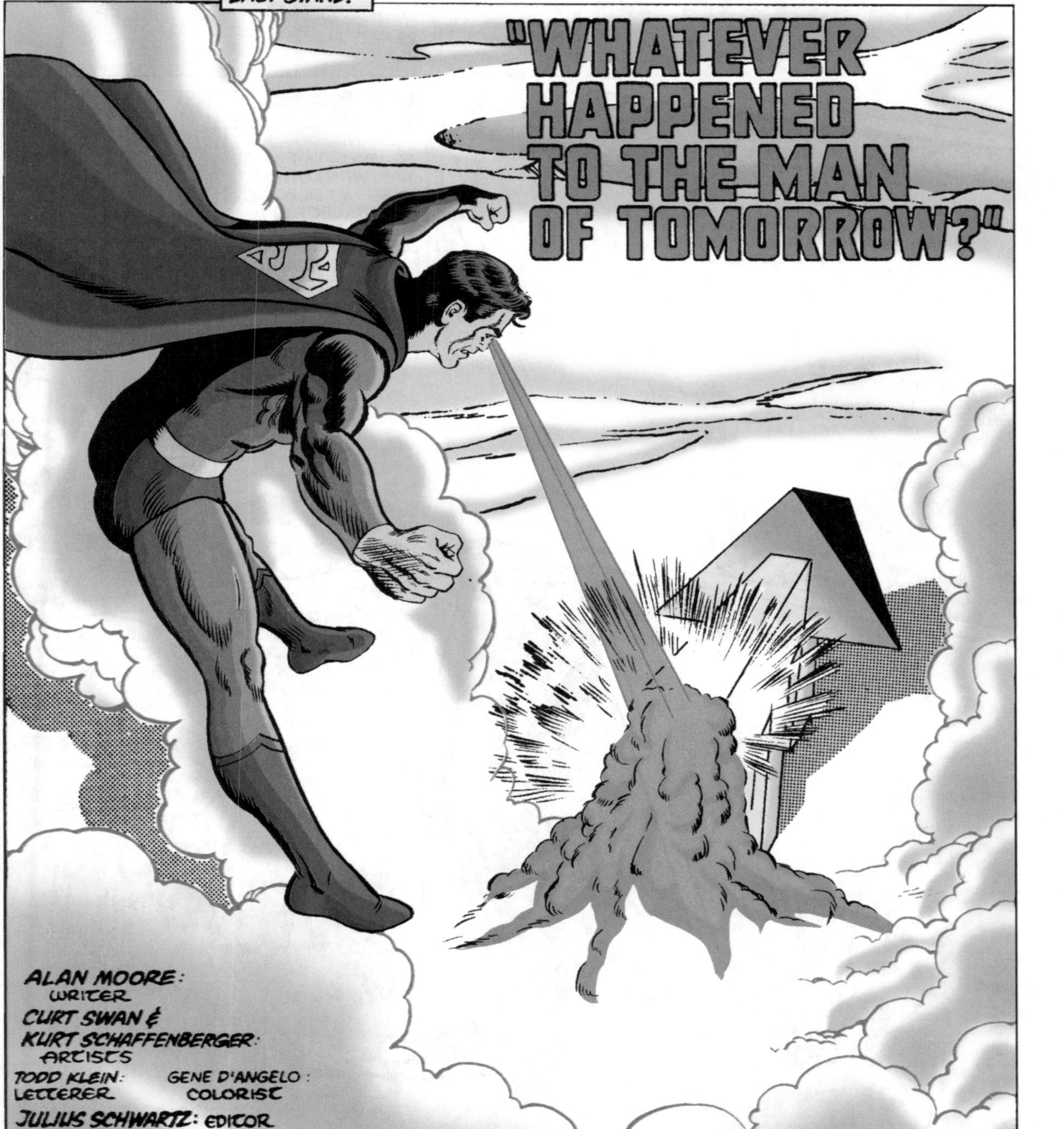
"WHATEVER HAPPENED TO THE MAN OF TOMORROW?"
ALAN MOORE: WRITER
CURT SWAN & KURT SCHAFFENBERGER: ARTISTS
TODD KLEIN: LETTERER
GENE D'ANGELO: COLORIST
JULIUS SCHWARTZ: EDITOR

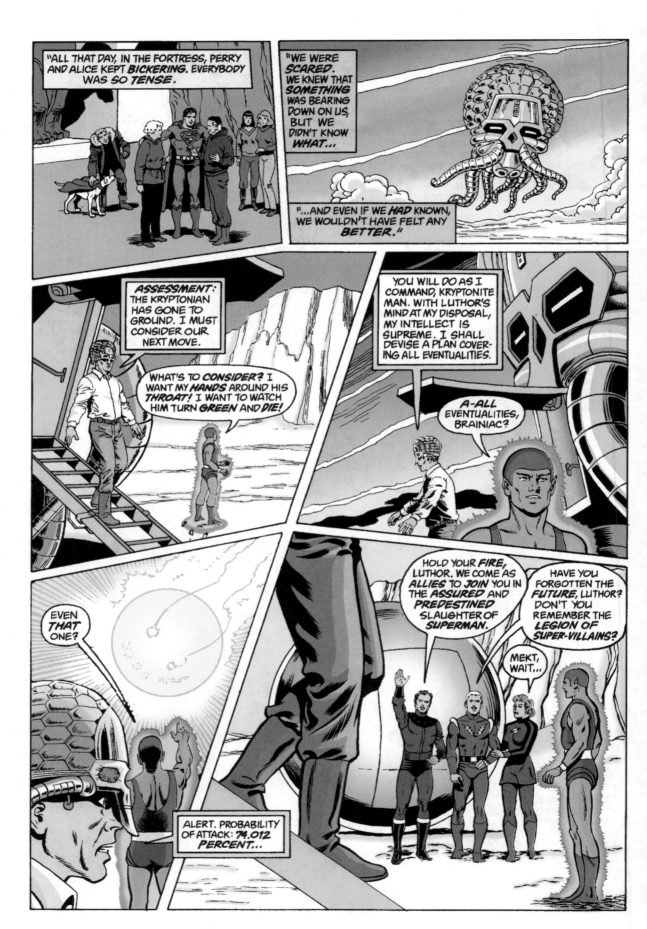

"ALL THAT DAY, IN THE FORTRESS, PERRY AND ALICE KEPT *BICKERING.* EVERYBODY WAS SO *TENSE.*

"WE WERE *SCARED.* WE KNEW THAT *SOMETHING* WAS BEARING DOWN ON US, BUT WE DIDN'T KNOW *WHAT...*

"...AND EVEN IF WE *HAD* KNOWN, WE WOULDN'T HAVE FELT ANY *BETTER.*"

ASSESSMENT: THE KRYPTONIAN HAS GONE TO GROUND. I MUST CONSIDER OUR NEXT MOVE.

WHAT'S TO *CONSIDER?* I WANT MY *HANDS* AROUND HIS *THROAT!* I WANT TO WATCH HIM TURN *GREEN* AND *DIE!*

YOU WILL DO AS I COMMAND, KRYPTONITE MAN. WITH LUTHOR'S MIND AT MY DISPOSAL, MY INTELLECT IS SUPREME. I SHALL DEVISE A PLAN COVERING ALL EVENTUALITIES.

A-ALL EVENTUALITIES, BRAINIAC?

EVEN *THAT* ONE?

HOLD YOUR *FIRE,* LUTHOR. WE COME AS *ALLIES* TO *JOIN* YOU IN THE *ASSURED* AND *PREDESTINED* SLAUGHTER OF *SUPERMAN.*

HAVE YOU FORGOTTEN THE *FUTURE,* LUTHOR? DON'T YOU REMEMBER THE *LEGION OF SUPER-VILLAINS?*

MEKT, WAIT...

ALERT. PROBABILITY OF ATTACK: *74.012 PERCENT...*

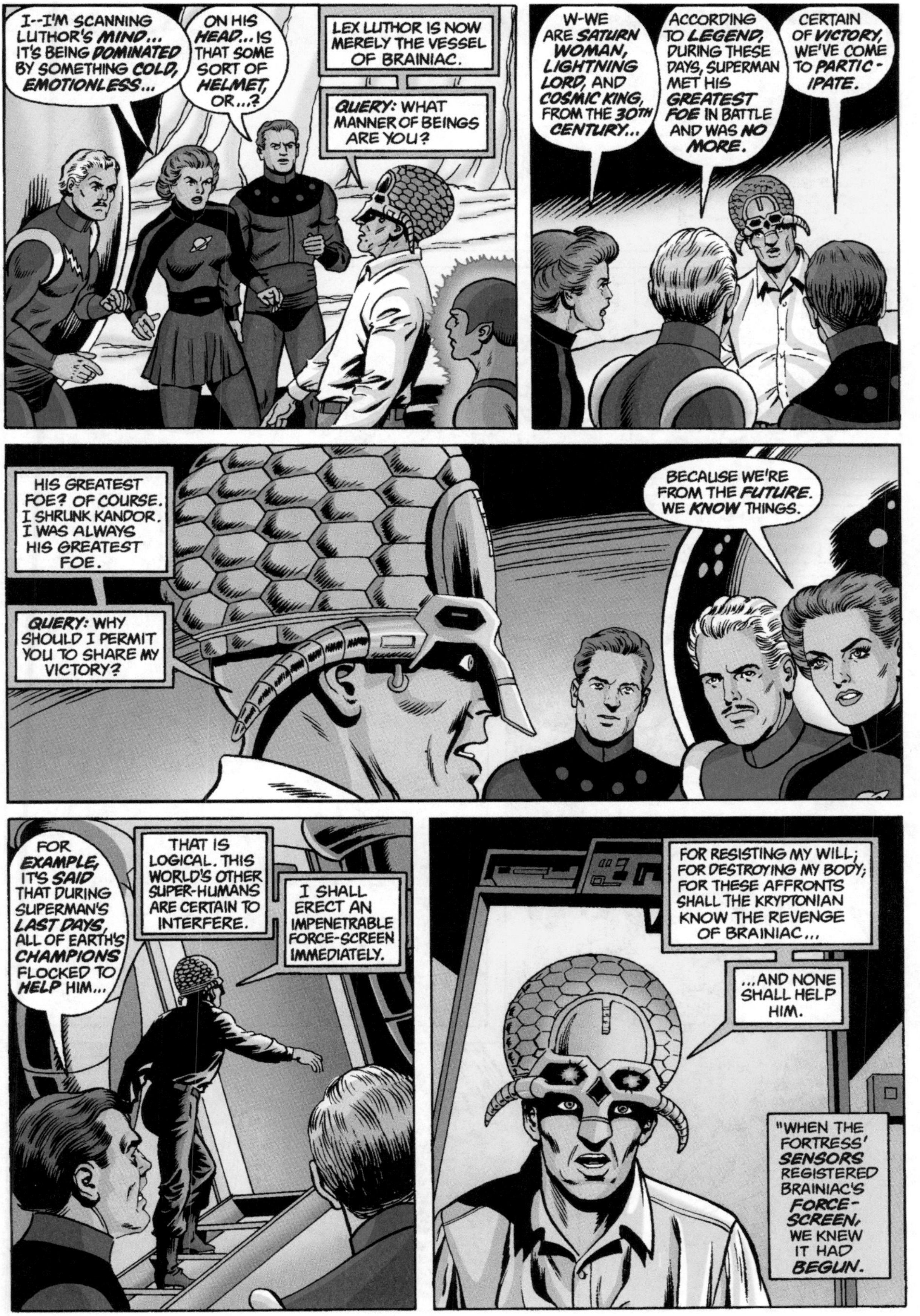
I--I'M SCANNING LUTHOR'S MIND... IT'S BEING DOMINATED BY SOMETHING COLD, EMOTIONLESS...
ON HIS HEAD... IS THAT SOME SORT OF HELMET, OR...?
LEX LUTHOR IS NOW MERELY THE VESSEL OF BRAINIAC.
QUERY: WHAT MANNER OF BEINGS ARE YOU?
W-WE ARE SATURN WOMAN, LIGHTNING LORD, AND COSMIC KING, FROM THE 30TH CENTURY...
ACCORDING TO LEGEND, DURING THESE DAYS, SUPERMAN MET HIS GREATEST FOE IN BATTLE AND WAS NO MORE.
CERTAIN OF VICTORY, WE'VE COME TO PARTIC-IPATE.
HIS GREATEST FOE? OF COURSE. I SHRUNK KANDOR. I WAS ALWAYS HIS GREATEST FOE.
QUERY: WHY SHOULD I PERMIT YOU TO SHARE MY VICTORY?
BECAUSE WE'RE FROM THE FUTURE. WE KNOW THINGS.
FOR EXAMPLE, IT'S SAID THAT DURING SUPERMAN'S LAST DAYS, ALL OF EARTH'S CHAMPIONS FLOCKED TO HELP HIM...
THAT IS LOGICAL. THIS WORLD'S OTHER SUPER-HUMANS ARE CERTAIN TO INTERFERE.
I SHALL ERECT AN IMPENETRABLE FORCE-SCREEN IMMEDIATELY.
FOR RESISTING MY WILL; FOR DESTROYING MY BODY; FOR THESE AFFRONTS SHALL THE KRYPTONIAN KNOW THE REVENGE OF BRAINIAC...
...AND NONE SHALL HELP HIM.
"WHEN THE FORTRESS' SENSORS REGISTERED BRAINIAC'S FORCE-SCREEN, WE KNEW IT HAD BEGUN.

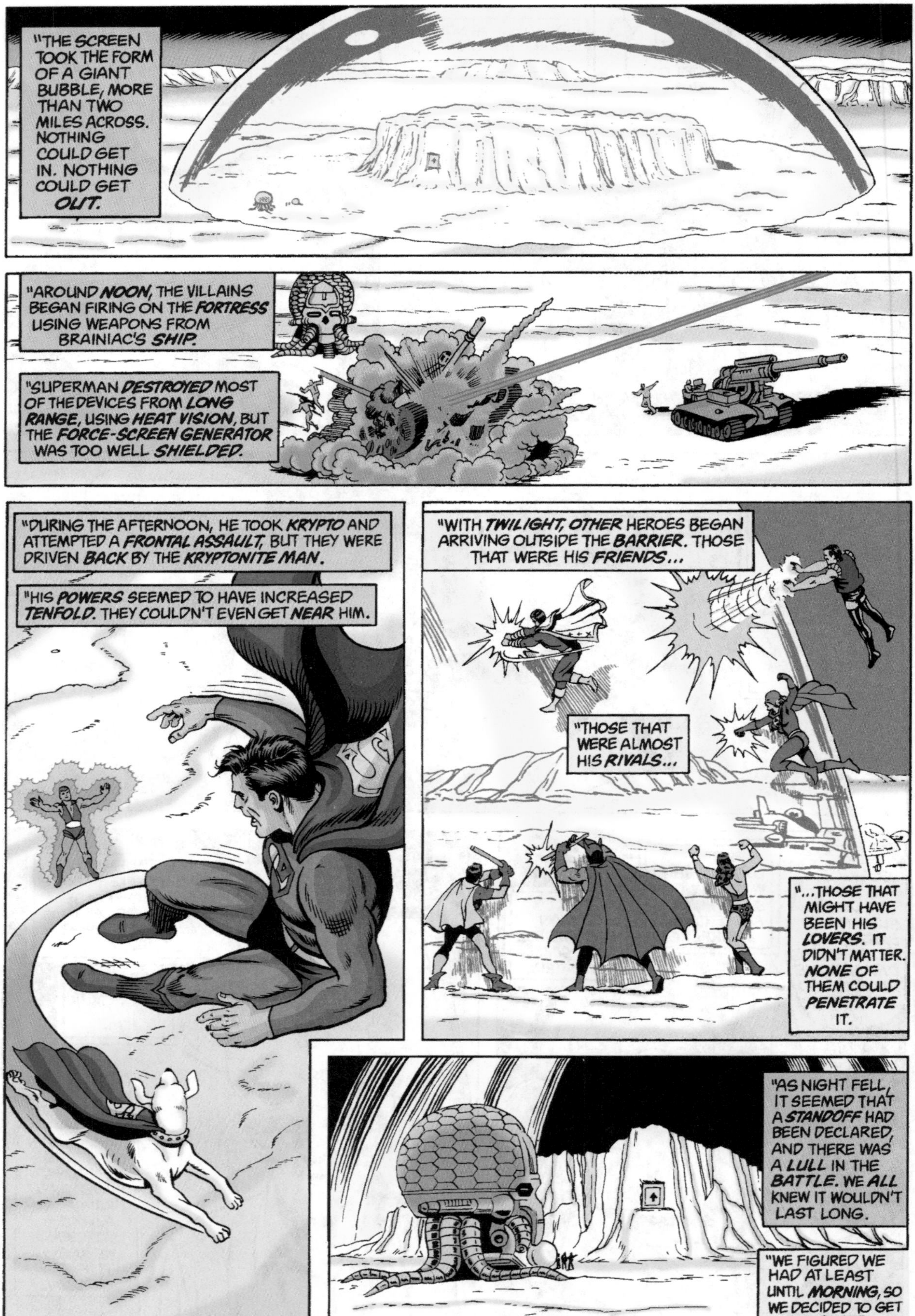
"THE SCREEN TOOK THE FORM OF A GIANT BUBBLE, MORE THAN TWO MILES ACROSS. NOTHING COULD GET IN. NOTHING COULD GET OUT.
"AROUND NOON, THE VILLAINS BEGAN FIRING ON THE FORTRESS USING WEAPONS FROM BRAINIAC'S SHIP.
"SUPERMAN DESTROYED MOST OF THE DEVICES FROM LONG RANGE, USING HEAT VISION, BUT THE FORCE-SCREEN GENERATOR WAS TOO WELL SHIELDED.
"DURING THE AFTERNOON, HE TOOK KRYPTO AND ATTEMPTED A FRONTAL ASSAULT, BUT THEY WERE DRIVEN BACK BY THE KRYPTONITE MAN.
"HIS POWERS SEEMED TO HAVE INCREASED TENFOLD. THEY COULDN'T EVEN GET NEAR HIM.
"WITH TWILIGHT, OTHER HEROES BEGAN ARRIVING OUTSIDE THE BARRIER. THOSE THAT WERE HIS FRIENDS...
"THOSE THAT WERE ALMOST HIS RIVALS...
"...THOSE THAT MIGHT HAVE BEEN HIS LOVERS. IT DIDN'T MATTER. NONE OF THEM COULD PENETRATE IT.
"AS NIGHT FELL, IT SEEMED THAT A STANDOFF HAD BEEN DECLARED, AND THERE WAS A LULL IN THE BATTLE. WE ALL KNEW IT WOULDN'T LAST LONG.
"WE FIGURED WE HAD AT LEAST UNTIL MORNING, SO WE DECIDED TO GET SOME SLEEP...

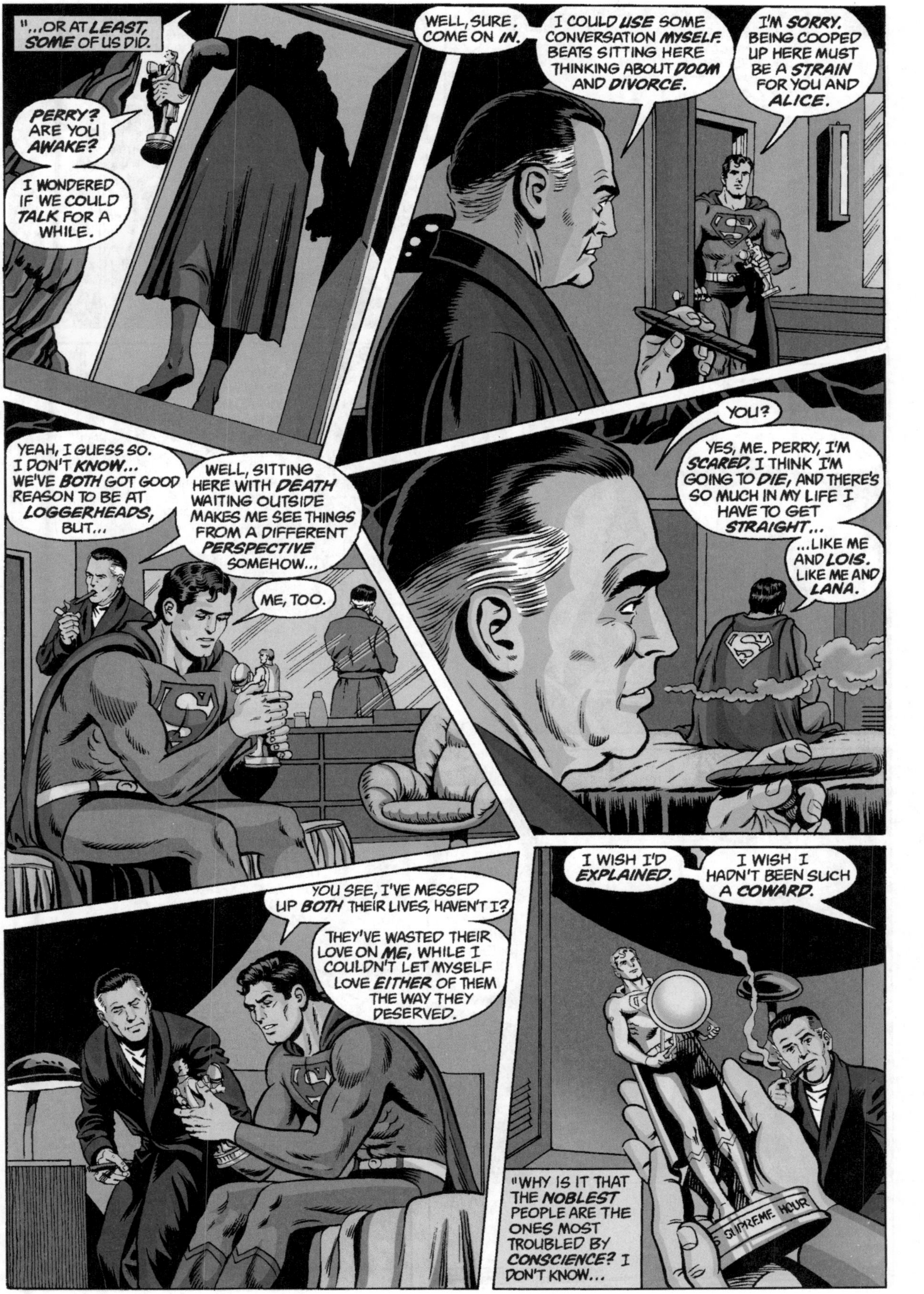
"...OR AT LEAST, SOME OF US DID.
PERRY? ARE YOU AWAKE?
I WONDERED IF WE COULD TALK FOR A WHILE.
WELL, SURE. COME ON IN.
I COULD USE SOME CONVERSATION MYSELF. BEATS SITTING HERE THINKING ABOUT DOOM AND DIVORCE.
I'M SORRY. BEING COOPED UP HERE MUST BE A STRAIN FOR YOU AND ALICE.
YEAH, I GUESS SO. I DON'T KNOW... WE'VE BOTH GOT GOOD REASON TO BE AT LOGGERHEADS, BUT...
WELL, SITTING HERE WITH DEATH WAITING OUTSIDE MAKES ME SEE THINGS FROM A DIFFERENT PERSPECTIVE SOMEHOW...
ME, TOO.
YOU?
YES, ME. PERRY, I'M SCARED. I THINK I'M GOING TO DIE, AND THERE'S SO MUCH IN MY LIFE I HAVE TO GET STRAIGHT...
...LIKE ME AND LOIS. LIKE ME AND LANA.
YOU SEE, I'VE MESSED UP BOTH THEIR LIVES, HAVEN'T I?
THEY'VE WASTED THEIR LOVE ON ME, WHILE I COULDN'T LET MYSELF LOVE EITHER OF THEM THE WAY THEY DESERVED.
I WISH I'D EXPLAINED.
I WISH I HADN'T BEEN SUCH A COWARD.
"WHY IS IT THAT THE NOBLEST PEOPLE ARE THE ONES MOST TROUBLED BY CONSCIENCE? I DON'T KNOW...
SUPREME HOUR

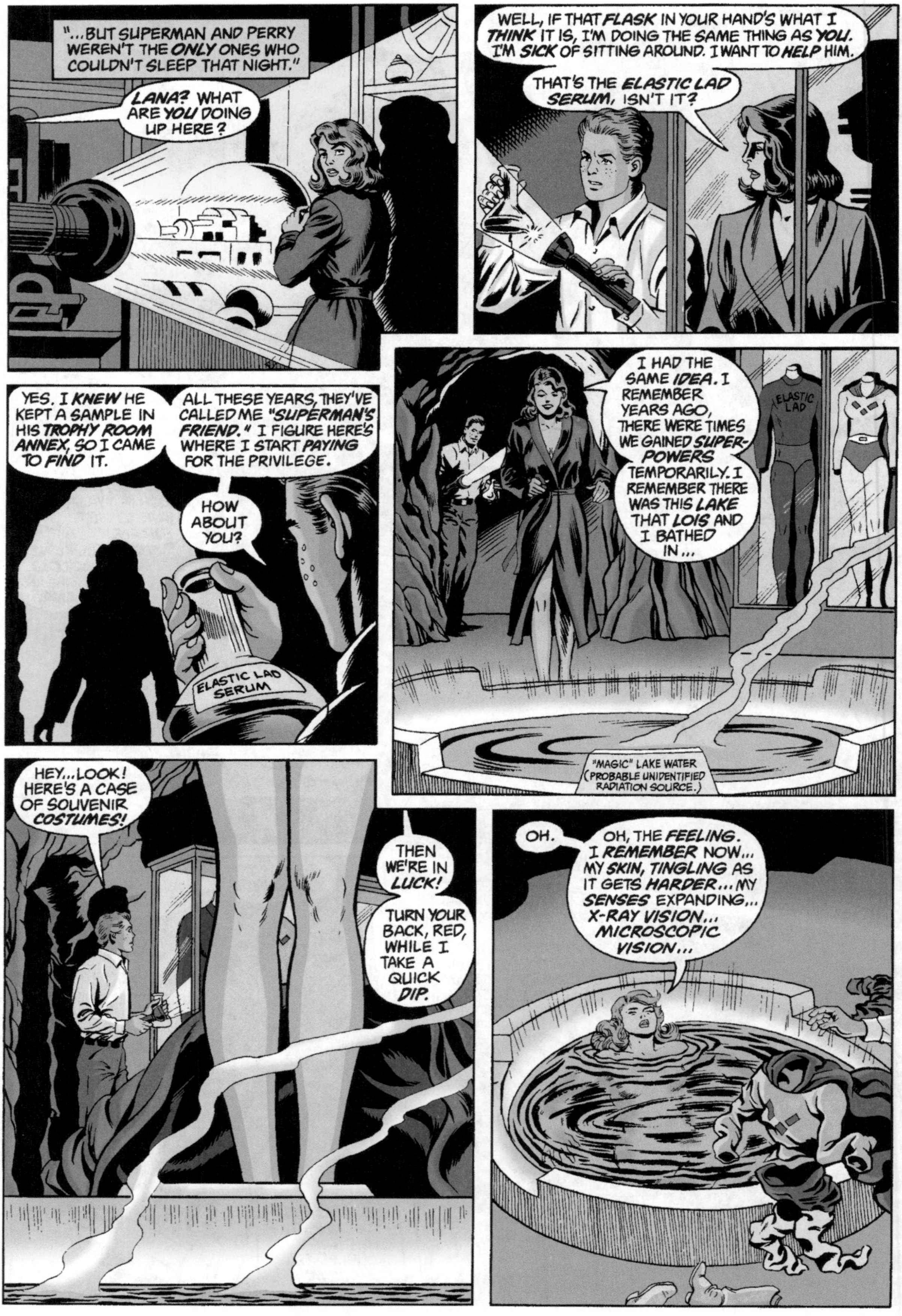
"...BUT SUPERMAN AND PERRY WEREN'T THE ONLY ONES WHO COULDN'T SLEEP THAT NIGHT."
LANA? WHAT ARE YOU DOING UP HERE?
WELL, IF THAT FLASK IN YOUR HAND'S WHAT I THINK IT IS, I'M DOING THE SAME THING AS YOU. I'M SICK OF SITTING AROUND. I WANT TO HELP HIM.
THAT'S THE ELASTIC LAD SERUM, ISN'T IT?
YES. I KNEW HE KEPT A SAMPLE IN HIS TROPHY ROOM ANNEX, SO I CAME TO FIND IT.
ALL THESE YEARS, THEY'VE CALLED ME "SUPERMAN'S FRIEND." I FIGURE HERE'S WHERE I START PAYING FOR THE PRIVILEGE.
HOW ABOUT YOU?
ELASTIC LAD SERUM
I HAD THE SAME IDEA. I REMEMBER YEARS AGO, THERE WERE TIMES WE GAINED SUPER-POWERS TEMPORARILY. I REMEMBER THERE WAS THIS LAKE THAT LOIS AND I BATHED IN...
ELASTIC LAD
"MAGIC" LAKE WATER (PROBABLE UNIDENTIFIED RADIATION SOURCE.)
HEY...LOOK! HERE'S A CASE OF SOUVENIR COSTUMES!
THEN WE'RE IN LUCK!
TURN YOUR BACK, RED, WHILE I TAKE A QUICK DIP.
OH.
OH, THE FEELING. I REMEMBER NOW... MY SKIN, TINGLING AS IT GETS HARDER... MY SENSES EXPANDING... X-RAY VISION... MICROSCOPIC VISION...

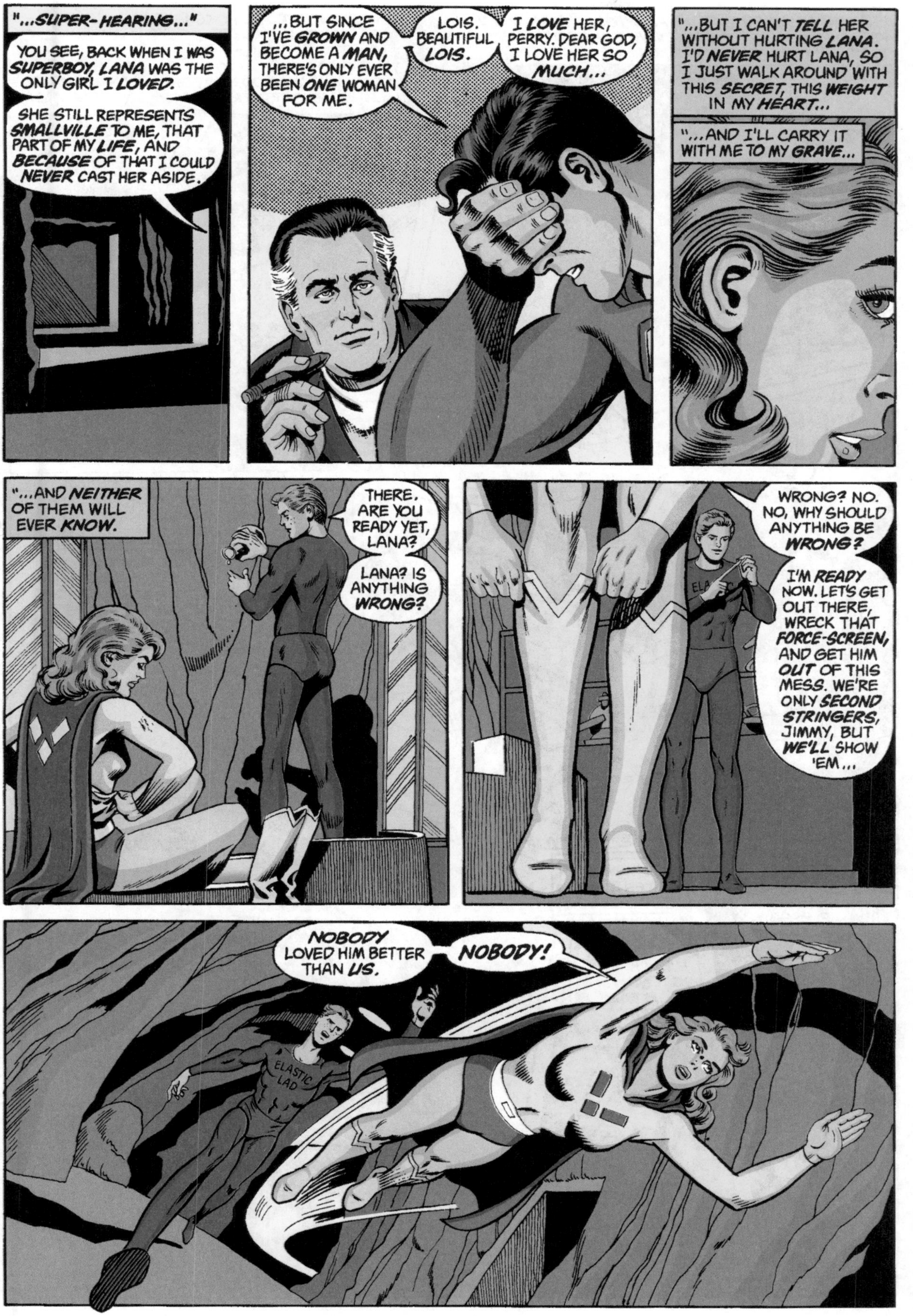
"...SUPER-HEARING..."
YOU SEE, BACK WHEN I WAS SUPERBOY, LANA WAS THE ONLY GIRL I LOVED.
SHE STILL REPRESENTS SMALLVILLE TO ME, THAT PART OF MY LIFE, AND BECAUSE OF THAT I COULD NEVER CAST HER ASIDE.
...BUT SINCE I'VE GROWN AND BECOME A MAN, THERE'S ONLY EVER BEEN ONE WOMAN FOR ME.
LOIS. BEAUTIFUL LOIS.
I LOVE HER, PERRY. DEAR GOD, I LOVE HER SO MUCH...
"...BUT I CAN'T TELL HER WITHOUT HURTING LANA. I'D NEVER HURT LANA, SO I JUST WALK AROUND WITH THIS SECRET, THIS WEIGHT IN MY HEART...
"...AND I'LL CARRY IT WITH ME TO MY GRAVE...
"...AND NEITHER OF THEM WILL EVER KNOW.
THERE. ARE YOU READY YET, LANA?
LANA? IS ANYTHING WRONG?
WRONG? NO. NO, WHY SHOULD ANYTHING BE WRONG?
I'M READY NOW. LET'S GET OUT THERE, WRECK THAT FORCE-SCREEN, AND GET HIM OUT OF THIS MESS. WE'RE ONLY SECOND STRINGERS, JIMMY, BUT WE'LL SHOW 'EM...
NOBODY LOVED HIM BETTER THAN US.
NOBODY!
ELASTIC LAD

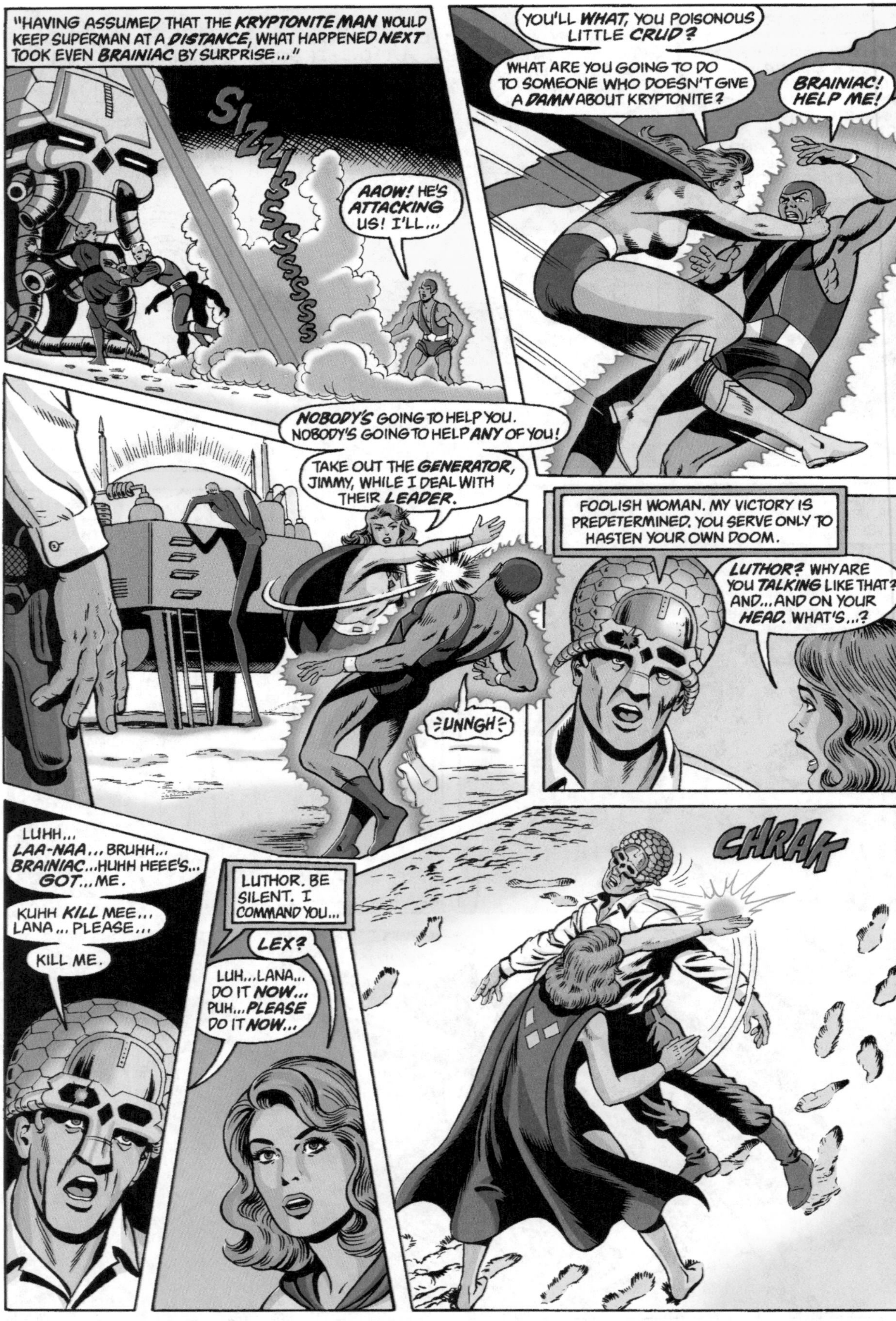
"HAVING ASSUMED THAT THE KRYPTONITE MAN WOULD KEEP SUPERMAN AT A DISTANCE, WHAT HAPPENED NEXT TOOK EVEN BRAINIAC BY SURPRISE..."
SIZZISSSSSSS
AAOW! HE'S ATTACKING US! I'LL...
YOU'LL WHAT, YOU POISONOUS LITTLE CRUD?
WHAT ARE YOU GOING TO DO TO SOMEONE WHO DOESN'T GIVE A DAMN ABOUT KRYPTONITE?
BRAINIAC! HELP ME!
NOBODY'S GOING TO HELP YOU. NOBODY'S GOING TO HELP ANY OF YOU!
TAKE OUT THE GENERATOR, JIMMY, WHILE I DEAL WITH THEIR LEADER.
UNNGH
FOOLISH WOMAN. MY VICTORY IS PREDETERMINED. YOU SERVE ONLY TO HASTEN YOUR OWN DOOM.
LUTHOR? WHY ARE YOU TALKING LIKE THAT? AND... AND ON YOUR HEAD. WHAT'S...?
LUHH... LAA-NAA... BRUHH... BRAINIAC...HUHH HEEE'S... GOT...ME.
KUHH KILL MEE... LANA... PLEASE...
KILL ME.
LUTHOR. BE SILENT. I COMMAND YOU...
LEX?
LUH...LANA... DO IT NOW... PUH...PLEASE DO IT NOW...
CHRAK

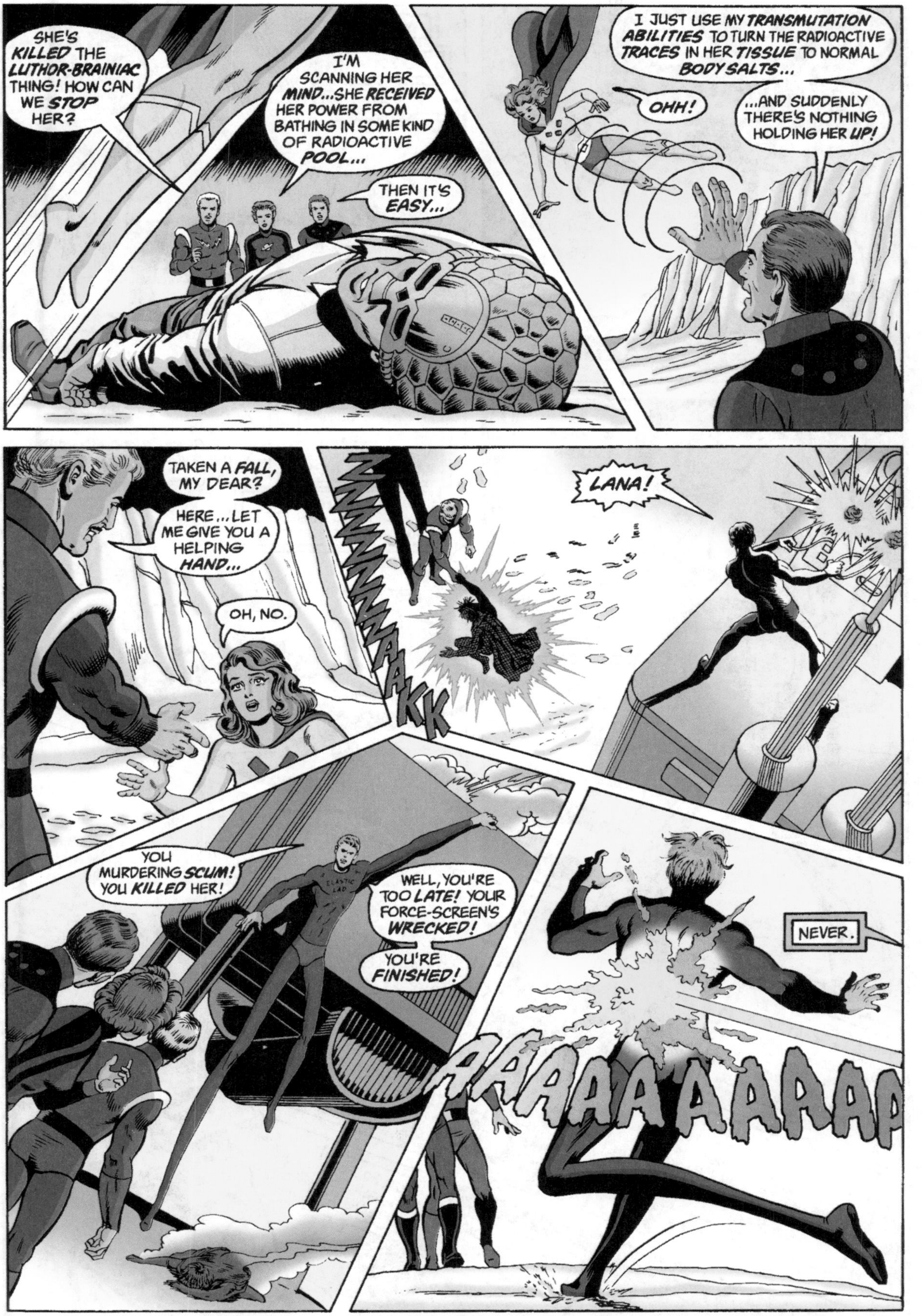
SHE'S KILLED THE LUTHOR-BRAINIAC THING! HOW CAN WE STOP HER?
I'M SCANNING HER MIND...SHE RECEIVED HER POWER FROM BATHING IN SOME KIND OF RADIOACTIVE POOL...
THEN IT'S EASY...
I JUST USE MY TRANSMUTATION ABILITIES TO TURN THE RADIOACTIVE TRACES IN HER TISSUE TO NORMAL BODY SALTS...
OHH!
...AND SUDDENLY THERE'S NOTHING HOLDING HER UP!
TAKEN A FALL, MY DEAR?
HERE... LET ME GIVE YOU A HELPING HAND...
OH, NO.
ZZZZZZZAAKK
LANA!
YOU MURDERING SCUM! YOU KILLED HER!
ELASTIC LAD
WELL, YOU'RE TOO LATE! YOUR FORCE-SCREEN'S WRECKED!
YOU'RE FINISHED!
NEVER.
AAAAAAAAAP

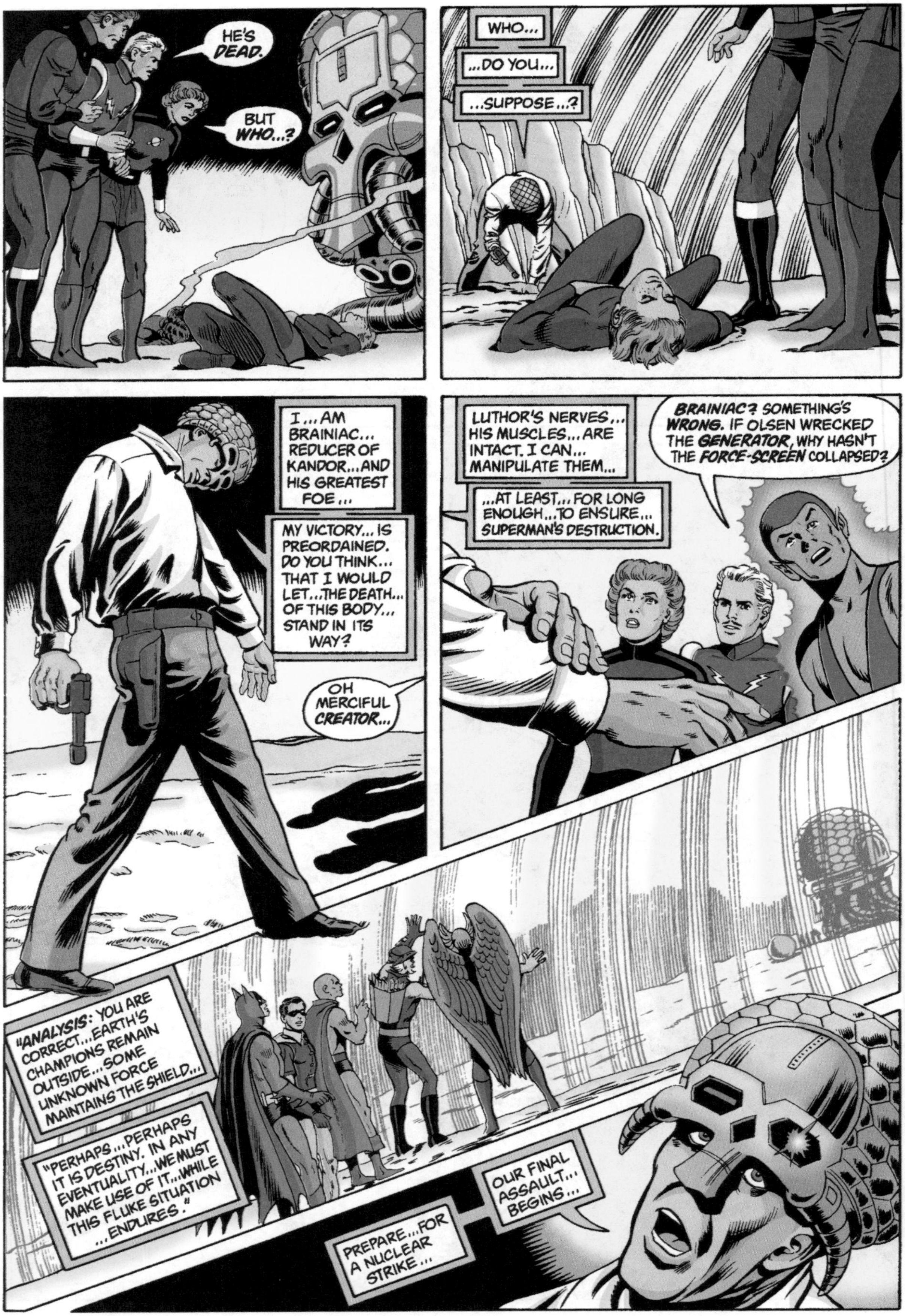
HE'S DEAD.
BUT WHO...?
WHO...
...DO YOU...
...SUPPOSE...?
I...AM BRAINIAC... REDUCER OF KANDOR...AND HIS GREATEST FOE...
MY VICTORY... IS PREORDAINED. DO YOU THINK... THAT I WOULD LET...THE DEATH... OF THIS BODY... STAND IN ITS WAY?
OH MERCIFUL CREATOR...
LUTHOR'S NERVES... HIS MUSCLES... ARE INTACT. I CAN... MANIPULATE THEM...
...AT LEAST... FOR LONG ENOUGH... TO ENSURE... SUPERMAN'S DESTRUCTION.
BRAINIAC? SOMETHING'S WRONG. IF OLSEN WRECKED THE GENERATOR, WHY HASN'T THE FORCE-SCREEN COLLAPSED?
"ANALYSIS: YOU ARE CORRECT... EARTH'S CHAMPIONS REMAIN OUTSIDE... SOME UNKNOWN FORCE MAINTAINS THE SHIELD...
"PERHAPS... PERHAPS IT IS DESTINY. IN ANY EVENTUALITY... WE MUST MAKE USE OF IT... WHILE THIS FLUKE SITUATION ...ENDURES."
OUR FINAL ASSAULT... BEGINS...
PREPARE... FOR A NUCLEAR STRIKE...

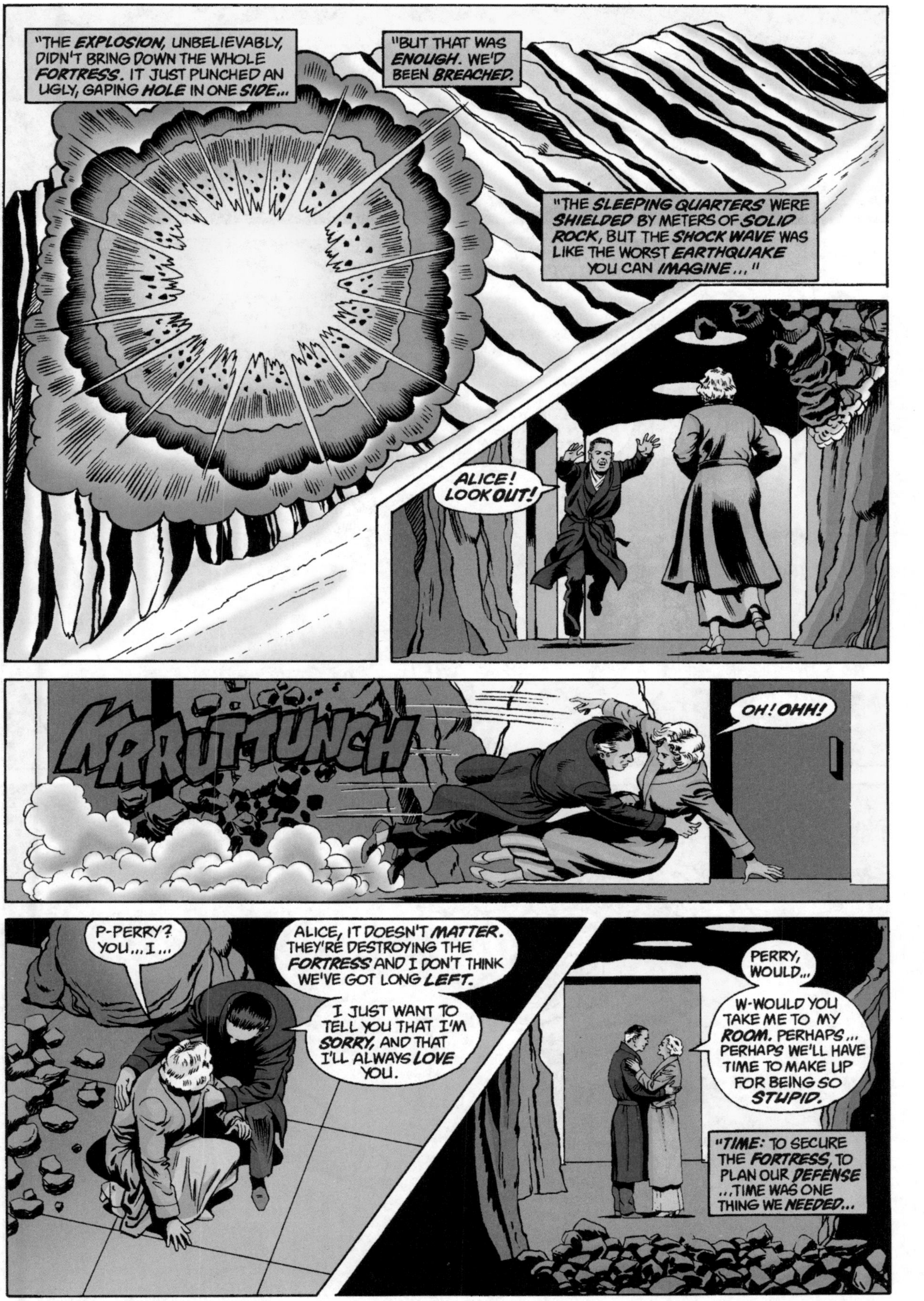
"THE EXPLOSION, UNBELIEVABLY, DIDN'T BRING DOWN THE WHOLE FORTRESS. IT JUST PUNCHED AN UGLY, GAPING HOLE IN ONE SIDE...
"BUT THAT WAS ENOUGH. WE'D BEEN BREACHED.
"THE SLEEPING QUARTERS WERE SHIELDED BY METERS OF SOLID ROCK, BUT THE SHOCK WAVE WAS LIKE THE WORST EARTHQUAKE YOU CAN IMAGINE..."
ALICE! LOOK OUT!
KRRUTTUNCH
OH! OHH!
P-PERRY? YOU... I...
ALICE, IT DOESN'T MATTER. THEY'RE DESTROYING THE FORTRESS AND I DON'T THINK WE'VE GOT LONG LEFT.
I JUST WANT TO TELL YOU THAT I'M SORRY, AND THAT I'LL ALWAYS LOVE YOU.
PERRY, WOULD...
W-WOULD YOU TAKE ME TO MY ROOM. PERHAPS... PERHAPS WE'LL HAVE TIME TO MAKE UP FOR BEING SO STUPID.
"TIME: TO SECURE THE FORTRESS, TO PLAN OUR DEFENSE ...TIME WAS ONE THING WE NEEDED...

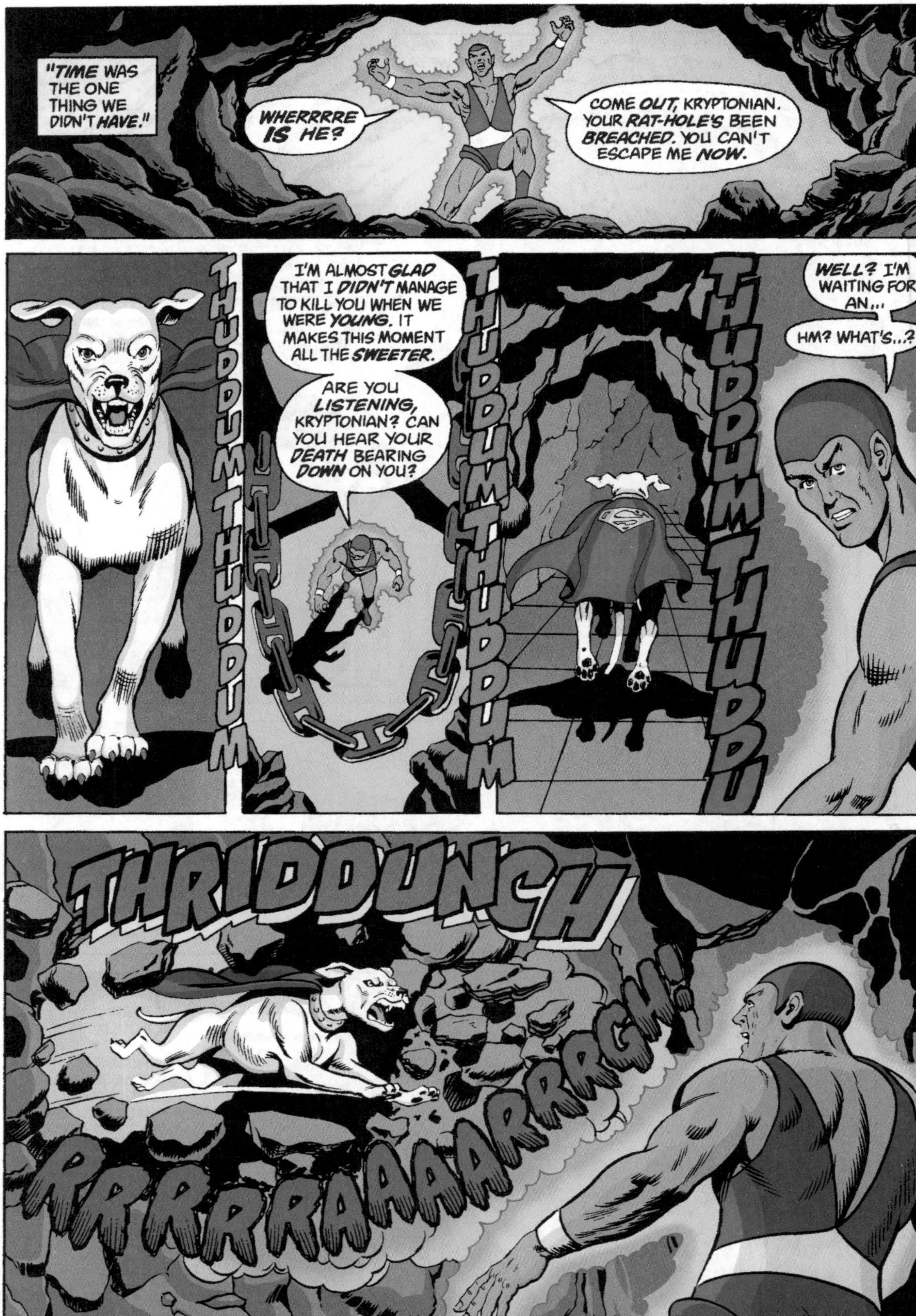
"TIME WAS THE ONE THING WE DIDN'T HAVE."
WHERRRRE IS HE?
COME OUT, KRYPTONIAN. YOUR RAT-HOLE'S BEEN BREACHED. YOU CAN'T ESCAPE ME NOW.
THUDDUMTHUDDUM
I'M ALMOST GLAD THAT I DIDN'T MANAGE TO KILL YOU WHEN WE WERE YOUNG. IT MAKES THIS MOMENT ALL THE SWEETER.
ARE YOU LISTENING, KRYPTONIAN? CAN YOU HEAR YOUR DEATH BEARING DOWN ON YOU?
THUDDUMTHUDDUM
THUDDUMTHUDDU
WELL? I'M WAITING FOR AN...
HM? WHAT'S...?
THRIDDUNCH
RRRRRAAAAARRRRGH!

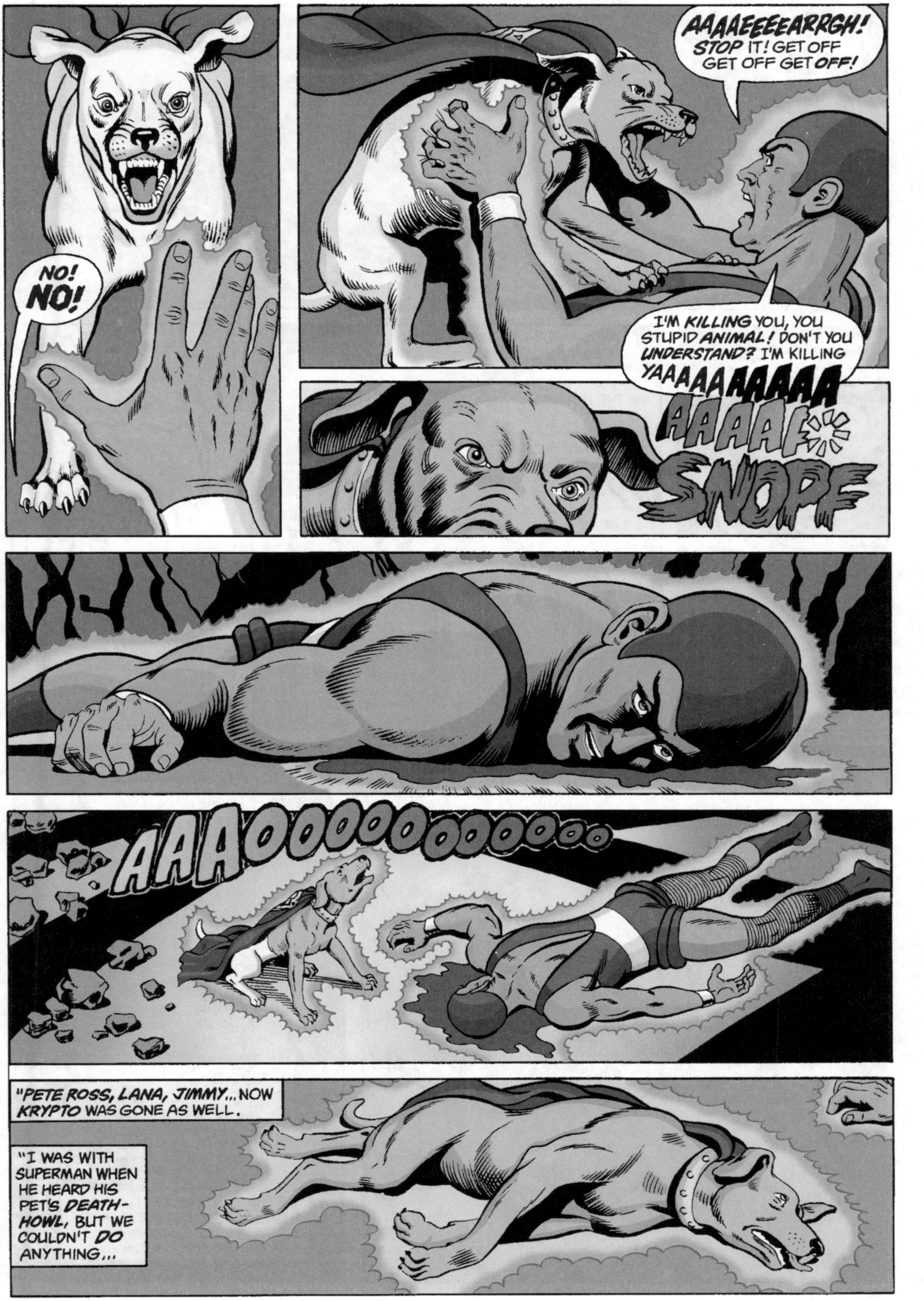
NO! NO!
AAAAEEEEARRGH! STOP IT! GET OFF GET OFF GET OFF!
I'M KILLING YOU, YOU STUPID ANIMAL! DON'T YOU UNDERSTAND? I'M KILLING YAAAAAAAAAAAAAAF
SNOPF
AAAOOOOOOOOoooo
"PETE ROSS, LANA, JIMMY... NOW KRYPTO WAS GONE AS WELL.
"I WAS WITH SUPERMAN WHEN HE HEARD HIS PET'S DEATH-HOWL, BUT WE COULDN'T DO ANYTHING...

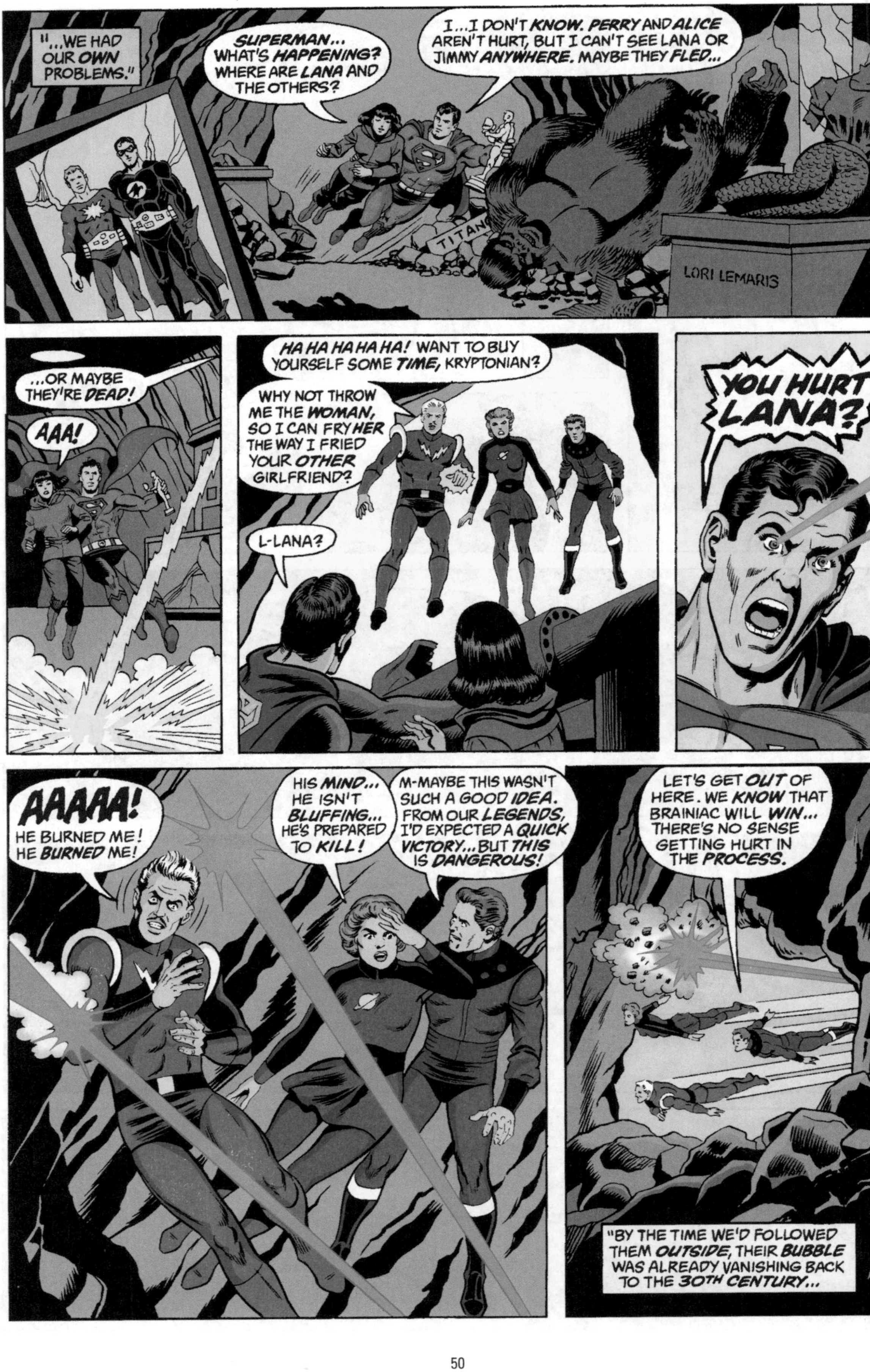
"...WE HAD OUR OWN PROBLEMS."
SUPERMAN... WHAT'S HAPPENING? WHERE ARE LANA AND THE OTHERS?
I...I DON'T KNOW. PERRY AND ALICE AREN'T HURT, BUT I CAN'T SEE LANA OR JIMMY ANYWHERE. MAYBE THEY FLED...
TITAN
LORI LEMARIS
...OR MAYBE THEY'RE DEAD!
AAA!
HA HA HA HA HA! WANT TO BUY YOURSELF SOME TIME, KRYPTONIAN?
WHY NOT THROW ME THE WOMAN, SO I CAN FRY HER THE WAY I FRIED YOUR OTHER GIRLFRIEND?
L-LANA?
YOU HURT LANA?
AAAAA! HE BURNED ME! HE BURNED ME!
HIS MIND... HE ISN'T BLUFFING... HE'S PREPARED TO KILL!
M-MAYBE THIS WASN'T SUCH A GOOD IDEA. FROM OUR LEGENDS, I'D EXPECTED A QUICK VICTORY... BUT THIS IS DANGEROUS!
LET'S GET OUT OF HERE. WE KNOW THAT BRAINIAC WILL WIN... THERE'S NO SENSE GETTING HURT IN THE PROCESS.
"BY THE TIME WE'D FOLLOWED THEM OUTSIDE, THEIR BUBBLE WAS ALREADY VANISHING BACK TO THE 30TH CENTURY...

"...AND THERE WAS ONLY ONE FOE LEFT TO *FACE*.

"OR MAYBE *TWO*."

ANALYSIS: STIFFENING,...OF LIMBS...DIFFICULTY...IN MOVEMENT. **ASSESSMENT:** ONSET...OF RIGOR MORTIS...IN HOST BODY...IMMINENT.

OH, GOD, *LOOK* AT IT!

BUT...THE VILLAINS FROM THE FUTURE...THEY SAID YOU WOULD MEET...YOUR GREATEST FOE IN BATTLE... AND BE NO MORE. ME. BRAINIAC. YOUR GREATEST FOE ...

I AM PREDESTINED,... TO DESTROY YOU ...

LOIS, GET *BACK*! HE'S *FALLING*!

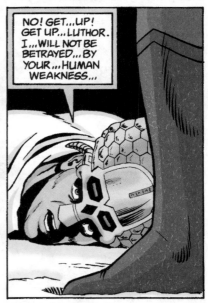

NO! GET...UP! GET UP...LUTHOR. I...WILL NOT BE BETRAYED...BY YOUR...HUMAN WEAKNESS...

WHERE...IS MY KRYPTONITE MAN...? WHY...IS MY FORCE-SCREEN...STILL STANDING...? I DON'T KNOW...I DON'T CARE ...

I...AM COMING FOR YOU... KRYPTONIAN... MY VICTORY...IS INEVITABLE ...

SUPERMAN? IT'S CRAWLING *OFF* HIM...

CLINK RINK PLITTINK

IT'S OKAY, LOIS. I... I DON'T THINK HE'S IN ANY CONDITION TO HARM US.

SHRING CHLINK KINGLE TLING

"THE DISINTEGRATING COLLECTION OF PLATES AND CIRCUITS CRAWLED A COUPLE OF INCHES, PROPELLED BY SHEER MALICE, THEN STOPPED MOVING.

"BRAINIAC WAS *DEAD*.

"IT WAS ALL OVER ...

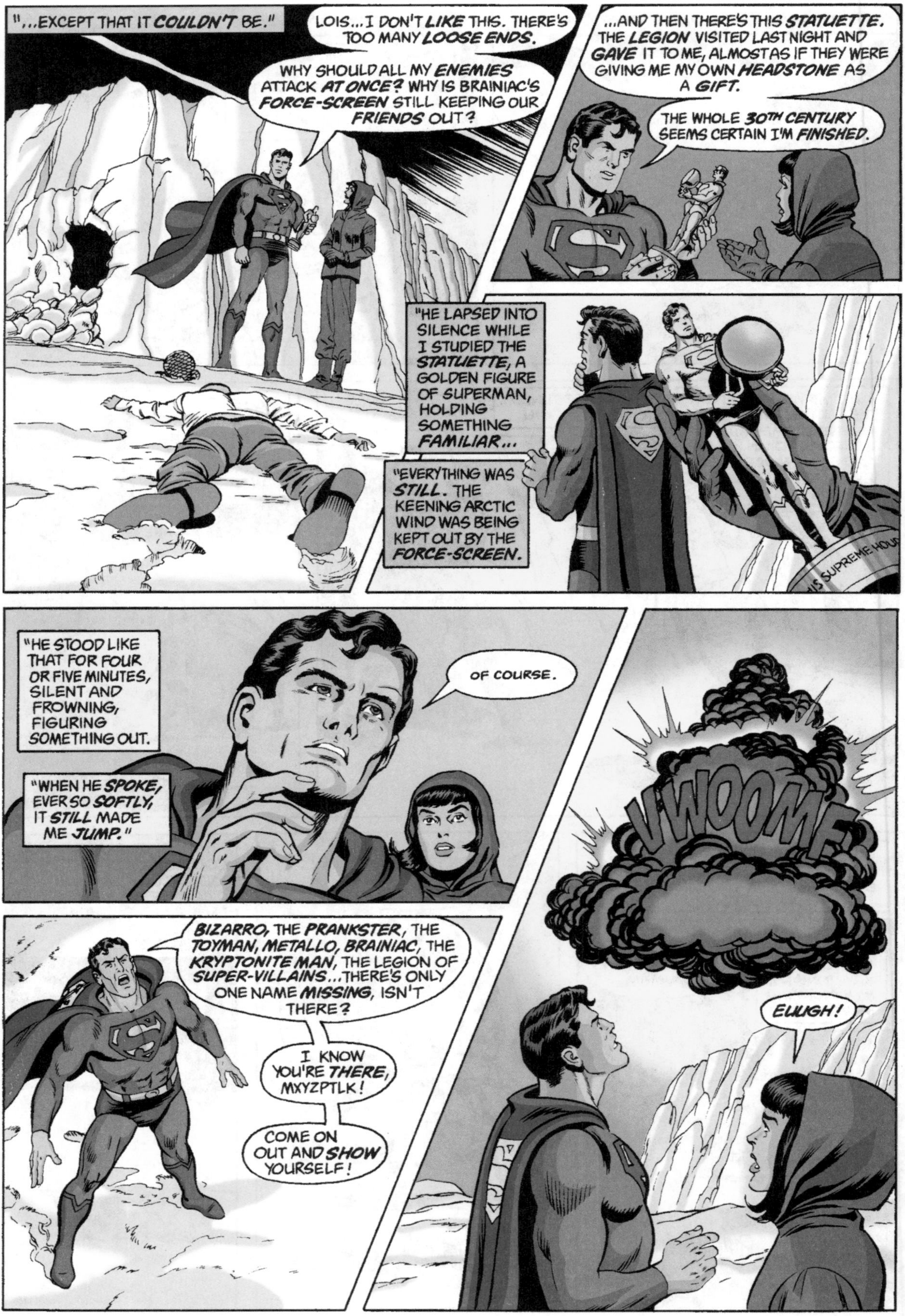
"...EXCEPT THAT IT COULDN'T BE."
LOIS... I DON'T LIKE THIS. THERE'S TOO MANY LOOSE ENDS.
WHY SHOULD ALL MY ENEMIES ATTACK AT ONCE? WHY IS BRAINIAC'S FORCE-SCREEN STILL KEEPING OUR FRIENDS OUT?
...AND THEN THERE'S THIS STATUETTE. THE LEGION VISITED LAST NIGHT AND GAVE IT TO ME, ALMOST AS IF THEY WERE GIVING ME MY OWN HEADSTONE AS A GIFT.
THE WHOLE 30TH CENTURY SEEMS CERTAIN I'M FINISHED.
"HE LAPSED INTO SILENCE WHILE I STUDIED THE STATUETTE, A GOLDEN FIGURE OF SUPERMAN, HOLDING SOMETHING FAMILIAR...
"EVERYTHING WAS STILL. THE KEENING ARCTIC WIND WAS BEING KEPT OUT BY THE FORCE-SCREEN.
"HE STOOD LIKE THAT FOR FOUR OR FIVE MINUTES, SILENT AND FROWNING, FIGURING SOMETHING OUT.
"WHEN HE SPOKE, EVER SO SOFTLY, IT STILL MADE ME JUMP."
OF COURSE.
BIZARRO, THE PRANKSTER, THE TOYMAN, METALLO, BRAINIAC, THE KRYPTONITE MAN, THE LEGION OF SUPER-VILLAINS... THERE'S ONLY ONE NAME MISSING, ISN'T THERE?
I KNOW YOU'RE THERE, MXYZPTLK!
COME ON OUT AND SHOW YOURSELF!
VWOOMF!
EUUGH!

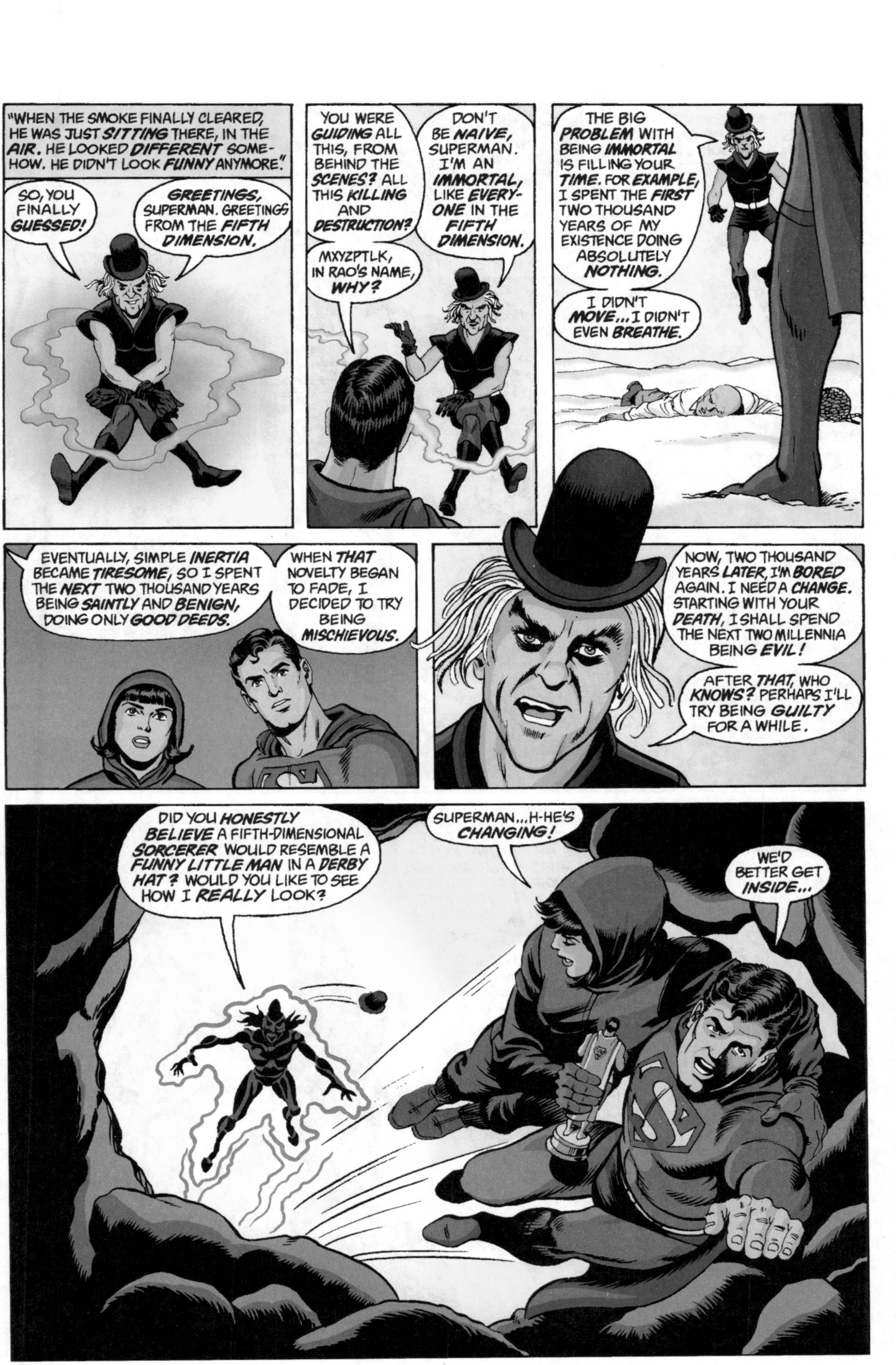
"WHEN THE SMOKE FINALLY CLEARED, HE WAS JUST SITTING THERE, IN THE AIR. HE LOOKED DIFFERENT SOMEHOW. HE DIDN'T LOOK FUNNY ANYMORE."
SO, YOU FINALLY GUESSED!
GREETINGS, SUPERMAN. GREETINGS FROM THE FIFTH DIMENSION.
YOU WERE GUIDING ALL THIS, FROM BEHIND THE SCENES? ALL THIS KILLING AND DESTRUCTION?
MXYZPTLK, IN RAO'S NAME, WHY?
DON'T BE NAIVE, SUPERMAN. I'M AN IMMORTAL, LIKE EVERYONE IN THE FIFTH DIMENSION.
THE BIG PROBLEM WITH BEING IMMORTAL IS FILLING YOUR TIME. FOR EXAMPLE, I SPENT THE FIRST TWO THOUSAND YEARS OF MY EXISTENCE DOING ABSOLUTELY NOTHING.
I DIDN'T MOVE... I DIDN'T EVEN BREATHE.
EVENTUALLY, SIMPLE INERTIA BECAME TIRESOME, SO I SPENT THE NEXT TWO THOUSAND YEARS BEING SAINTLY AND BENIGN, DOING ONLY GOOD DEEDS.
WHEN THAT NOVELTY BEGAN TO FADE, I DECIDED TO TRY BEING MISCHIEVOUS.
NOW, TWO THOUSAND YEARS LATER, I'M BORED AGAIN. I NEED A CHANGE. STARTING WITH YOUR DEATH, I SHALL SPEND THE NEXT TWO MILLENNIA BEING EVIL!
AFTER THAT, WHO KNOWS? PERHAPS I'LL TRY BEING GUILTY FOR A WHILE.
DID YOU HONESTLY BELIEVE A FIFTH-DIMENSIONAL SORCERER WOULD RESEMBLE A FUNNY LITTLE MAN IN A DERBY HAT? WOULD YOU LIKE TO SEE HOW I REALLY LOOK?
SUPERMAN... H-HE'S CHANGING!
WE'D BETTER GET INSIDE...

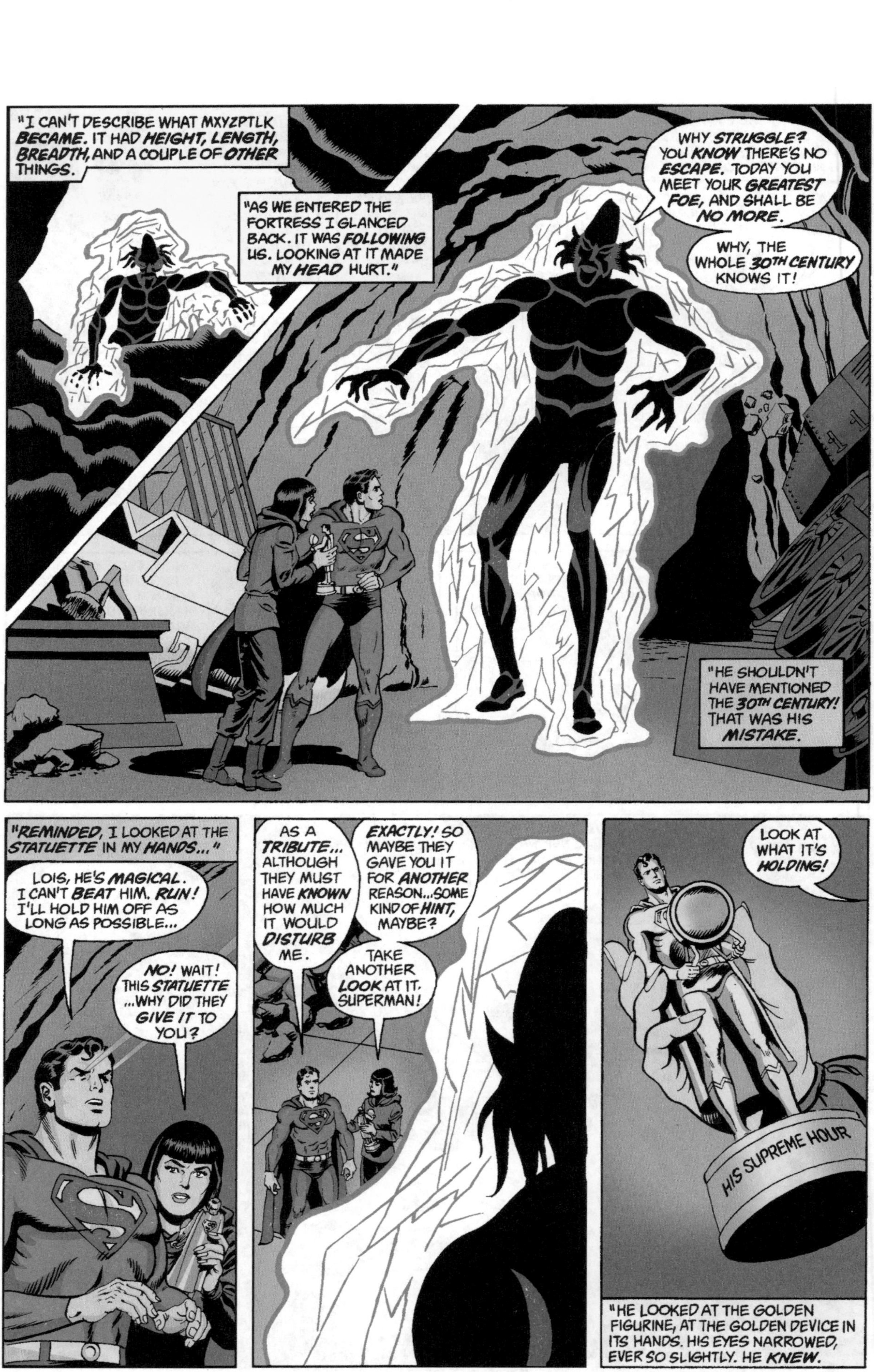
"I CAN'T DESCRIBE WHAT MXYZPTLK BECAME. IT HAD HEIGHT, LENGTH, BREADTH, AND A COUPLE OF OTHER THINGS.
"AS WE ENTERED THE FORTRESS I GLANCED BACK. IT WAS FOLLOWING US. LOOKING AT IT MADE MY HEAD HURT."
WHY STRUGGLE? YOU KNOW THERE'S NO ESCAPE. TODAY YOU MEET YOUR GREATEST FOE, AND SHALL BE NO MORE.
WHY, THE WHOLE 30TH CENTURY KNOWS IT!
"HE SHOULDN'T HAVE MENTIONED THE 30TH CENTURY! THAT WAS HIS MISTAKE.
"REMINDED, I LOOKED AT THE STATUETTE IN MY HANDS..."
LOIS, HE'S MAGICAL. I CAN'T BEAT HIM. RUN! I'LL HOLD HIM OFF AS LONG AS POSSIBLE...
NO! WAIT! THIS STATUETTE ...WHY DID THEY GIVE IT TO YOU?
AS A TRIBUTE... ALTHOUGH THEY MUST HAVE KNOWN HOW MUCH IT WOULD DISTURB ME.
EXACTLY! SO MAYBE THEY GAVE YOU IT FOR ANOTHER REASON...SOME KIND OF HINT, MAYBE?
TAKE ANOTHER LOOK AT IT, SUPERMAN!
LOOK AT WHAT IT'S HOLDING!
HIS SUPREME HOUR
"HE LOOKED AT THE GOLDEN FIGURINE, AT THE GOLDEN DEVICE IN ITS HANDS. HIS EYES NARROWED, EVER SO SLIGHTLY. HE KNEW.

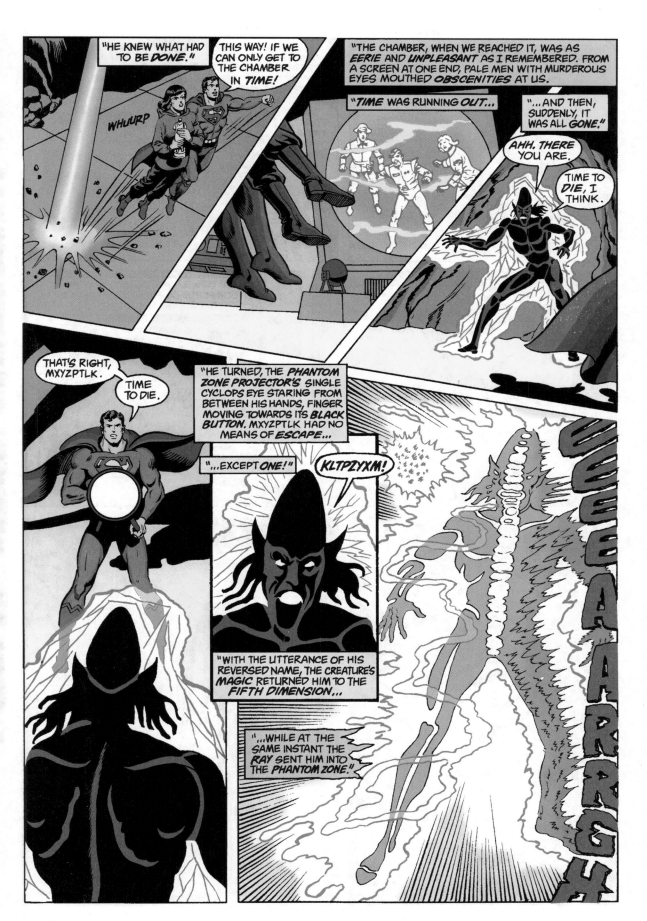

"HE KNEW WHAT HAD TO BE *DONE.*"

THIS WAY! IF WE CAN ONLY GET TO THE CHAMBER IN *TIME!*

WHUURP

"THE CHAMBER, WHEN WE REACHED IT, WAS AS *EERIE* AND *UNPLEASANT* AS I REMEMBERED. FROM A SCREEN AT ONE END, PALE MEN WITH MURDEROUS EYES MOUTHED *OBSCENITIES* AT US."

"*TIME* WAS RUNNING *OUT...*"

"...AND THEN, SUDDENLY, IT WAS ALL *GONE.*"

AHH. THERE YOU ARE.

TIME TO *DIE,* I THINK.

THAT'S RIGHT, *MXYZPTLK.*

TIME TO DIE.

"HE TURNED, THE *PHANTOM ZONE PROJECTOR'S* SINGLE CYCLOPS EYE STARING FROM BETWEEN HIS HANDS, FINGER MOVING TOWARDS ITS *BLACK BUTTON.* MXYZPTLK HAD NO MEANS OF *ESCAPE...*"

"...EXCEPT *ONE!*"

KLTPZYXM!

"WITH THE UTTERANCE OF HIS *REVERSED* NAME, THE CREATURE'S *MAGIC* RETURNED HIM TO THE *FIFTH DIMENSION...*"

"...WHILE AT THE SAME INSTANT THE *RAY* SENT HIM INTO THE *PHANTOM ZONE.*"

EEEAARRGH

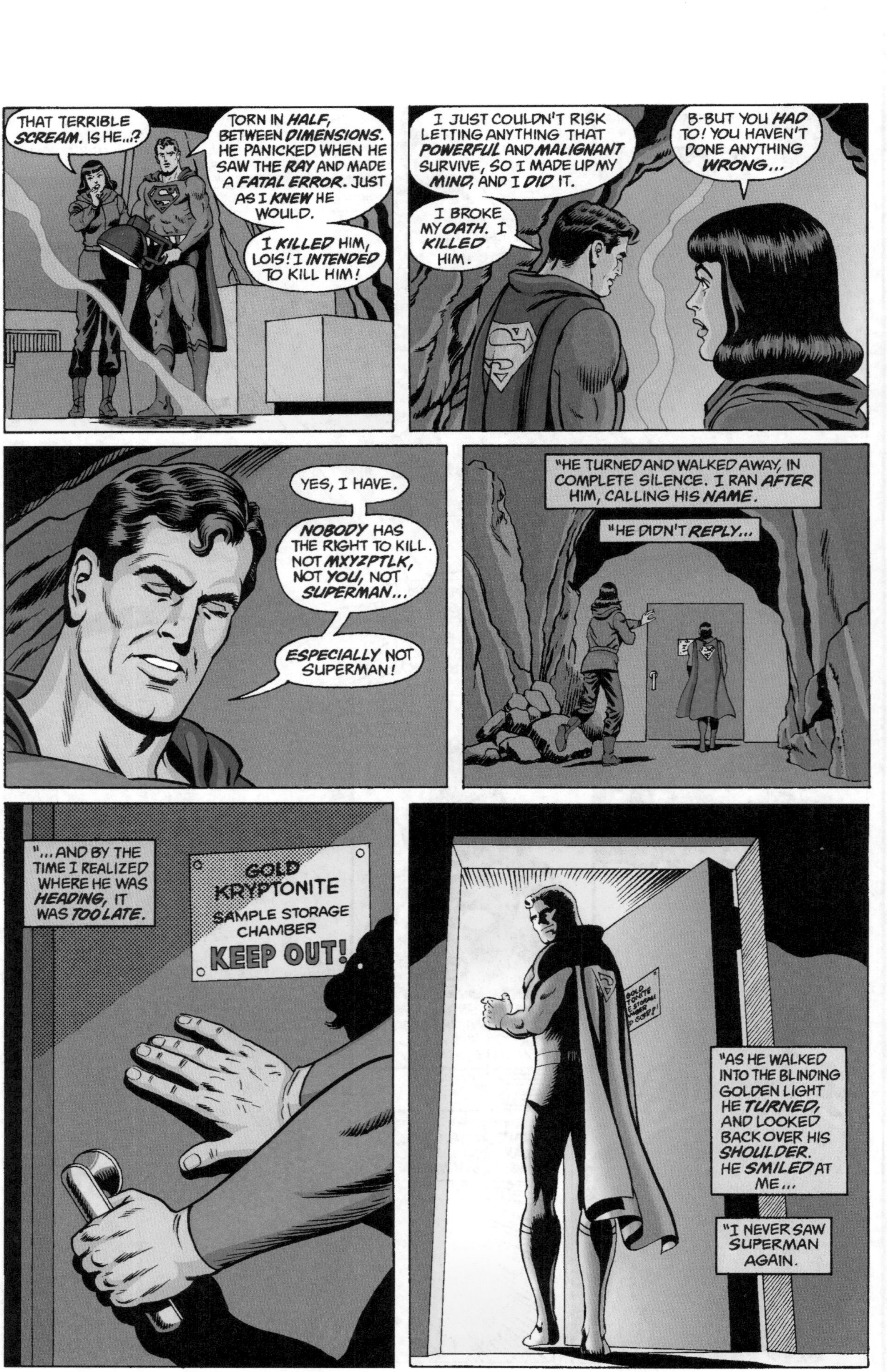
THAT TERRIBLE SCREAM. IS HE...?
TORN IN HALF, BETWEEN DIMENSIONS. HE PANICKED WHEN HE SAW THE RAY AND MADE A FATAL ERROR. JUST AS I KNEW HE WOULD.
I KILLED HIM, LOIS! I INTENDED TO KILL HIM!
I JUST COULDN'T RISK LETTING ANYTHING THAT POWERFUL AND MALIGNANT SURVIVE, SO I MADE UP MY MIND, AND I DID IT.
I BROKE MY OATH. I KILLED HIM.
B-BUT YOU HAD TO! YOU HAVEN'T DONE ANYTHING WRONG...
YES, I HAVE.
NOBODY HAS THE RIGHT TO KILL. NOT MXYZPTLK, NOT YOU, NOT SUPERMAN...
ESPECIALLY NOT SUPERMAN!
"HE TURNED AND WALKED AWAY, IN COMPLETE SILENCE. I RAN AFTER HIM, CALLING HIS NAME.
"HE DIDN'T REPLY...
"...AND BY THE TIME I REALIZED WHERE HE WAS HEADING, IT WAS TOO LATE.
GOLD KRYPTONITE SAMPLE STORAGE CHAMBER KEEP OUT!
"AS HE WALKED INTO THE BLINDING GOLDEN LIGHT HE TURNED, AND LOOKED BACK OVER HIS SHOULDER. HE SMILED AT ME...
"I NEVER SAW SUPERMAN AGAIN.

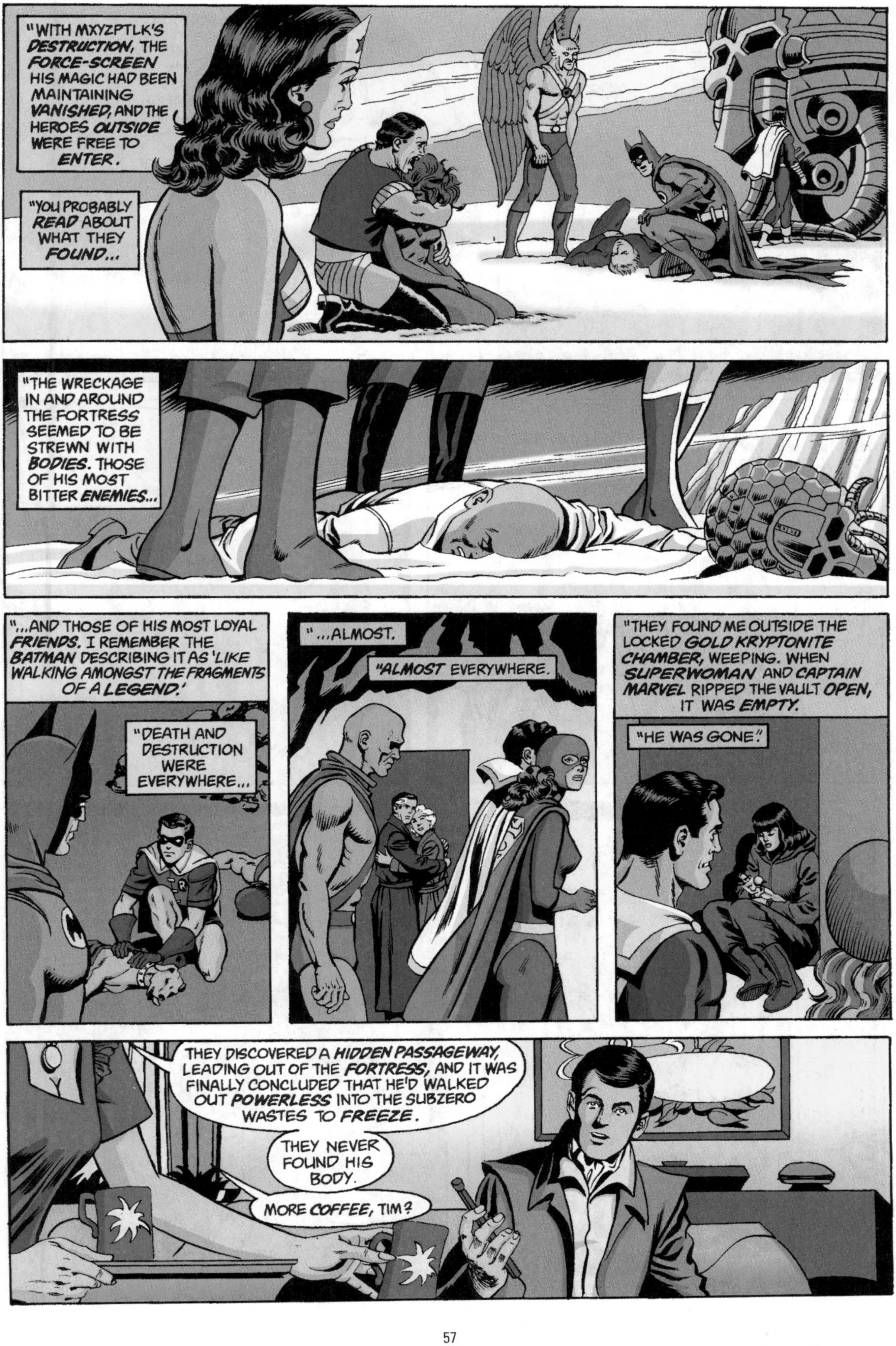
"WITH MXYZPTLK'S DESTRUCTION, THE FORCE-SCREEN HIS MAGIC HAD BEEN MAINTAINING VANISHED, AND THE HEROES OUTSIDE WERE FREE TO ENTER.
"YOU PROBABLY READ ABOUT WHAT THEY FOUND...
"THE WRECKAGE IN AND AROUND THE FORTRESS SEEMED TO BE STREWN WITH BODIES. THOSE OF HIS MOST BITTER ENEMIES...
"...AND THOSE OF HIS MOST LOYAL FRIENDS. I REMEMBER THE BATMAN DESCRIBING IT AS 'LIKE WALKING AMONGST THE FRAGMENTS OF A LEGEND.'
"DEATH AND DESTRUCTION WERE EVERYWHERE...
"...ALMOST.
"ALMOST EVERYWHERE.
"THEY FOUND ME OUTSIDE THE LOCKED GOLD KRYPTONITE CHAMBER, WEEPING. WHEN SUPERWOMAN AND CAPTAIN MARVEL RIPPED THE VAULT OPEN, IT WAS EMPTY.
"HE WAS GONE."
THEY DISCOVERED A HIDDEN PASSAGEWAY, LEADING OUT OF THE FORTRESS, AND IT WAS FINALLY CONCLUDED THAT HE'D WALKED OUT POWERLESS INTO THE SUBZERO WASTES TO FREEZE.
THEY NEVER FOUND HIS BODY.
MORE COFFEE, TIM?

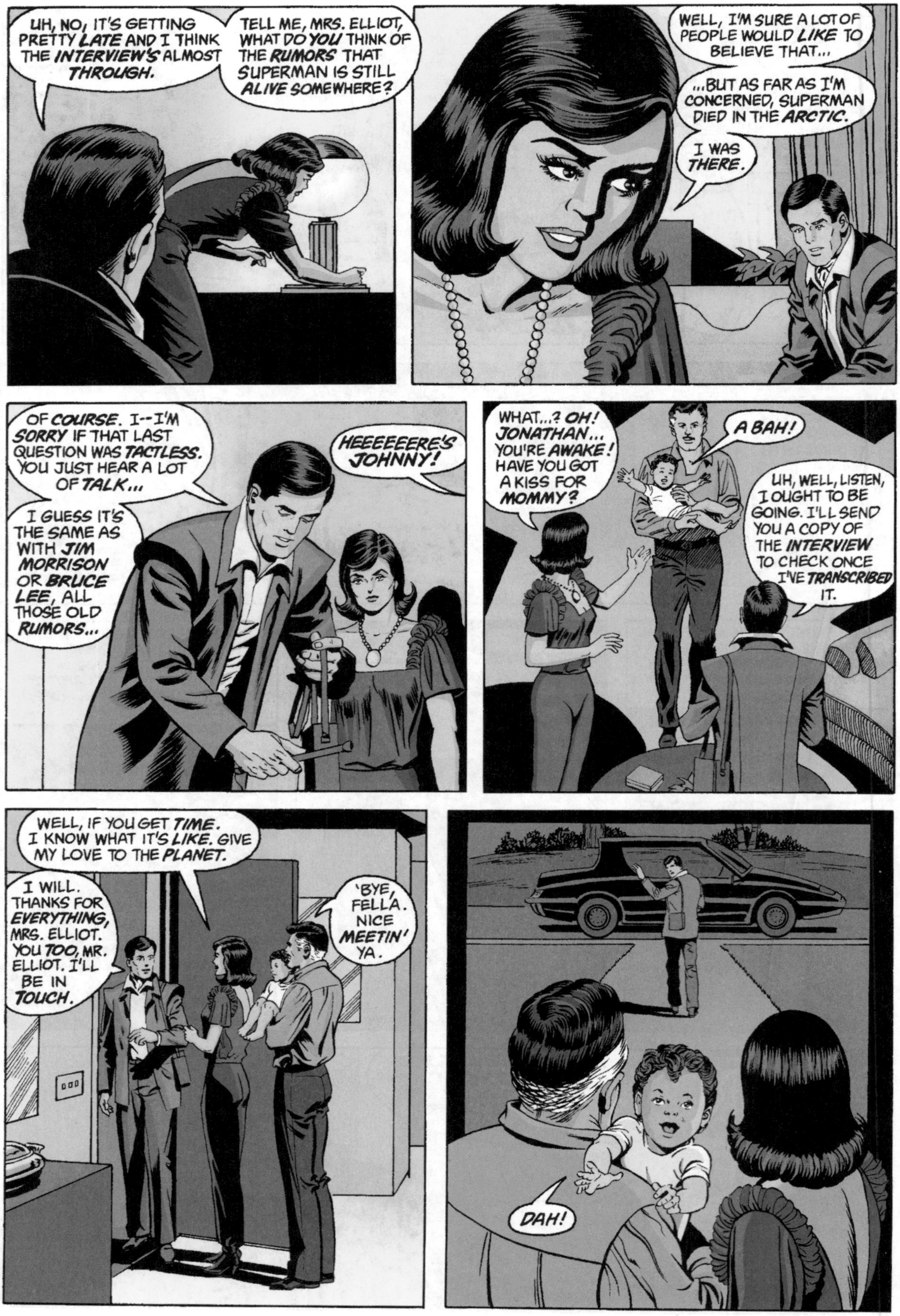
UH, NO, IT'S GETTING PRETTY LATE AND I THINK THE INTERVIEW'S ALMOST THROUGH.
TELL ME, MRS. ELLIOT, WHAT DO YOU THINK OF THE RUMORS THAT SUPERMAN IS STILL ALIVE SOMEWHERE?
WELL, I'M SURE A LOT OF PEOPLE WOULD LIKE TO BELIEVE THAT...
...BUT AS FAR AS I'M CONCERNED, SUPERMAN DIED IN THE ARCTIC.
I WAS THERE.
OF COURSE. I--I'M SORRY IF THAT LAST QUESTION WAS TACTLESS. YOU JUST HEAR A LOT OF TALK...
I GUESS IT'S THE SAME AS WITH JIM MORRISON OR BRUCE LEE, ALL THOSE OLD RUMORS...
HEEEEEERE'S JOHNNY!
WHAT...? OH! JONATHAN... YOU'RE AWAKE! HAVE YOU GOT A KISS FOR MOMMY?
A BAH!
UH, WELL, LISTEN, I OUGHT TO BE GOING. I'LL SEND YOU A COPY OF THE INTERVIEW TO CHECK ONCE I'VE TRANSCRIBED IT.
WELL, IF YOU GET TIME. I KNOW WHAT IT'S LIKE. GIVE MY LOVE TO THE PLANET.
I WILL. THANKS FOR EVERYTHING, MRS. ELLIOT. YOU TOO, MR. ELLIOT. I'LL BE IN TOUCH.
'BYE, FELLA. NICE MEETIN' YA.
DAH!

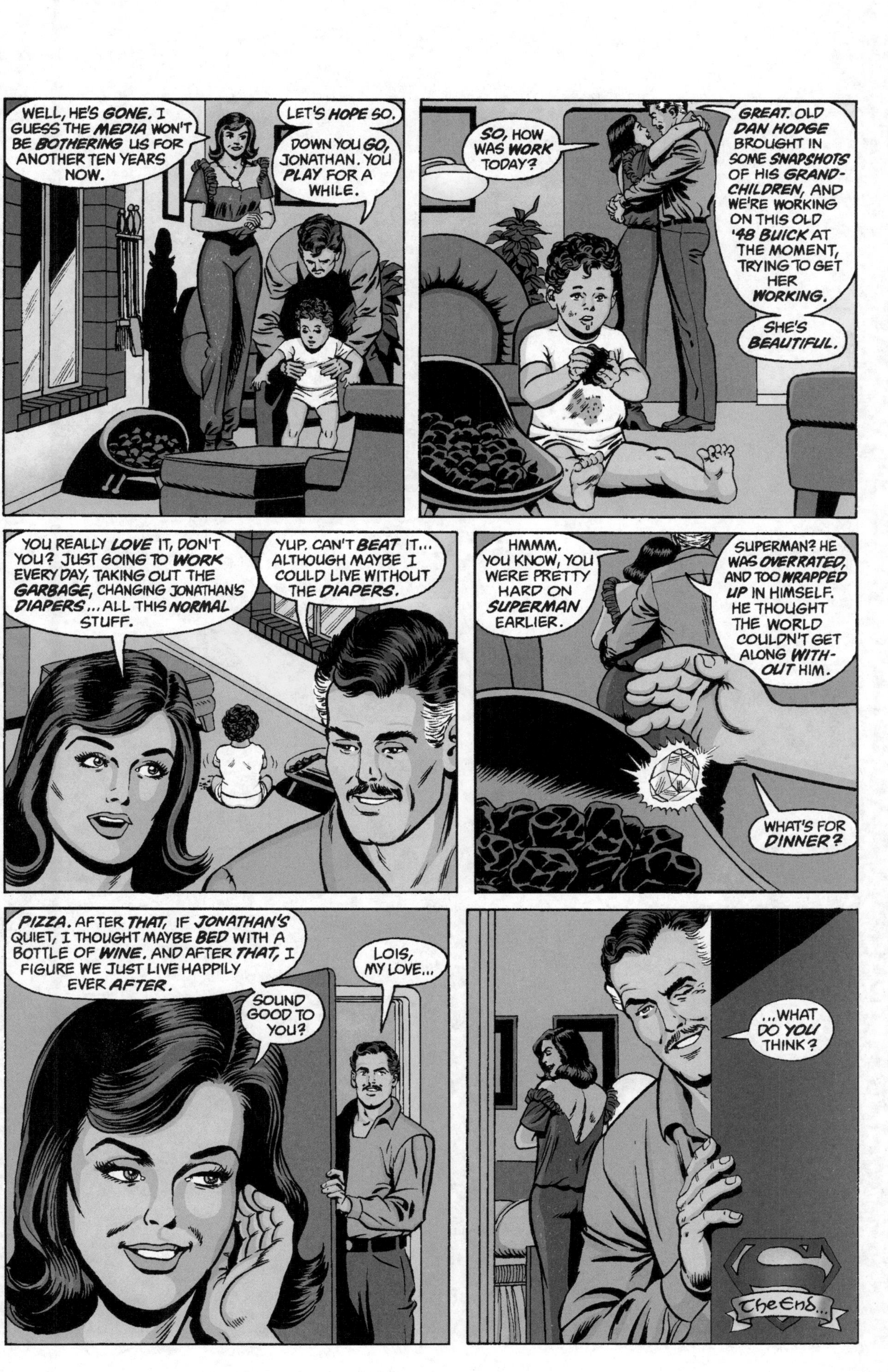

WELL, HE'S GONE. I GUESS THE MEDIA WON'T BE BOTHERING US FOR ANOTHER TEN YEARS NOW.
LET'S HOPE SO.
DOWN YOU GO, JONATHAN. YOU PLAY FOR A WHILE.
SO, HOW WAS WORK TODAY?
GREAT. OLD DAN HODGE BROUGHT IN SOME SNAPSHOTS OF HIS GRANDCHILDREN, AND WE'RE WORKING ON THIS OLD '48 BUICK AT THE MOMENT, TRYING TO GET HER WORKING.
SHE'S BEAUTIFUL.
YOU REALLY LOVE IT, DON'T YOU? JUST GOING TO WORK EVERY DAY, TAKING OUT THE GARBAGE, CHANGING JONATHAN'S DIAPERS... ALL THIS NORMAL STUFF.
YUP. CAN'T BEAT IT... ALTHOUGH MAYBE I COULD LIVE WITHOUT THE DIAPERS.
HMMM. YOU KNOW, YOU WERE PRETTY HARD ON SUPERMAN EARLIER.
SUPERMAN? HE WAS OVERRATED, AND TOO WRAPPED UP IN HIMSELF. HE THOUGHT THE WORLD COULDN'T GET ALONG WITHOUT HIM.
WHAT'S FOR DINNER?
PIZZA. AFTER THAT, IF JONATHAN'S QUIET, I THOUGHT MAYBE BED WITH A BOTTLE OF WINE. AND AFTER THAT, I FIGURE WE JUST LIVE HAPPILY EVER AFTER.
SOUND GOOD TO YOU?
LOIS, MY LOVE...
...WHAT DO YOU THINK?
The End...

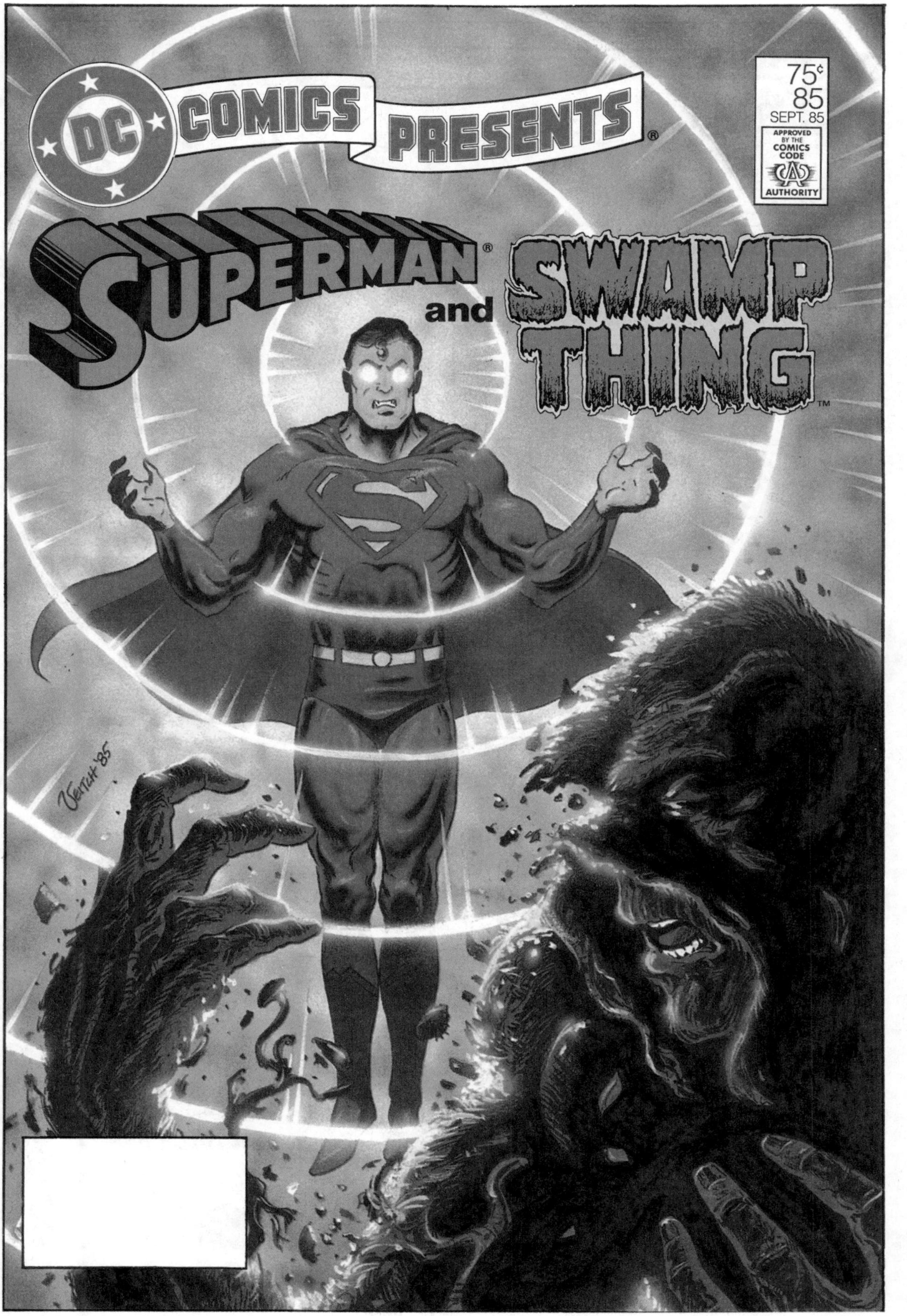
DC COMICS PRESENTS
75¢
85
SEPT. 85
APPROVED BY THE COMICS CODE AUTHORITY
SUPERMAN
and
SWAMP THING
VEITCH '85

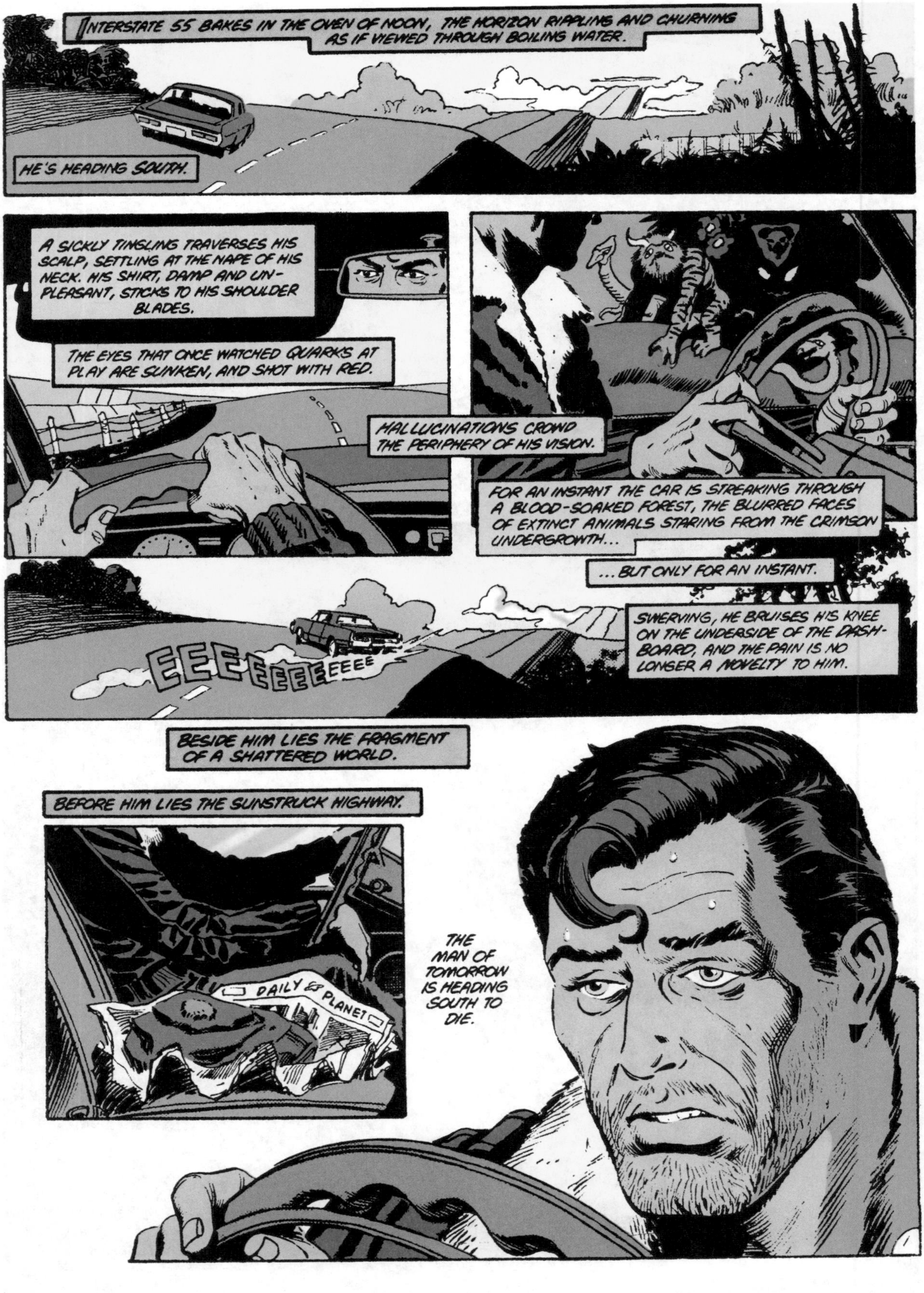
INTERSTATE 55 BAKES IN THE OVEN OF NOON, THE HORIZON RIPPLING AND CHURNING AS IF VIEWED THROUGH BOILING WATER.
HE'S HEADING SOUTH.
A SICKLY TINGLING TRAVERSES HIS SCALP, SETTLING AT THE NAPE OF HIS NECK. HIS SHIRT, DAMP AND UNPLEASANT, STICKS TO HIS SHOULDER BLADES.
THE EYES THAT ONCE WATCHED QUARKS AT PLAY ARE SUNKEN, AND SHOT WITH RED.
HALLUCINATIONS CROWD THE PERIPHERY OF HIS VISION.
FOR AN INSTANT THE CAR IS STREAKING THROUGH A BLOOD-SOAKED FOREST, THE BLURRED FACES OF EXTINCT ANIMALS STARING FROM THE CRIMSON UNDERGROWTH...
...BUT ONLY FOR AN INSTANT.
EEEEEEEEEEEE
SWERVING, HE BRUISES HIS KNEE ON THE UNDERSIDE OF THE DASHBOARD, AND THE PAIN IS NO LONGER A NOVELTY TO HIM.
BESIDE HIM LIES THE FRAGMENT OF A SHATTERED WORLD.
BEFORE HIM LIES THE SUNSTRUCK HIGHWAY.
DAILY PLANET
THE MAN OF TOMORROW IS HEADING SOUTH TO DIE.

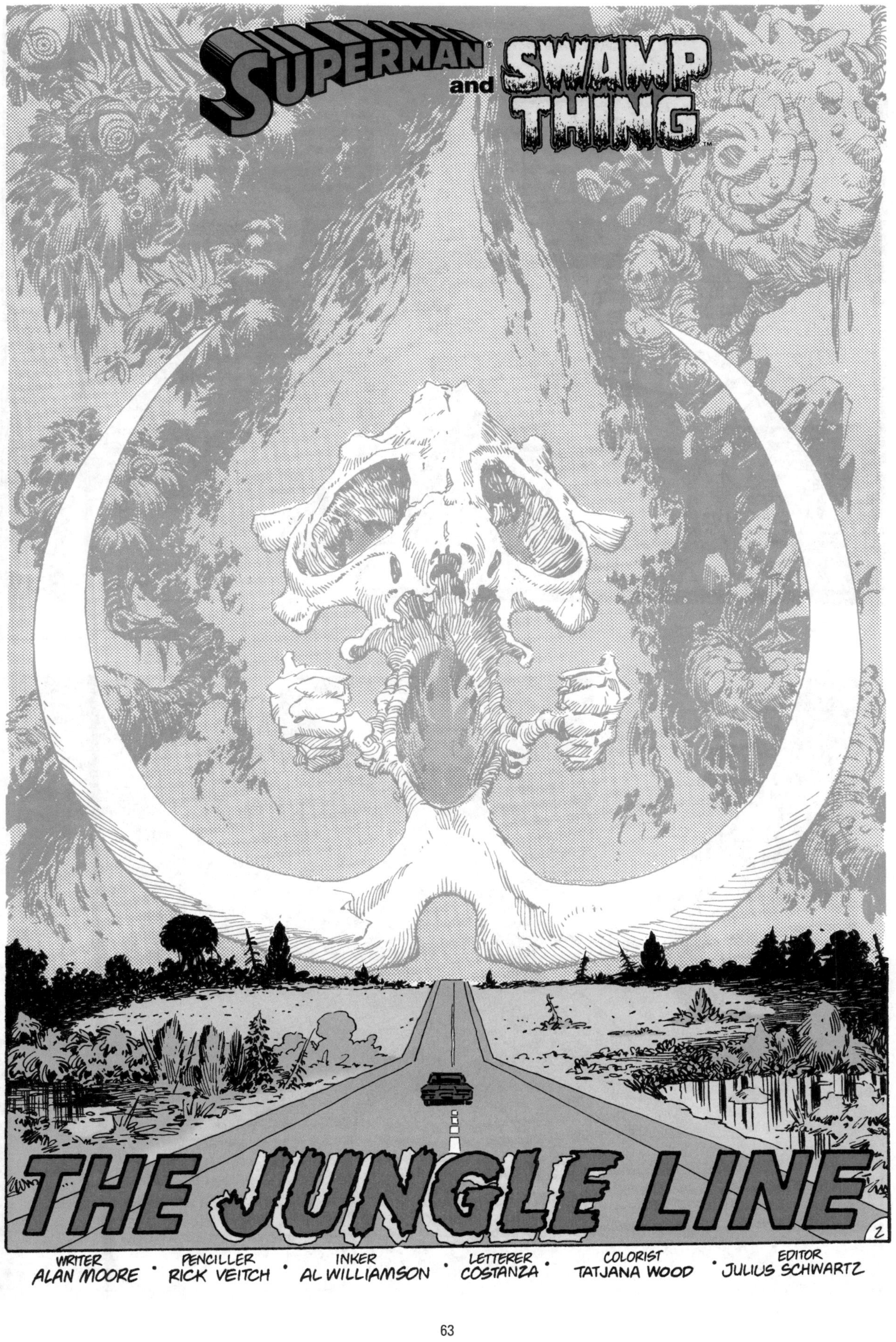
SUPERMAN® and SWAMP THING™
THE JUNGLE LINE
2

WRITER ALAN MOORE · PENCILLER RICK VEITCH · INKER AL WILLIAMSON · LETTERER COSTANZA · COLORIST TATJANA WOOD · EDITOR JULIUS SCHWARTZ

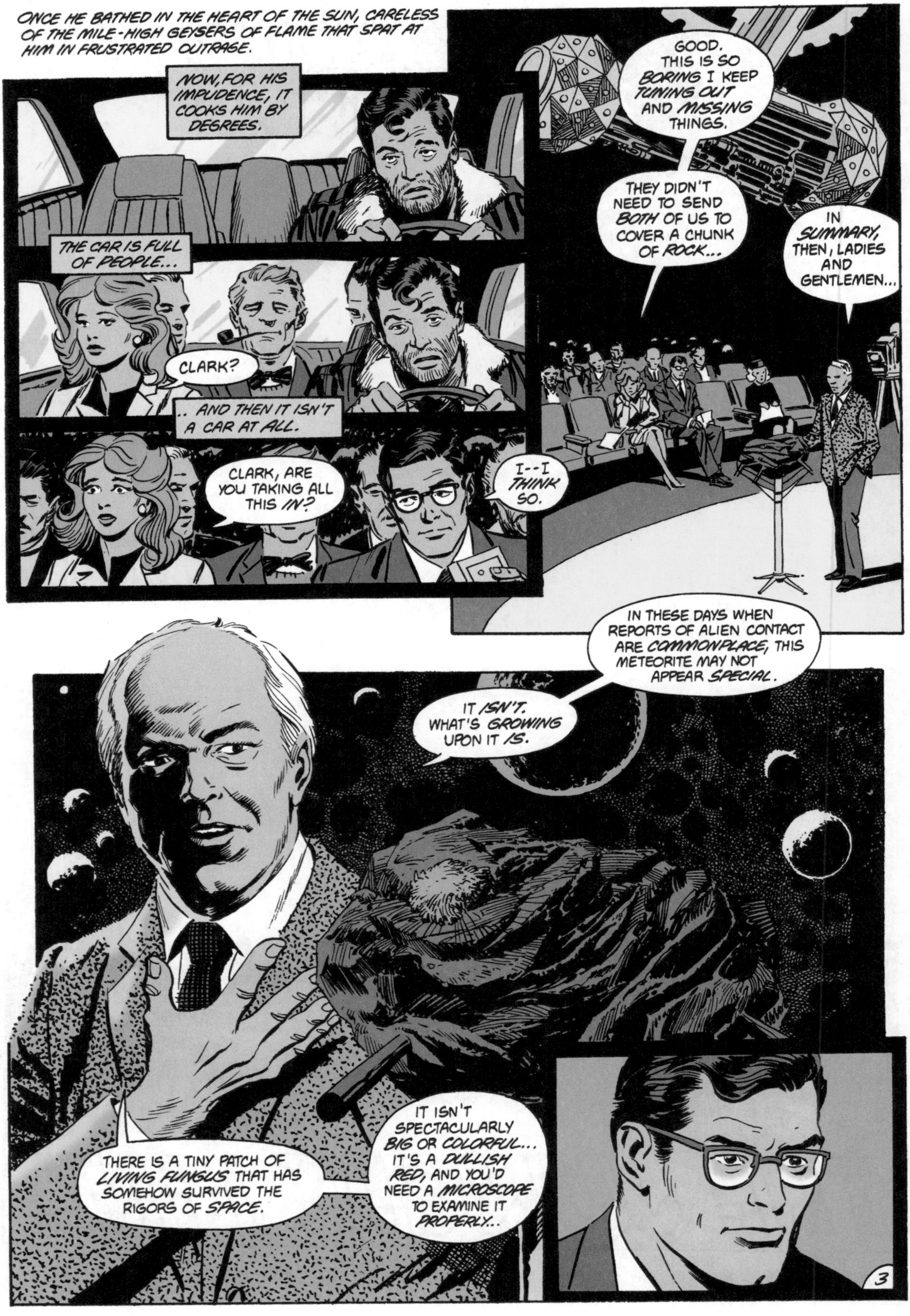
ONCE HE BATHED IN THE HEART OF THE SUN, CARELESS OF THE MILE-HIGH GEYSERS OF FLAME THAT SPAT AT HIM IN FRUSTRATED OUTRAGE.
NOW, FOR HIS IMPUDENCE, IT COOKS HIM BY DEGREES.
THE CAR IS FULL OF PEOPLE...
CLARK?
.. AND THEN IT ISN'T A CAR AT ALL.
CLARK, ARE YOU TAKING ALL THIS IN?
I--I THINK SO.
GOOD. THIS IS SO BORING I KEEP TUNING OUT AND MISSING THINGS.
THEY DIDN'T NEED TO SEND BOTH OF US TO COVER A CHUNK OF ROCK...
IN SUMMARY, THEN, LADIES AND GENTLEMEN...
IN THESE DAYS WHEN REPORTS OF ALIEN CONTACT ARE COMMONPLACE, THIS METEORITE MAY NOT APPEAR SPECIAL.
IT ISN'T. WHAT'S GROWING UPON IT IS.
THERE IS A TINY PATCH OF LIVING FUNGUS THAT HAS SOMEHOW SURVIVED THE RIGORS OF SPACE.
IT ISN'T SPECTACULARLY BIG OR COLORFUL... IT'S A DULLISH RED, AND YOU'D NEED A MICROSCOPE TO EXAMINE IT PROPERLY..
3

HOWEVER...THIS *LIFE FORM* HAS SURVIVED *DECADES*... POSSIBLY *CENTURIES*... IN AN *ABSOLUTE FRIGID VACUUM*.

TO *SCIENCE*, THIS IS AN *UN-PRECEDENTED* DISCOVERY.

DOES ANYONE HAVE ANY *QUESTIONS*?

YES? MS. *LANG*, I BELIEVE?

DR. *EVERETT*, IS THIS FIND *REALLY* THAT IMPORTANT?

AFTER ALL, FOR OVER *TWENTY YEARS* WE'VE HAD A LIVING ALIEN *JUST* AS INDESTRUCTIBLE UPON OUR PLANET.

AHH, YOU'RE TALKING ABOUT *SUPERMAN.*

WELL, THE *DIFFERENCE* IS THAT UNLIKE THIS *FUNGUS*, SUPERMAN COULD NOT BE EXPECTED TO LIE STILL THROUGH-OUT WHAT MAY BE *YEARS OF THOROUGH RESEARCH.*

ANY *OTHER* QUESTIONS?

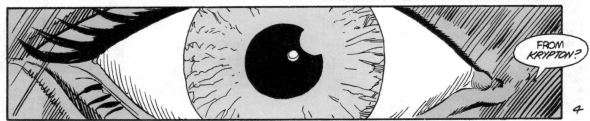

FROM *KRYPTON*?

4

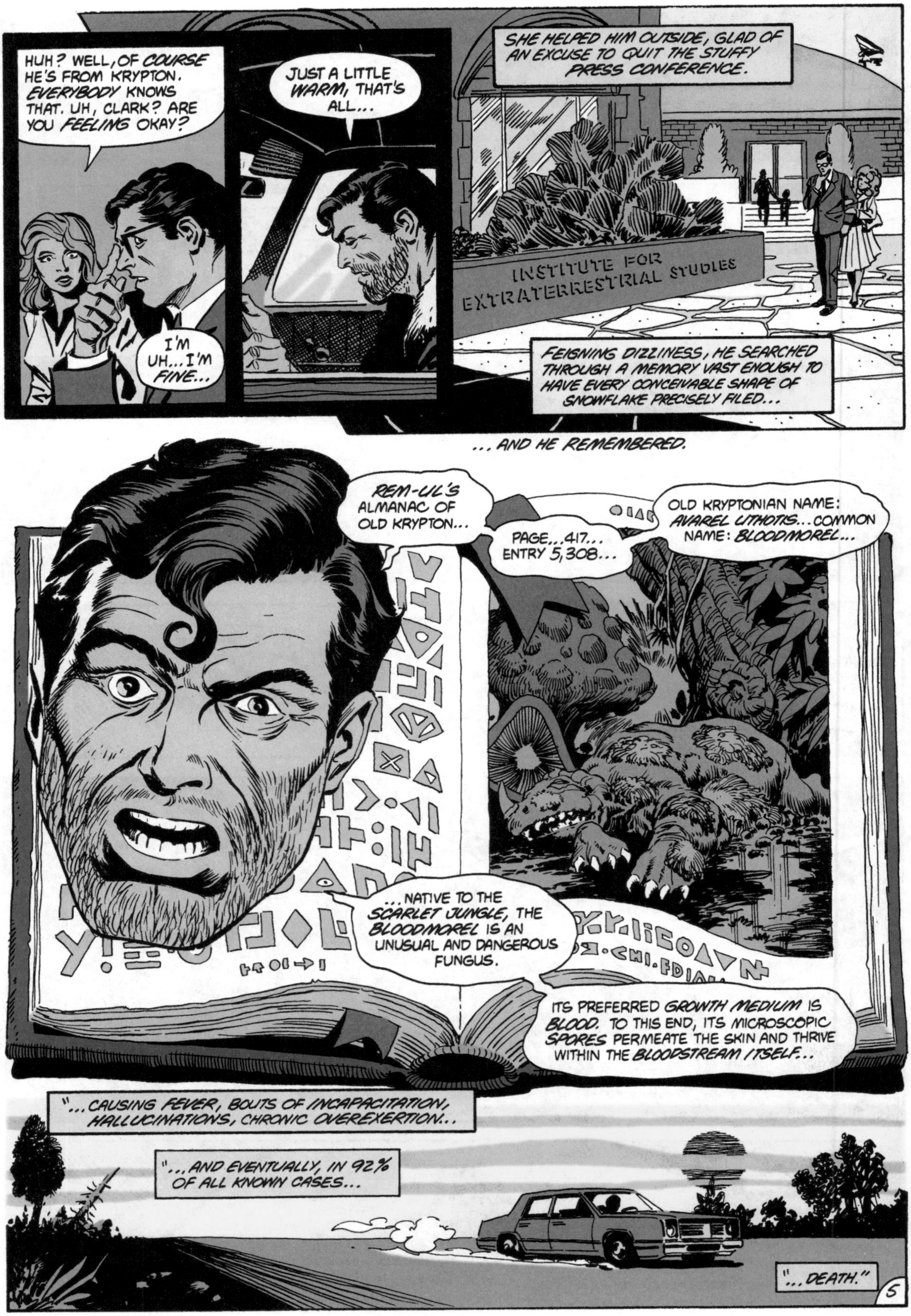
HUH? WELL, OF COURSE HE'S FROM KRYPTON. EVERYBODY KNOWS THAT. UH, CLARK? ARE YOU FEELING OKAY?
I'M UH... I'M FINE...
JUST A LITTLE WARM, THAT'S ALL...
SHE HELPED HIM OUTSIDE, GLAD OF AN EXCUSE TO QUIT THE STUFFY PRESS CONFERENCE.
INSTITUTE FOR EXTRATERRESTRIAL STUDIES
FEIGNING DIZZINESS, HE SEARCHED THROUGH A MEMORY VAST ENOUGH TO HAVE EVERY CONCEIVABLE SHAPE OF SNOWFLAKE PRECISELY FILED...
... AND HE REMEMBERED.
REM-UL'S ALMANAC OF OLD KRYPTON...
PAGE... 417... ENTRY 5,308...
OLD KRYPTONIAN NAME: AVAREL UTHOTIS... COMMON NAME: BLOODMOREL...
... NATIVE TO THE SCARLET JUNGLE, THE BLOODMOREL IS AN UNUSUAL AND DANGEROUS FUNGUS.
ITS PREFERRED GROWTH MEDIUM IS BLOOD. TO THIS END, ITS MICROSCOPIC SPORES PERMEATE THE SKIN AND THRIVE WITHIN THE BLOODSTREAM ITSELF...
"... CAUSING FEVER, BOUTS OF INCAPACITATION, HALLUCINATIONS, CHRONIC OVEREXERTION...
"... AND EVENTUALLY, IN 92% OF ALL KNOWN CASES...
"... DEATH."
5

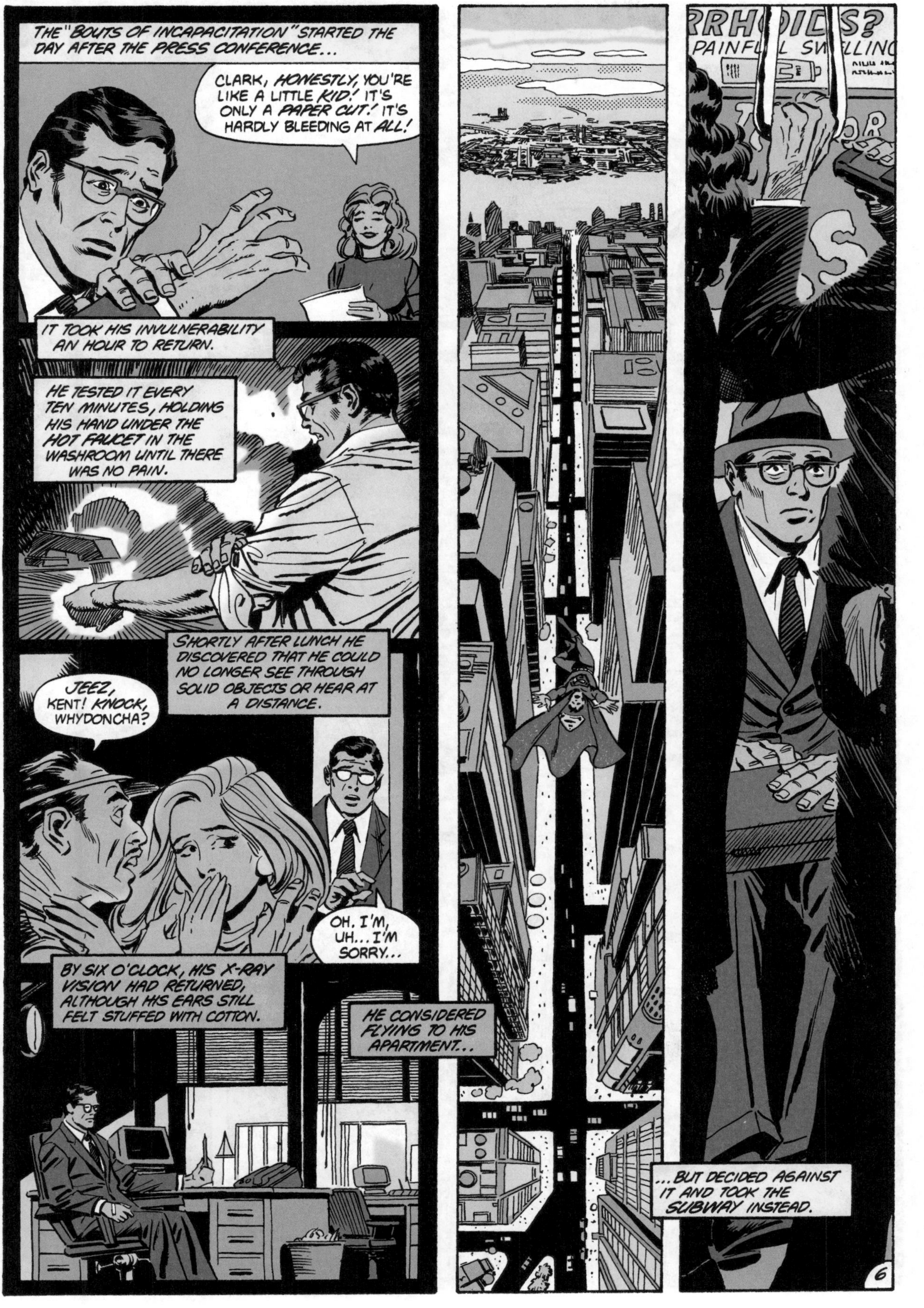

THE "BOUTS OF INCAPACITATION" STARTED THE DAY AFTER THE PRESS CONFERENCE...
CLARK, HONESTLY, YOU'RE LIKE A LITTLE KID! IT'S ONLY A PAPER CUT! IT'S HARDLY BLEEDING AT ALL!
IT TOOK HIS INVULNERABILITY AN HOUR TO RETURN.
HE TESTED IT EVERY TEN MINUTES, HOLDING HIS HAND UNDER THE HOT FAUCET IN THE WASHROOM UNTIL THERE WAS NO PAIN.
SHORTLY AFTER LUNCH HE DISCOVERED THAT HE COULD NO LONGER SEE THROUGH SOLID OBJECTS OR HEAR AT A DISTANCE.
JEEZ, KENT! KNOCK, WHYDONCHA?
OH. I'M, UH... I'M SORRY...
BY SIX O'CLOCK, HIS X-RAY VISION HAD RETURNED, ALTHOUGH HIS EARS STILL FELT STUFFED WITH COTTON.
HE CONSIDERED FLYING TO HIS APARTMENT...
RRHOIDS?
...BUT DECIDED AGAINST IT AND TOOK THE SUBWAY INSTEAD.
6

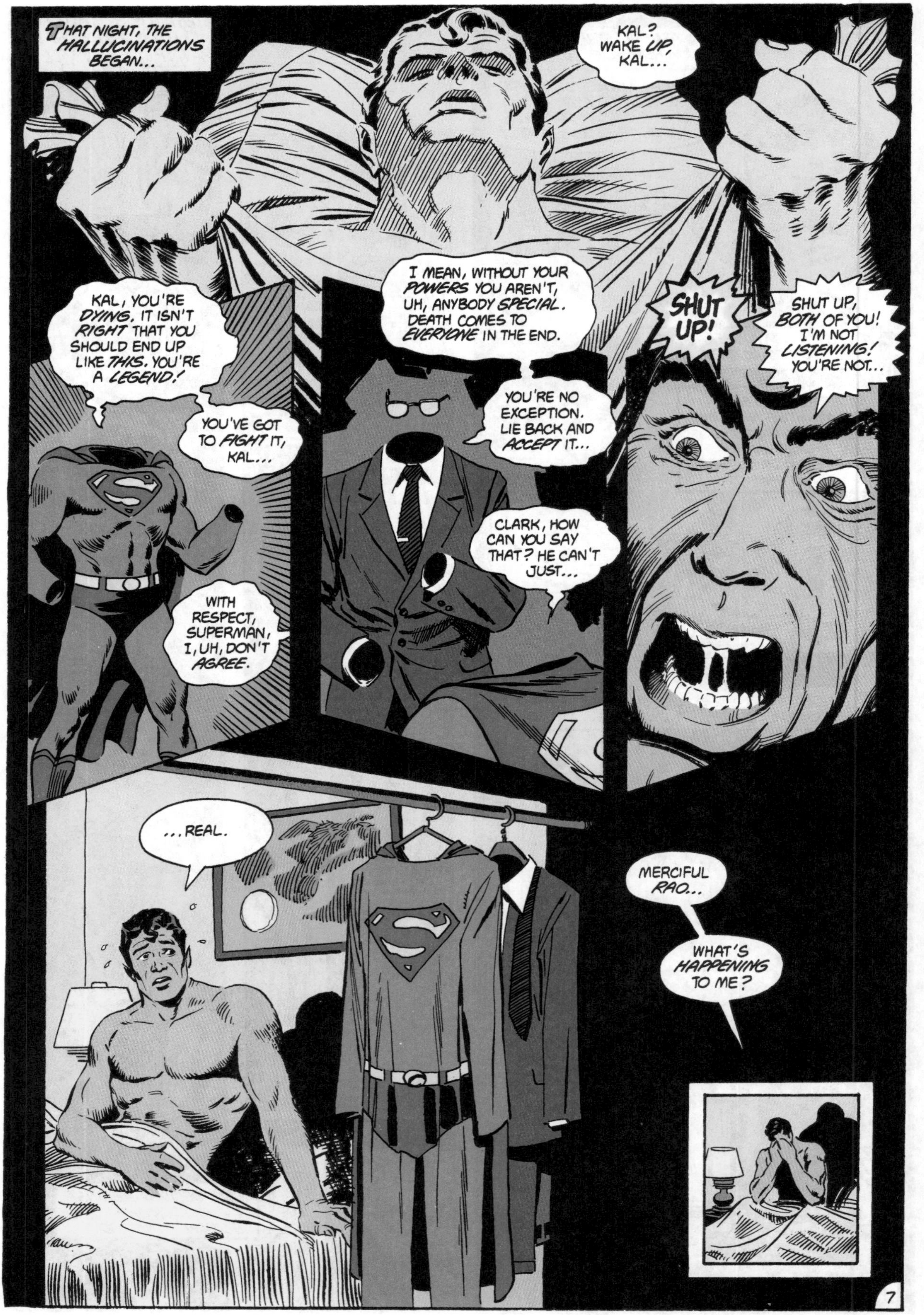
THAT NIGHT, THE HALLUCINATIONS BEGAN...
KAL? WAKE UP, KAL...
KAL, YOU'RE DYING. IT ISN'T RIGHT THAT YOU SHOULD END UP LIKE THIS. YOU'RE A LEGEND!
YOU'VE GOT TO FIGHT IT, KAL...
WITH RESPECT, SUPERMAN, I, UH, DON'T AGREE.
I MEAN, WITHOUT YOUR POWERS YOU AREN'T, UH, ANYBODY SPECIAL. DEATH COMES TO EVERYONE IN THE END.
YOU'RE NO EXCEPTION. LIE BACK AND ACCEPT IT...
CLARK, HOW CAN YOU SAY THAT? HE CAN'T JUST...
SHUT UP!
SHUT UP, BOTH OF YOU! I'M NOT LISTENING! YOU'RE NOT...
...REAL.
MERCIFUL RAO...
WHAT'S HAPPENING TO ME?
7

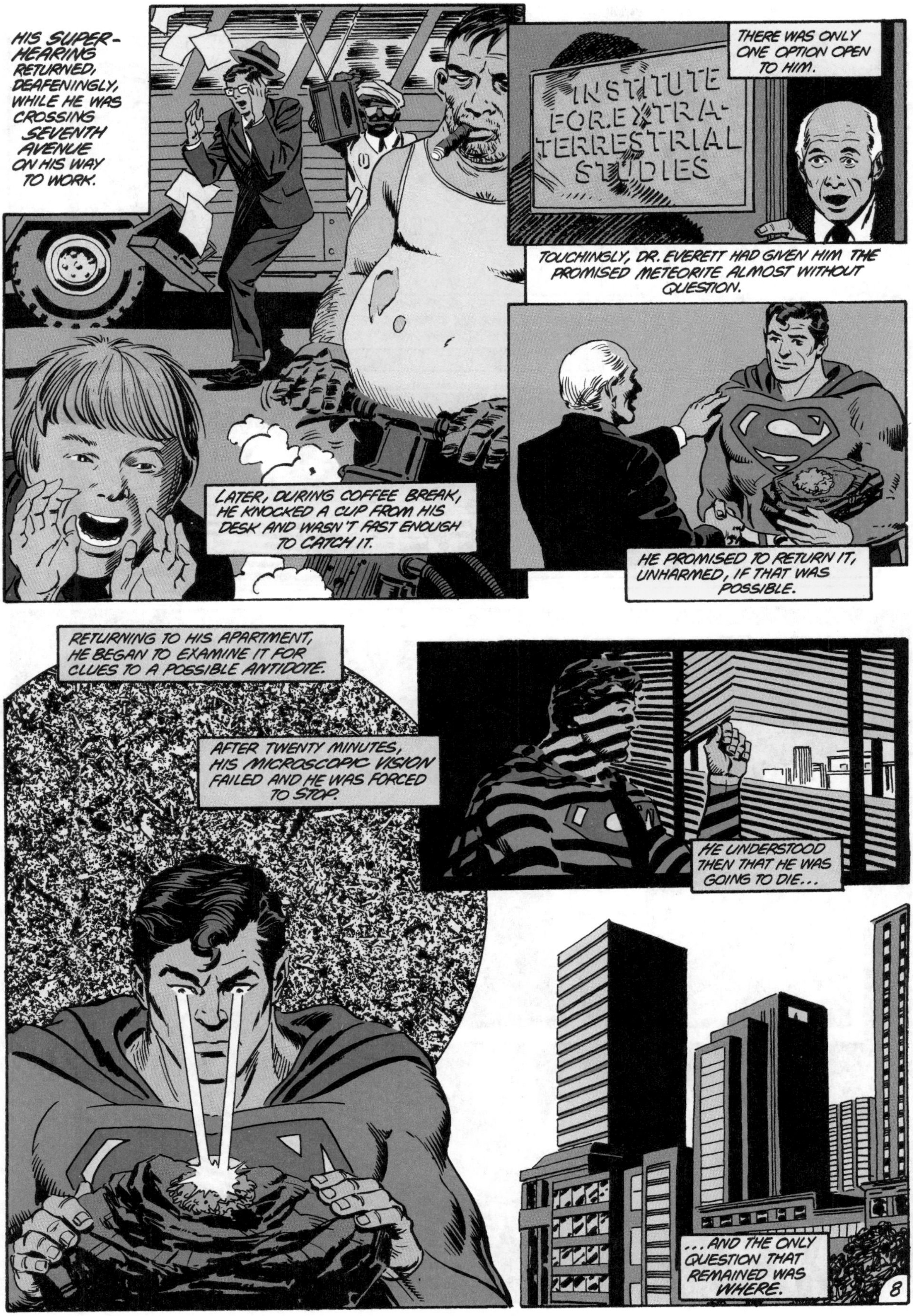
HIS SUPER-HEARING RETURNED, DEAFENINGLY, WHILE HE WAS CROSSING SEVENTH AVENUE ON HIS WAY TO WORK.
LATER, DURING COFFEE BREAK, HE KNOCKED A CUP FROM HIS DESK AND WASN'T FAST ENOUGH TO CATCH IT.
THERE WAS ONLY ONE OPTION OPEN TO HIM.
INSTITUTE FOR EXTRA-TERRESTRIAL STUDIES
TOUCHINGLY, DR. EVERETT HAD GIVEN HIM THE PROMISED METEORITE ALMOST WITHOUT QUESTION.
HE PROMISED TO RETURN IT, UNHARMED, IF THAT WAS POSSIBLE.
RETURNING TO HIS APARTMENT, HE BEGAN TO EXAMINE IT FOR CLUES TO A POSSIBLE ANTIDOTE.
AFTER TWENTY MINUTES, HIS MICROSCOPIC VISION FAILED AND HE WAS FORCED TO STOP.
HE UNDERSTOOD THEN THAT HE WAS GOING TO DIE...
...AND THE ONLY QUESTION THAT REMAINED WAS WHERE.
8

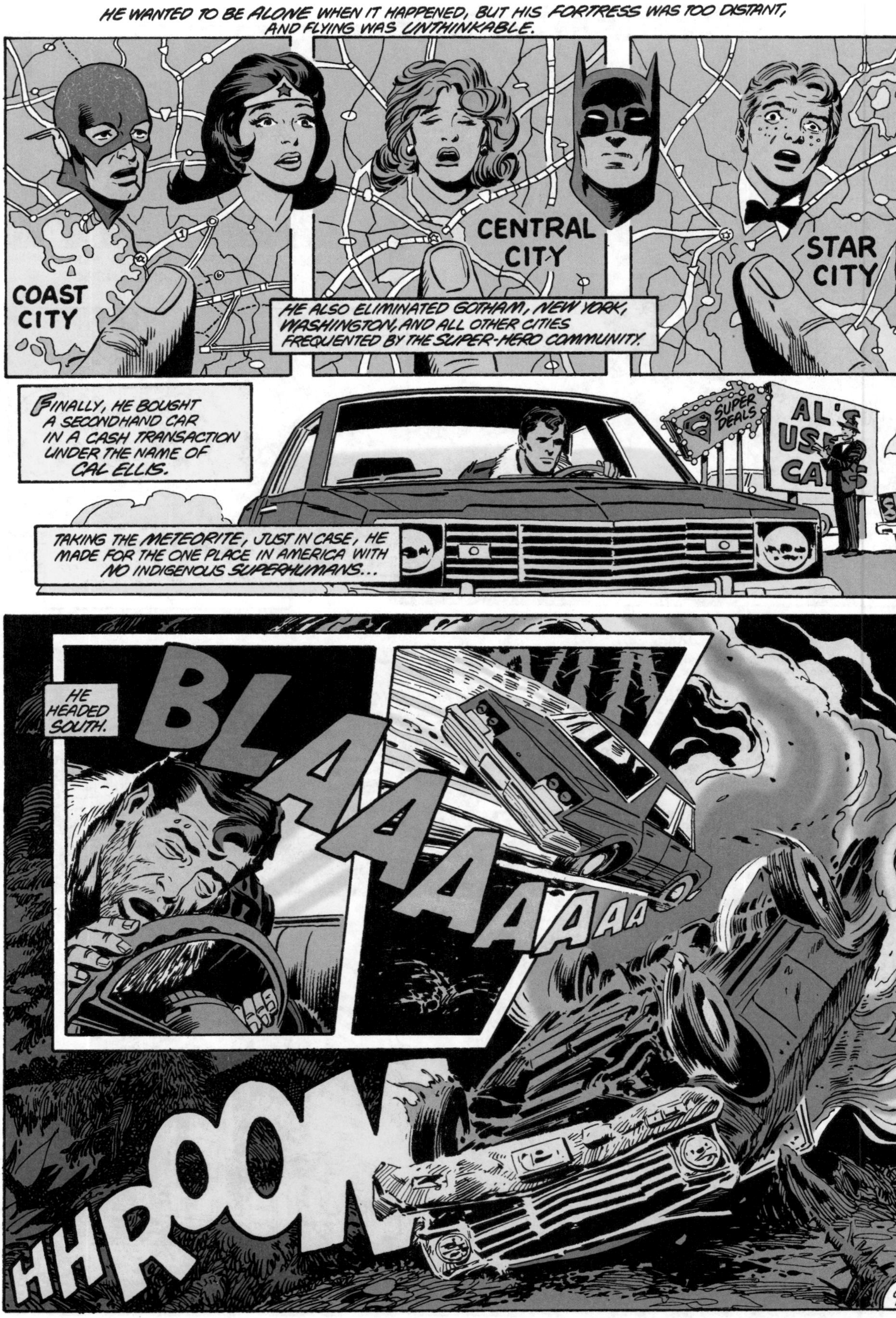
HE WANTED TO BE ALONE WHEN IT HAPPENED, BUT HIS FORTRESS WAS TOO DISTANT, AND FLYING WAS UNTHINKABLE.
COAST CITY
CENTRAL CITY
HE ALSO ELIMINATED GOTHAM, NEW YORK, WASHINGTON, AND ALL OTHER CITIES FREQUENTED BY THE SUPER-HERO COMMUNITY.
STAR CITY
FINALLY, HE BOUGHT A SECONDHAND CAR IN A CASH TRANSACTION UNDER THE NAME OF CAL ELLIS.
SUPER DEALS
TAKING THE METEORITE, JUST IN CASE, HE MADE FOR THE ONE PLACE IN AMERICA WITH NO INDIGENOUS SUPERHUMANS...
HE HEADED SOUTH.
BLAAAAAAAA
HHROOM
9

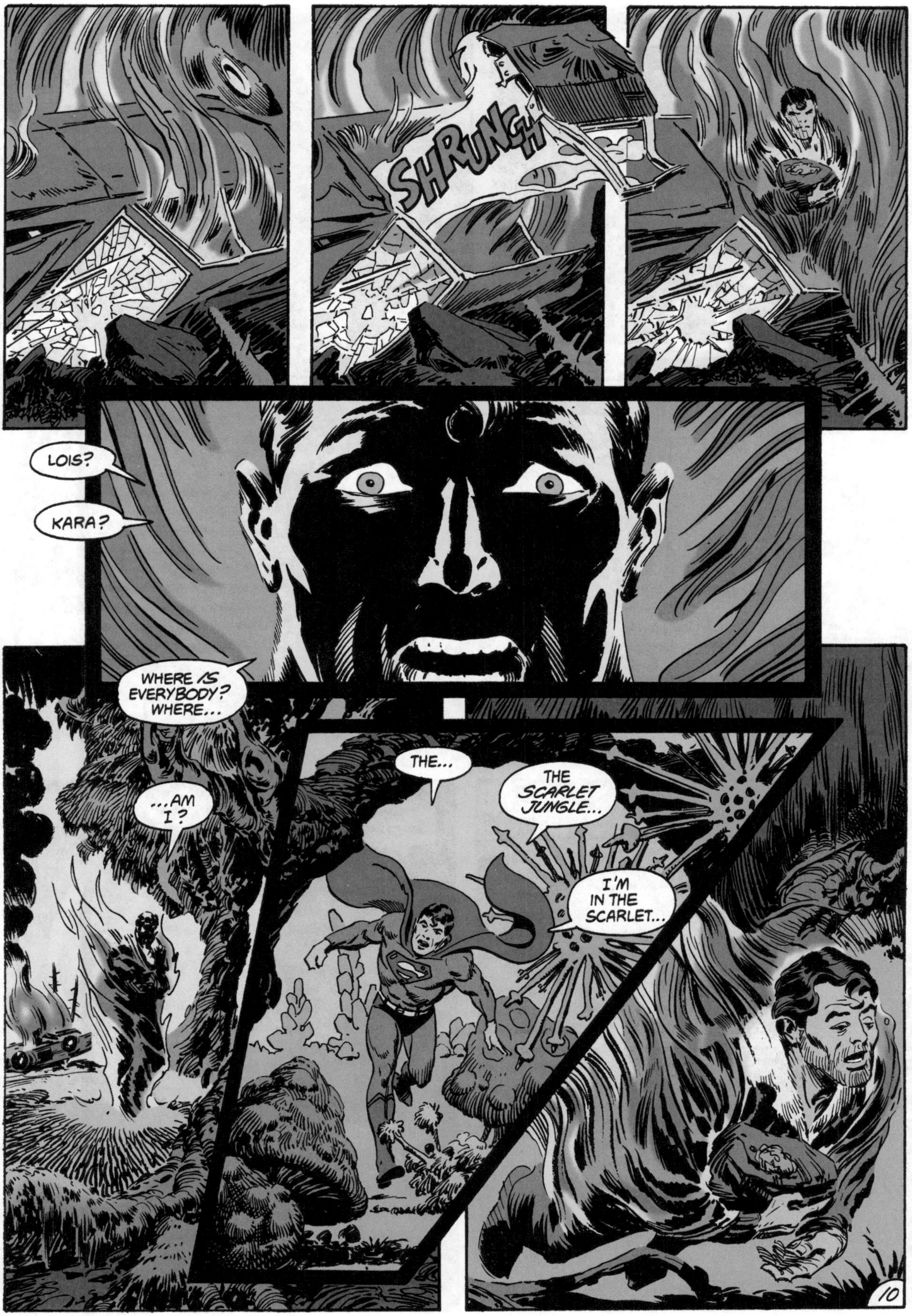
SHRUNCH
LOIS?
KARA?
WHERE IS EVERYBODY? WHERE...
...AM I?
THE...
THE SCARLET JUNGLE...
I'M IN THE SCARLET...
10

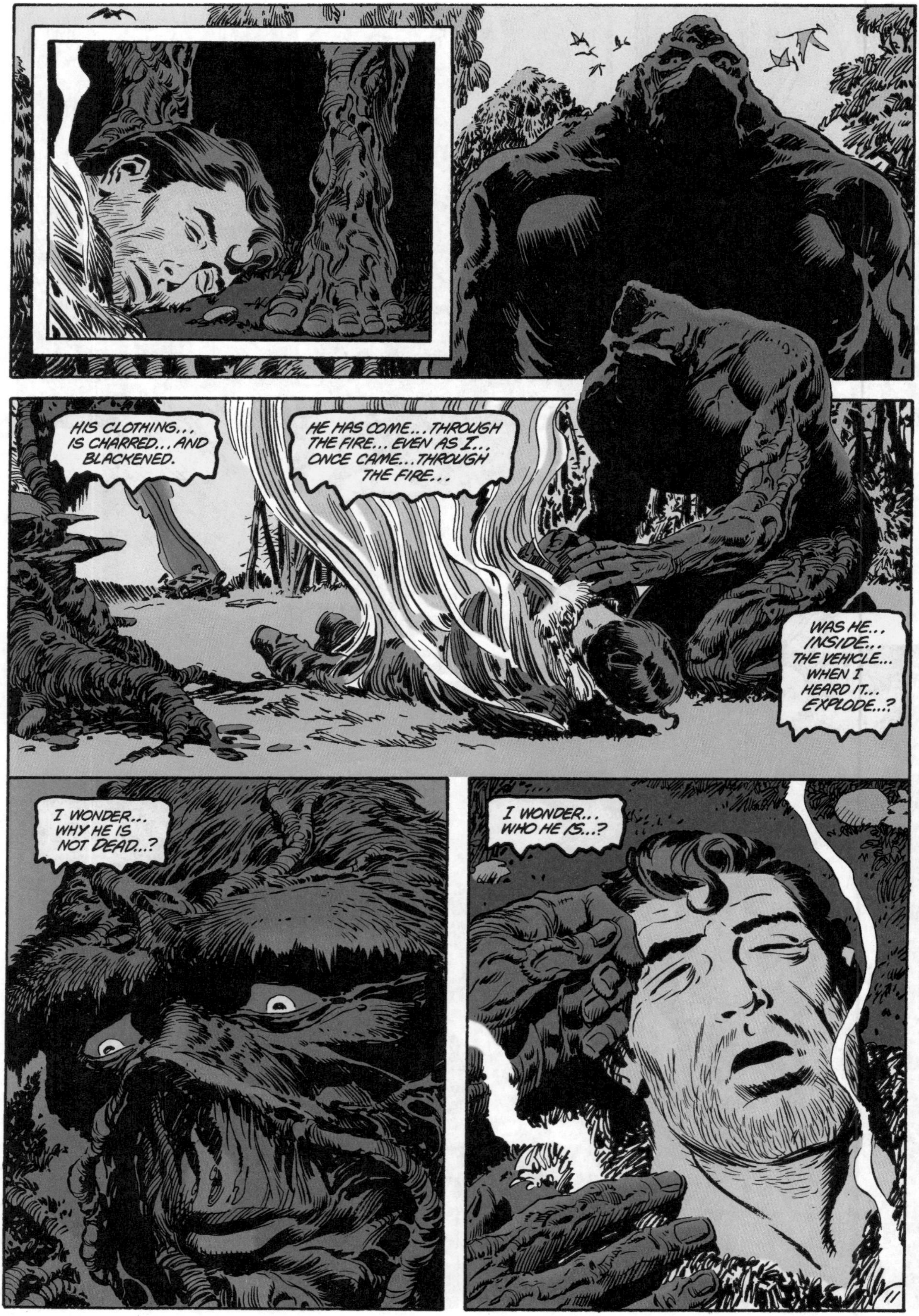
HIS CLOTHING... IS CHARRED... AND BLACKENED.
HE HAS COME... THROUGH THE FIRE... EVEN AS I... ONCE CAME... THROUGH THE FIRE...
WAS HE... INSIDE... THE VEHICLE... WHEN I HEARD IT... EXPLODE...?
I WONDER... WHY HE IS NOT DEAD...?
I WONDER... WHO HE IS...?

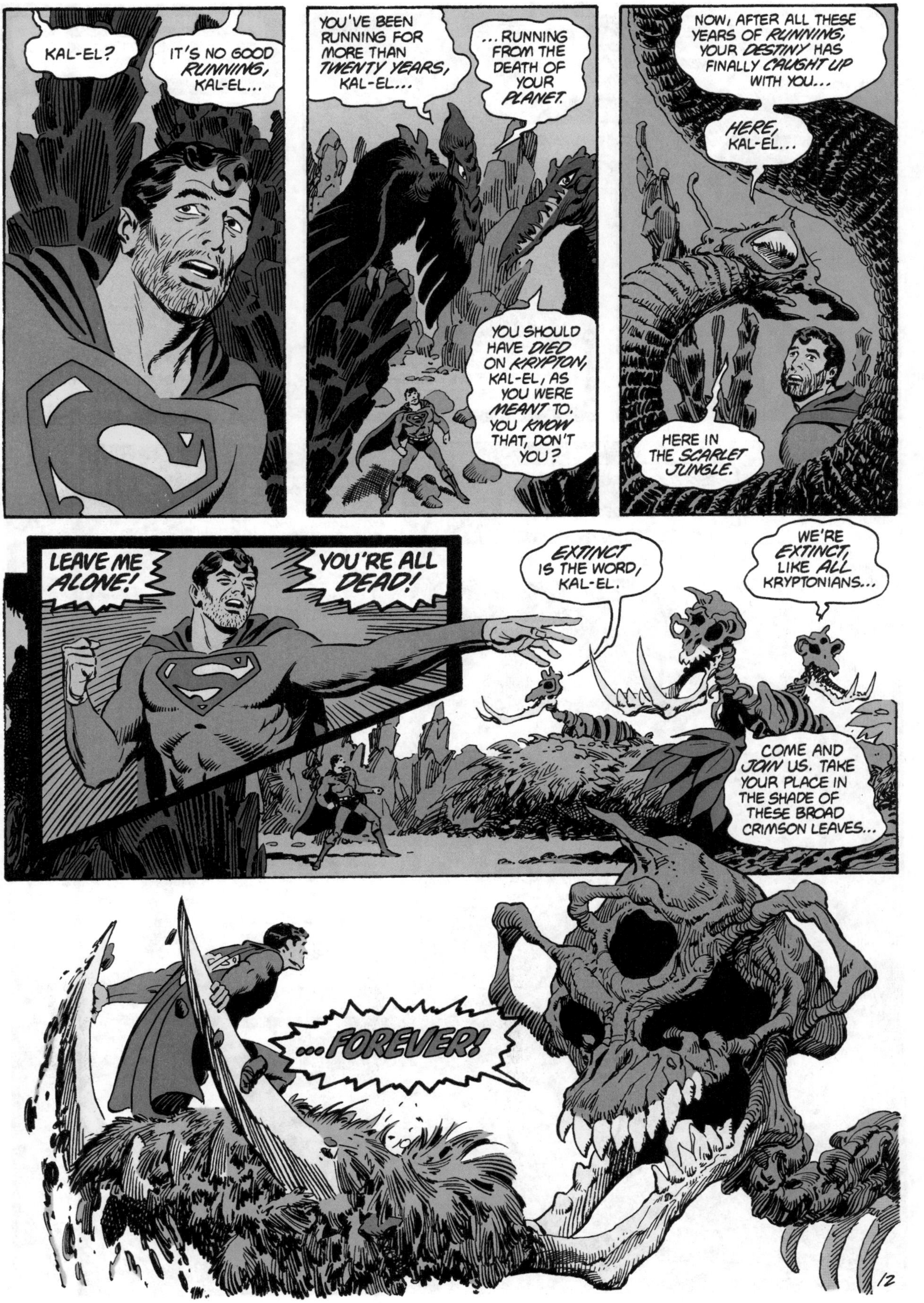
KAL-EL?
IT'S NO GOOD RUNNING, KAL-EL...
YOU'VE BEEN RUNNING FOR MORE THAN TWENTY YEARS, KAL-EL...
...RUNNING FROM THE DEATH OF YOUR PLANET.
YOU SHOULD HAVE DIED ON KRYPTON, KAL-EL, AS YOU WERE MEANT TO. YOU KNOW THAT, DON'T YOU?
NOW, AFTER ALL THESE YEARS OF RUNNING, YOUR DESTINY HAS FINALLY CAUGHT UP WITH YOU...
HERE, KAL-EL...
HERE IN THE SCARLET JUNGLE.
LEAVE ME ALONE!
YOU'RE ALL DEAD!
EXTINCT IS THE WORD, KAL-EL.
WE'RE EXTINCT, LIKE ALL KRYPTONIANS...
COME AND JOIN US. TAKE YOUR PLACE IN THE SHADE OF THESE BROAD CRIMSON LEAVES...
...FOREVER!
12

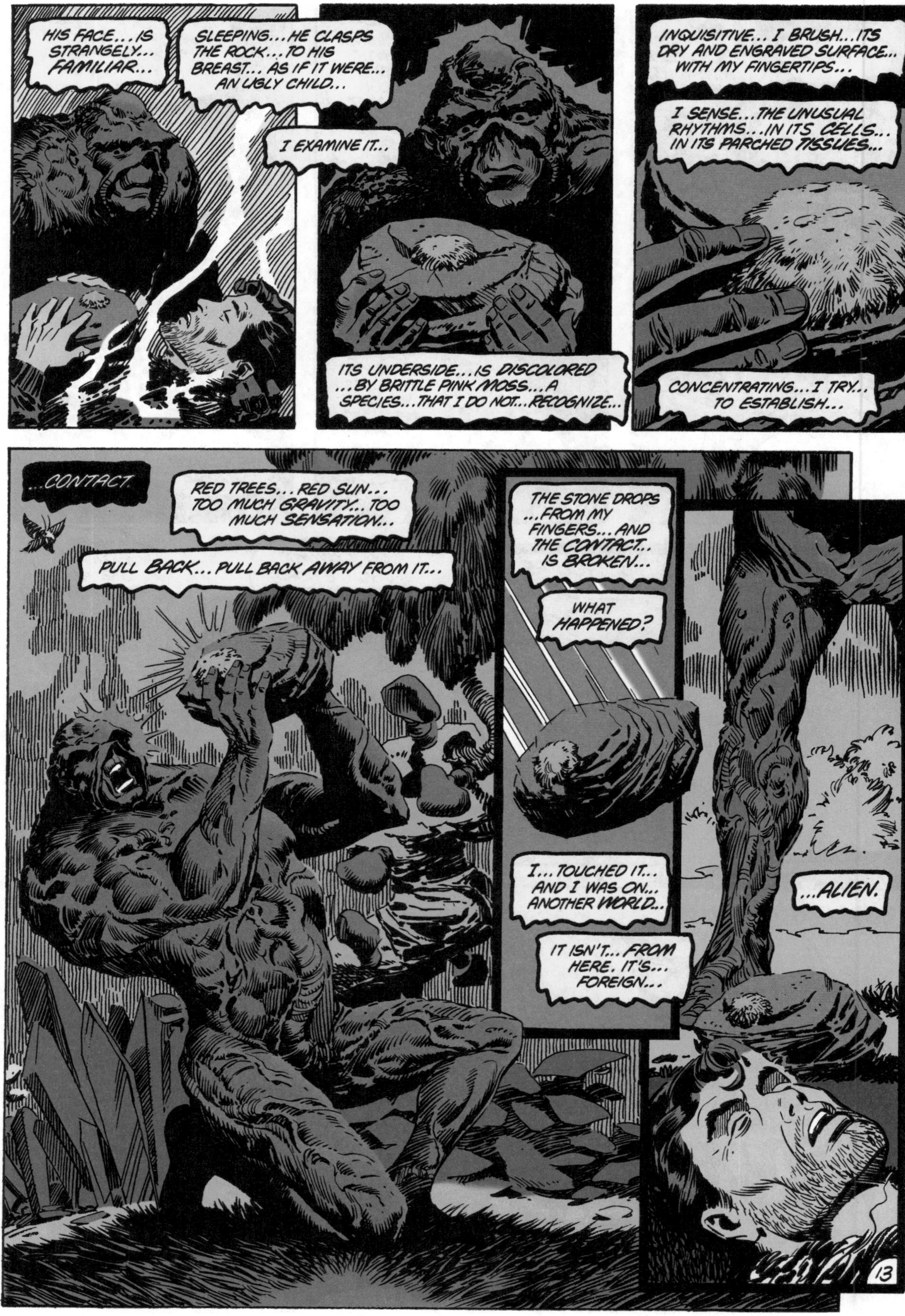
HIS FACE... IS STRANGELY... FAMILIAR...
SLEEPING... HE CLASPS THE ROCK... TO HIS BREAST... AS IF IT WERE... AN UGLY CHILD...
I EXAMINE IT...
ITS UNDERSIDE... IS DISCOLORED ...BY BRITTLE PINK MOSS... A SPECIES... THAT I DO NOT... RECOGNIZE...
INQUISITIVE... I BRUSH... ITS DRY AND ENGRAVED SURFACE... WITH MY FINGERTIPS...
I SENSE... THE UNUSUAL RHYTHMS... IN ITS CELLS... IN ITS PARCHED TISSUES...
CONCENTRATING... I TRY... TO ESTABLISH...
...CONTACT.
RED TREES... RED SUN... TOO MUCH GRAVITY... TOO MUCH SENSATION...
PULL BACK... PULL BACK AWAY FROM IT...
THE STONE DROPS ...FROM MY FINGERS... AND THE CONTACT... IS BROKEN...
WHAT HAPPENED?
I... TOUCHED IT... AND I WAS ON... ANOTHER WORLD...
IT ISN'T... FROM HERE. IT'S... FOREIGN...
...ALIEN.
13

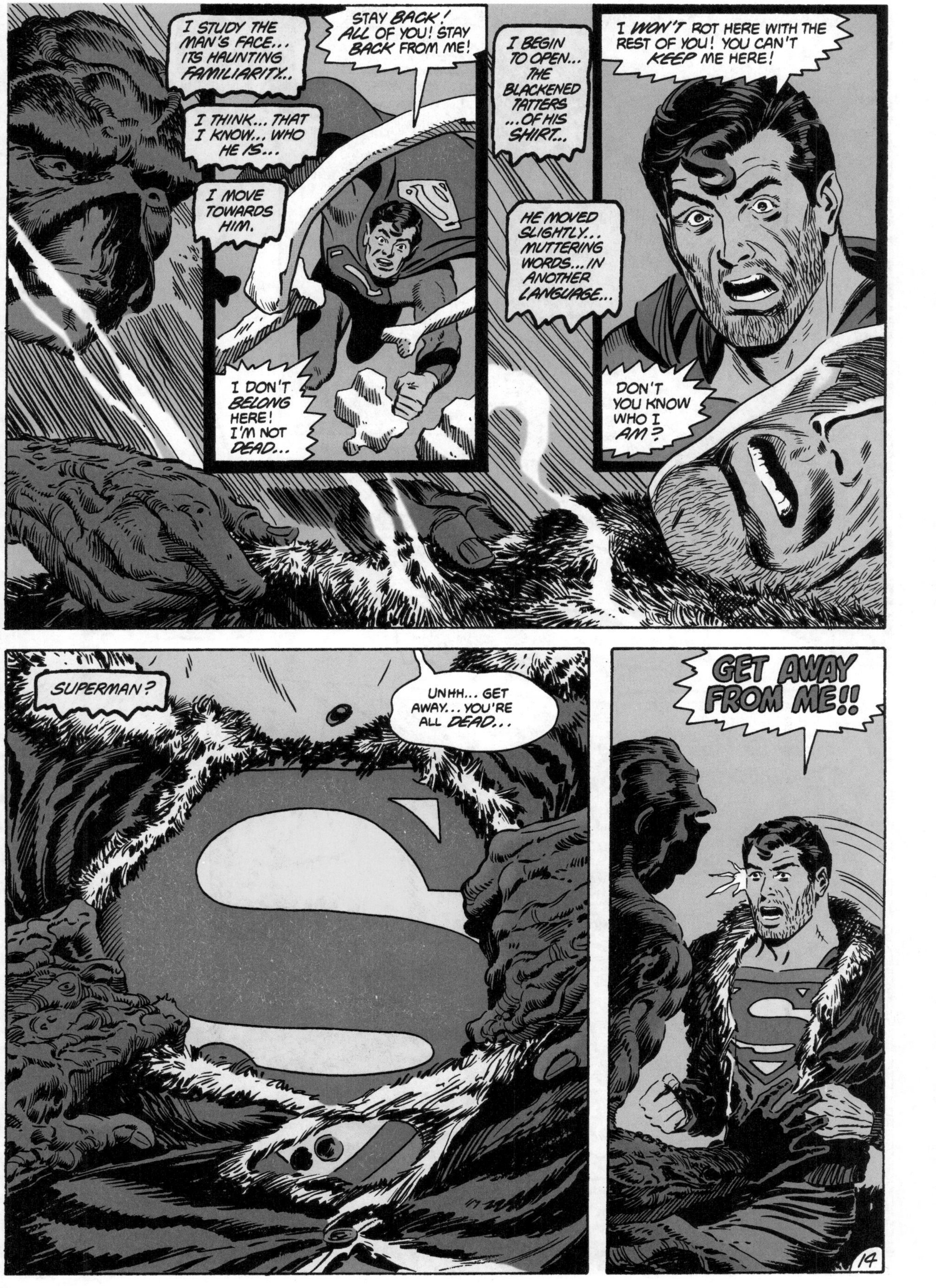

I STUDY THE MAN'S FACE... ITS HAUNTING FAMILIARITY...
I THINK... THAT I KNOW... WHO HE IS...
I MOVE TOWARDS HIM.
STAY BACK! ALL OF YOU! STAY BACK FROM ME!
I DON'T BELONG HERE! I'M NOT DEAD...
I BEGIN TO OPEN... THE BLACKENED TATTERS ...OF HIS SHIRT...
HE MOVED SLIGHTLY... MUTTERING WORDS... IN ANOTHER LANGUAGE...
I WON'T ROT HERE WITH THE REST OF YOU! YOU CAN'T KEEP ME HERE!
DON'T YOU KNOW WHO I AM?
SUPERMAN?
UNHH... GET AWAY... YOU'RE ALL DEAD...
GET AWAY FROM ME!!
14

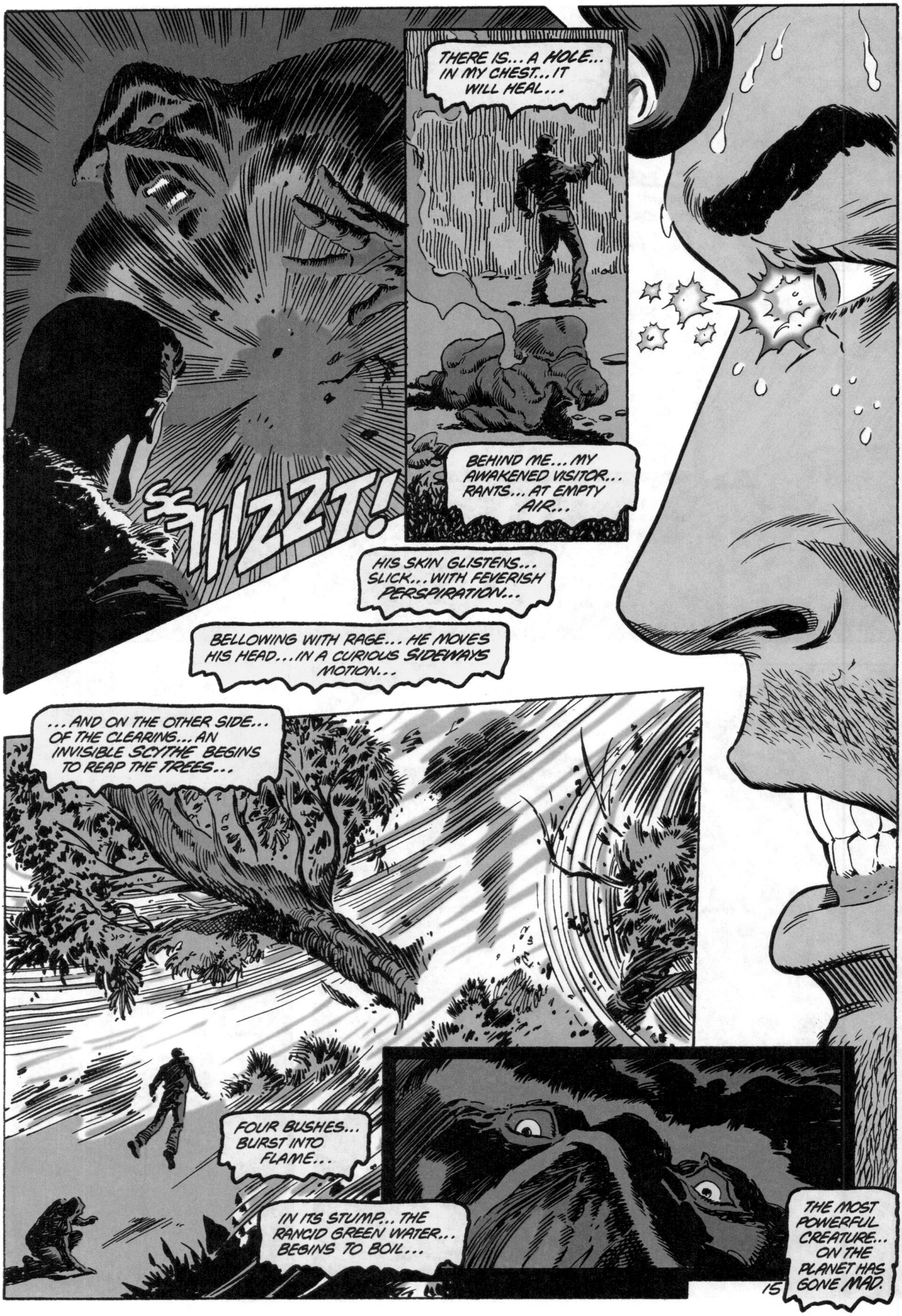
THERE IS... A HOLE... IN MY CHEST... IT WILL HEAL...
SSSSSSIZZZT!
BEHIND ME... MY AWAKENED VISITOR... RANTS... AT EMPTY AIR...
HIS SKIN GLISTENS... SLICK... WITH FEVERISH PERSPIRATION...
BELLOWING WITH RAGE... HE MOVES HIS HEAD... IN A CURIOUS SIDEWAYS MOTION...
...AND ON THE OTHER SIDE... OF THE CLEARING... AN INVISIBLE SCYTHE BEGINS TO REAP THE TREES...
FOUR BUSHES... BURST INTO FLAME...
IN ITS STUMP... THE RANCID GREEN WATER... BEGINS TO BOIL...
THE MOST POWERFUL CREATURE... ON THE PLANET HAS GONE MAD.
15

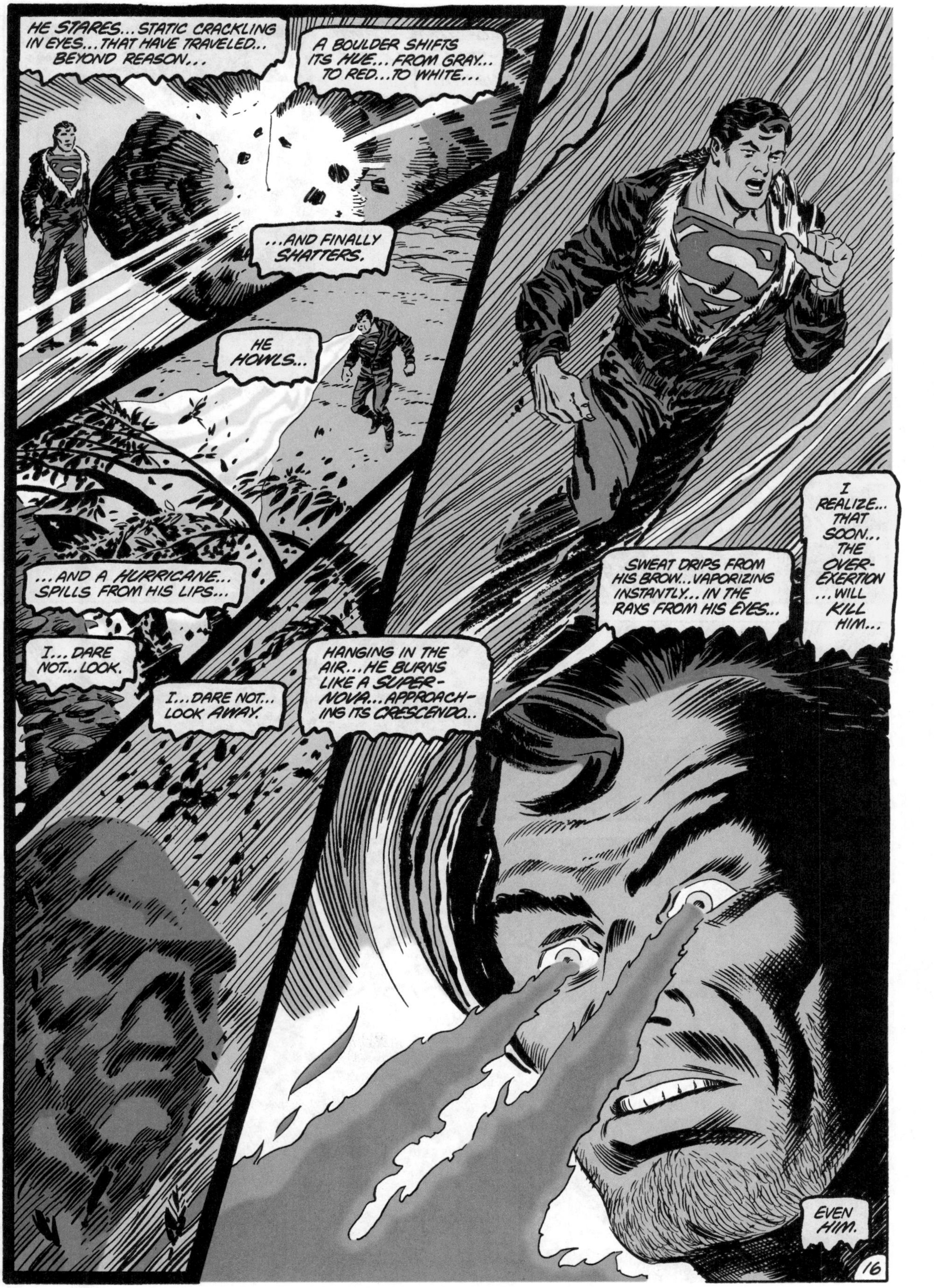
HE STARES... STATIC CRACKLING IN EYES... THAT HAVE TRAVELED... BEYOND REASON...
A BOULDER SHIFTS ITS HUE... FROM GRAY... TO RED... TO WHITE...
...AND FINALLY SHATTERS.
HE HOWLS...
...AND A HURRICANE... SPILLS FROM HIS LIPS...
I... DARE NOT... LOOK.
I... DARE NOT... LOOK AWAY.
HANGING IN THE AIR... HE BURNS LIKE A SUPER-NOVA... APPROACH-ING ITS CRESCENDO...
SWEAT DRIPS FROM HIS BROW... VAPORIZING INSTANTLY... IN THE RAYS FROM HIS EYES...
I REALIZE... THAT SOON... THE OVER-EXERTION ...WILL KILL HIM...
EVEN HIM.
16

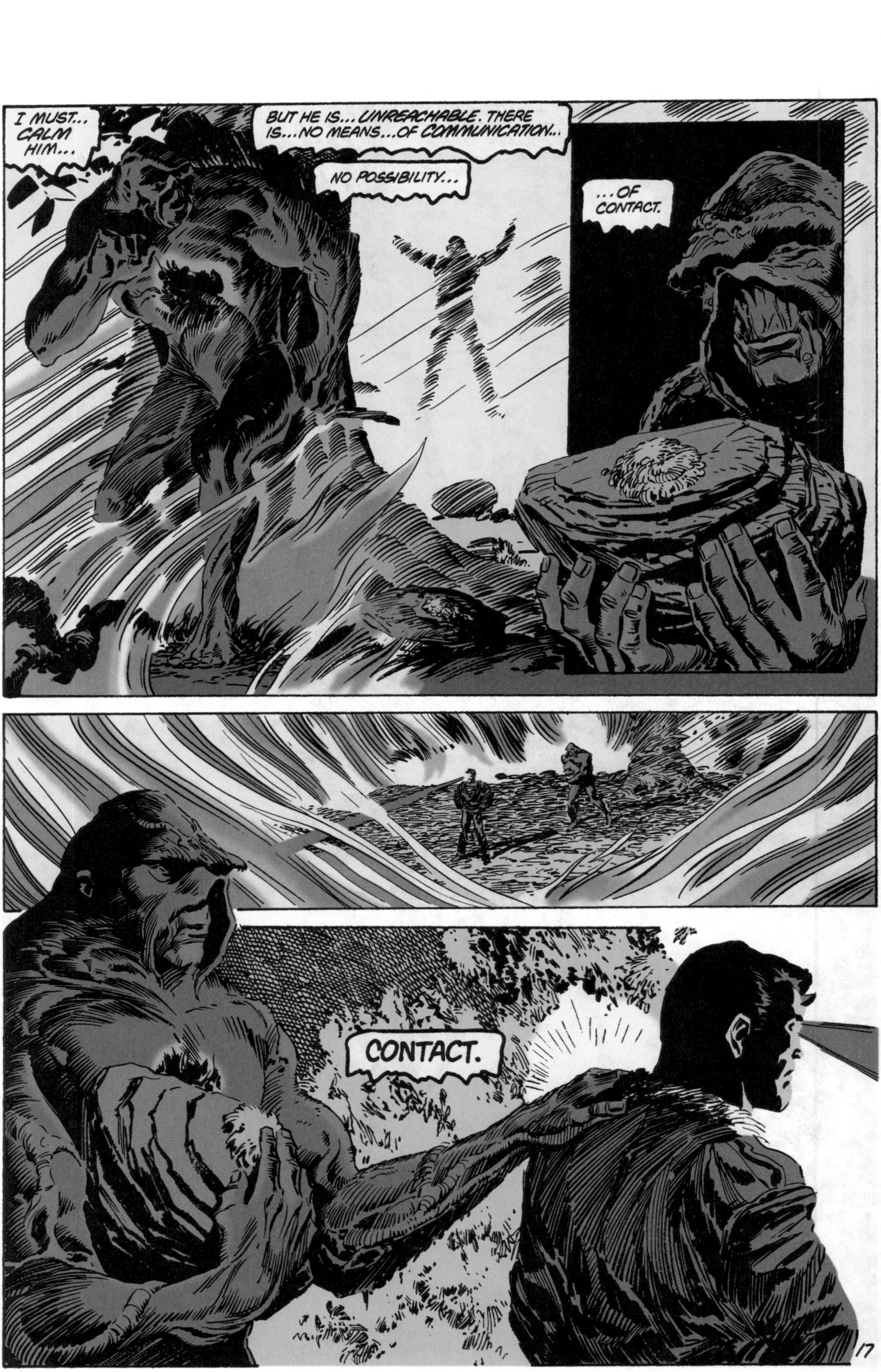

I MUST... CALM HIM...
BUT HE IS... UNREACHABLE. THERE IS... NO MEANS... OF COMMUNICATION...
NO POSSIBILITY...
...OF CONTACT.
CONTACT.
17

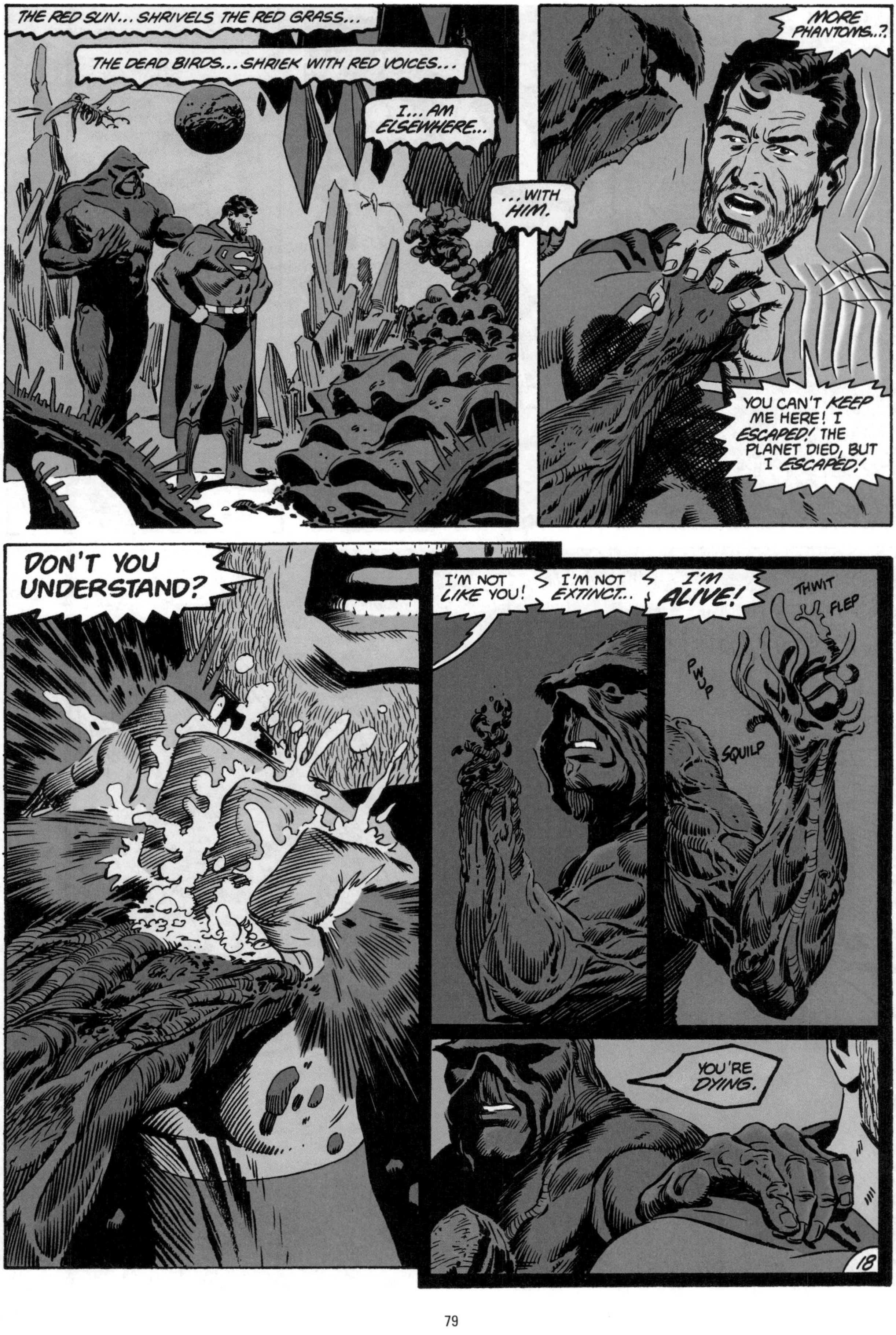
THE RED SUN... SHRIVELS THE RED GRASS...
THE DEAD BIRDS... SHRIEK WITH RED VOICES...
I... AM ELSEWHERE...
...WITH HIM.
MORE PHANTOMS..?
YOU CAN'T KEEP ME HERE! I ESCAPED! THE PLANET DIED, BUT I ESCAPED!
DON'T YOU UNDERSTAND?
I'M NOT LIKE YOU!
I'M NOT EXTINCT...
I'M ALIVE!
THWIT
FLEP
PWUP
SQUILP
YOU'RE DYING.
18

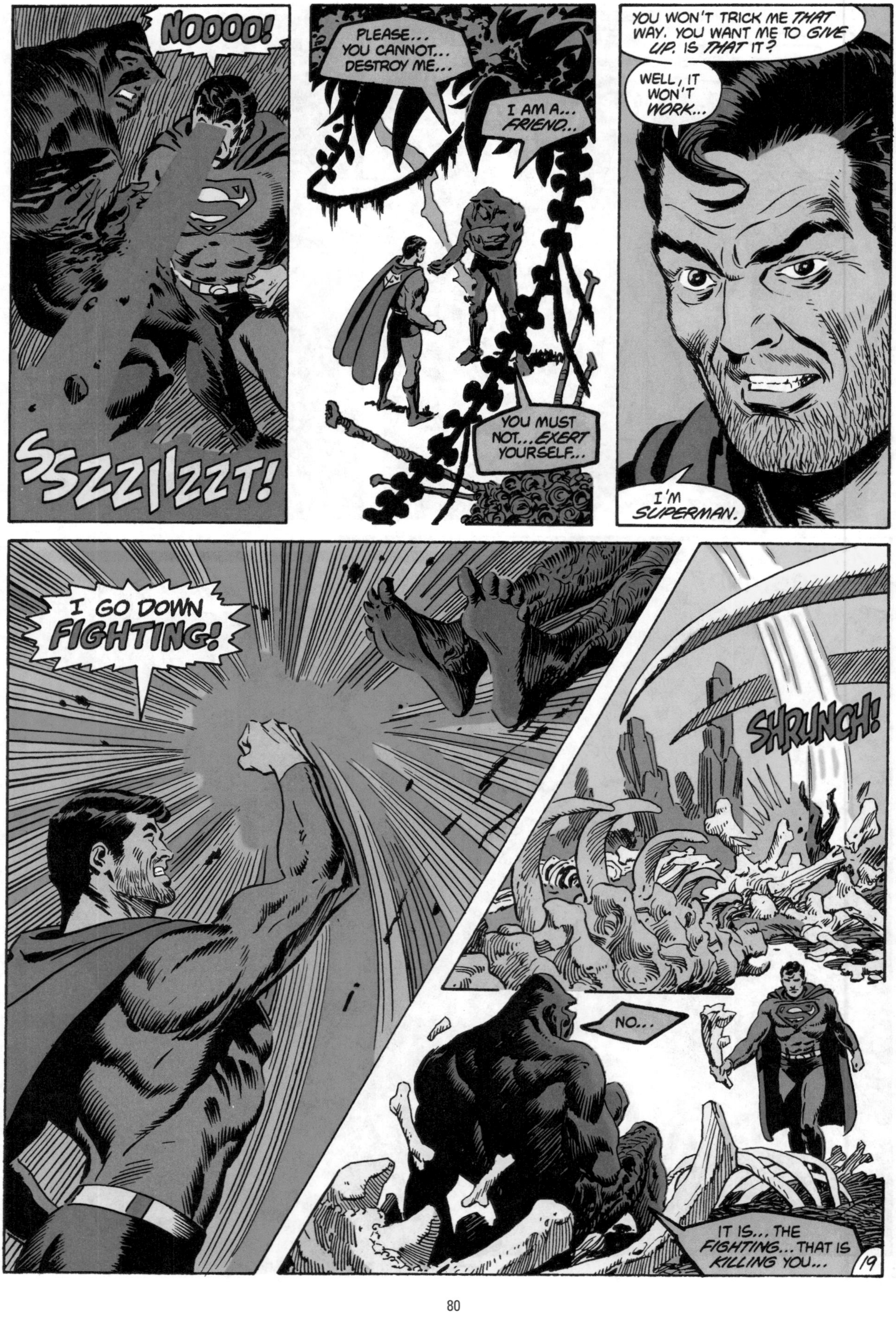
NOOOO!
SSZZIIZZT!
PLEASE... YOU CANNOT... DESTROY ME...
I AM A... FRIEND...
YOU MUST NOT... EXERT YOURSELF...
YOU WON'T TRICK ME THAT WAY. YOU WANT ME TO GIVE UP. IS THAT IT?
WELL, IT WON'T WORK...
I'M SUPERMAN.
I GO DOWN FIGHTING!
SHRUNCH!
NO...
IT IS... THE FIGHTING... THAT IS KILLING YOU...
19

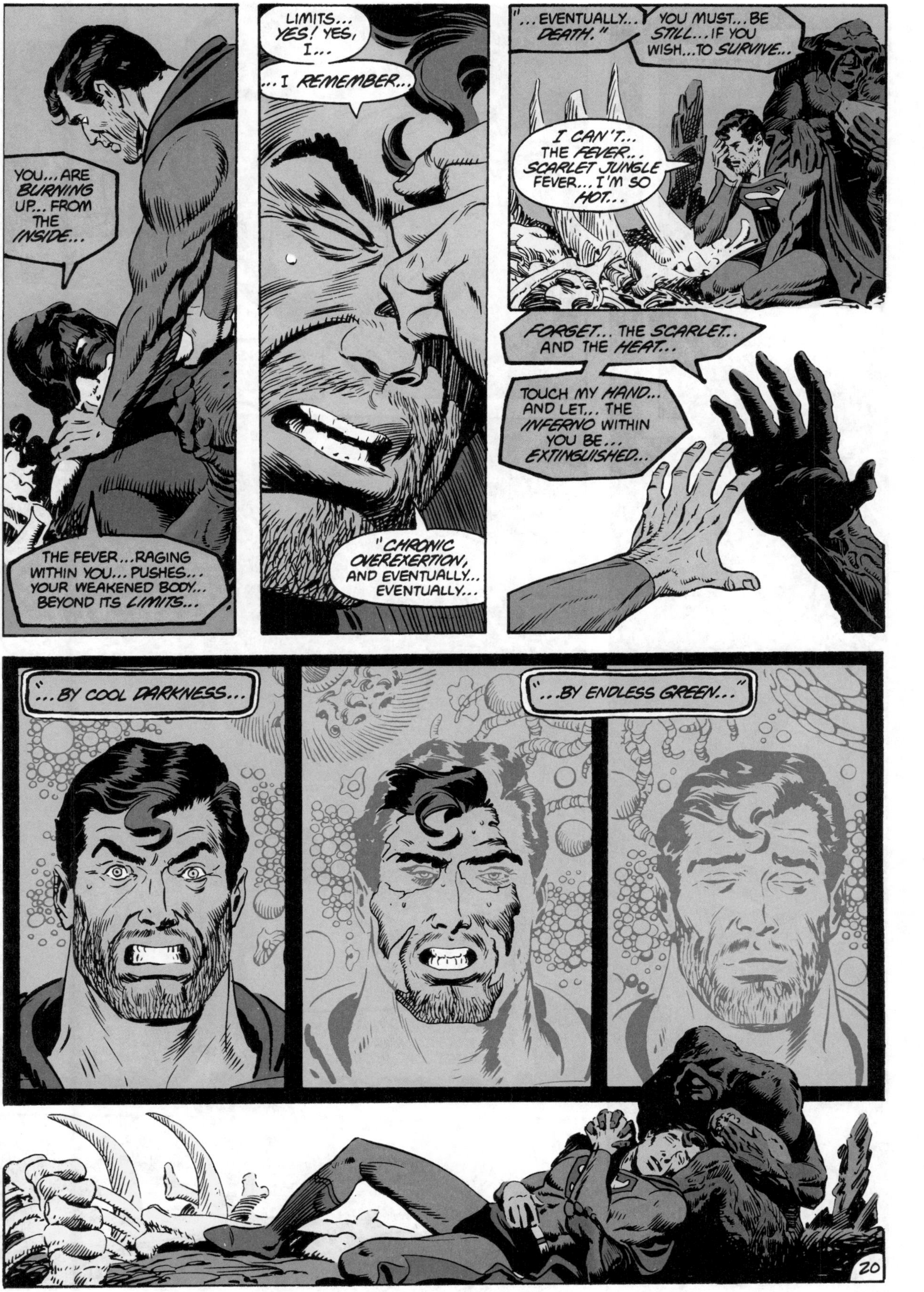
YOU... ARE BURNING UP... FROM THE INSIDE...
THE FEVER... RAGING WITHIN YOU... PUSHES... YOUR WEAKENED BODY... BEYOND ITS LIMITS...
LIMITS... YES! YES, I...
...I REMEMBER...
"CHRONIC OVEREXERTION, AND EVENTUALLY... EVENTUALLY...
"...EVENTUALLY... DEATH."
YOU MUST... BE STILL... IF YOU WISH... TO SURVIVE...
I CAN'T... THE FEVER... SCARLET JUNGLE FEVER... I'M SO HOT...
FORGET... THE SCARLET... AND THE HEAT...
TOUCH MY HAND... AND LET... THE INFERNO WITHIN YOU BE... EXTINGUISHED...
"...BY COOL DARKNESS...
"...BY ENDLESS GREEN..."
20

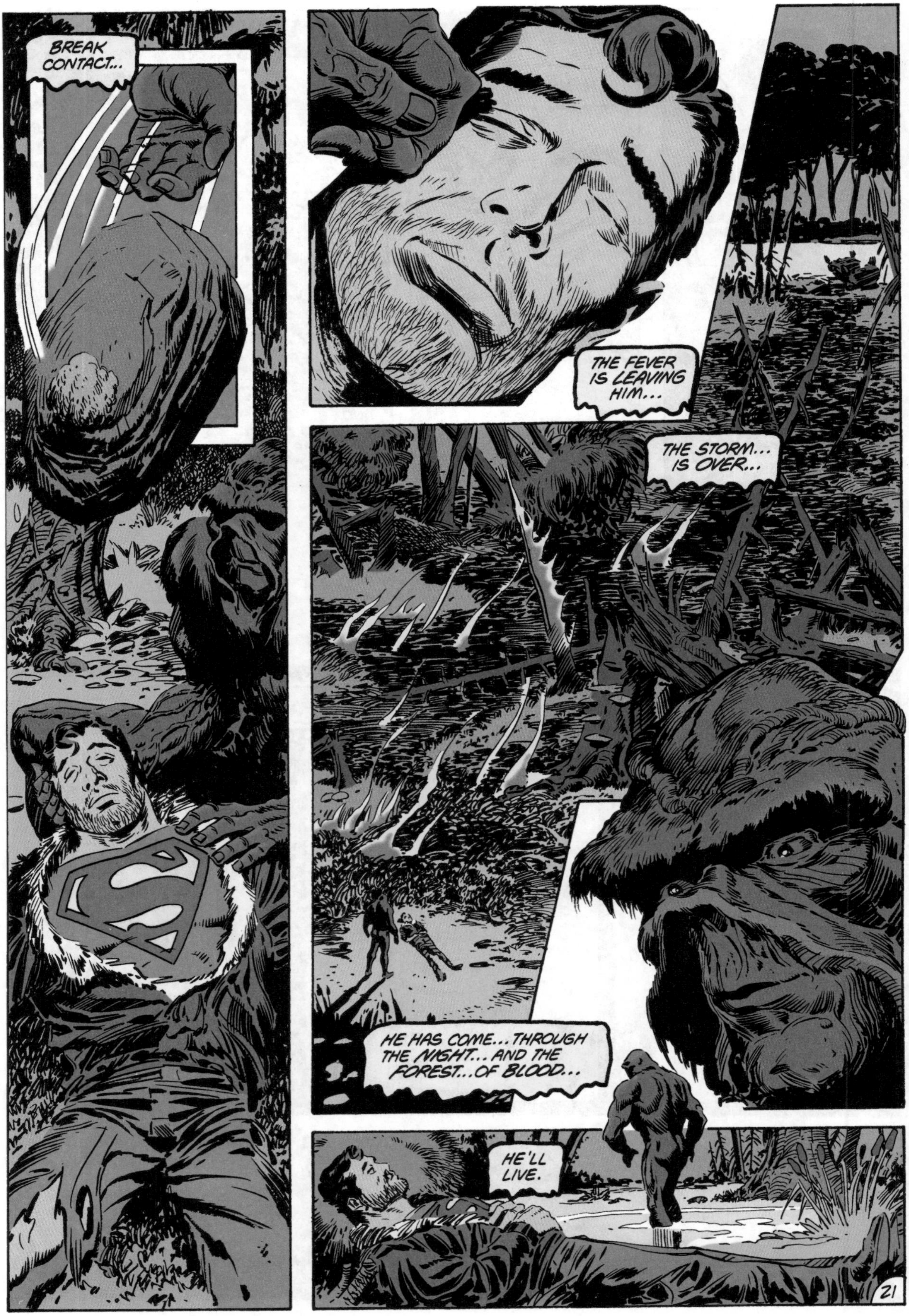
BREAK CONTACT...
THE FEVER IS LEAVING HIM...
THE STORM... IS OVER...
HE HAS COME... THROUGH THE NIGHT... AND THE FOREST... OF BLOOD...
HE'LL LIVE.
21

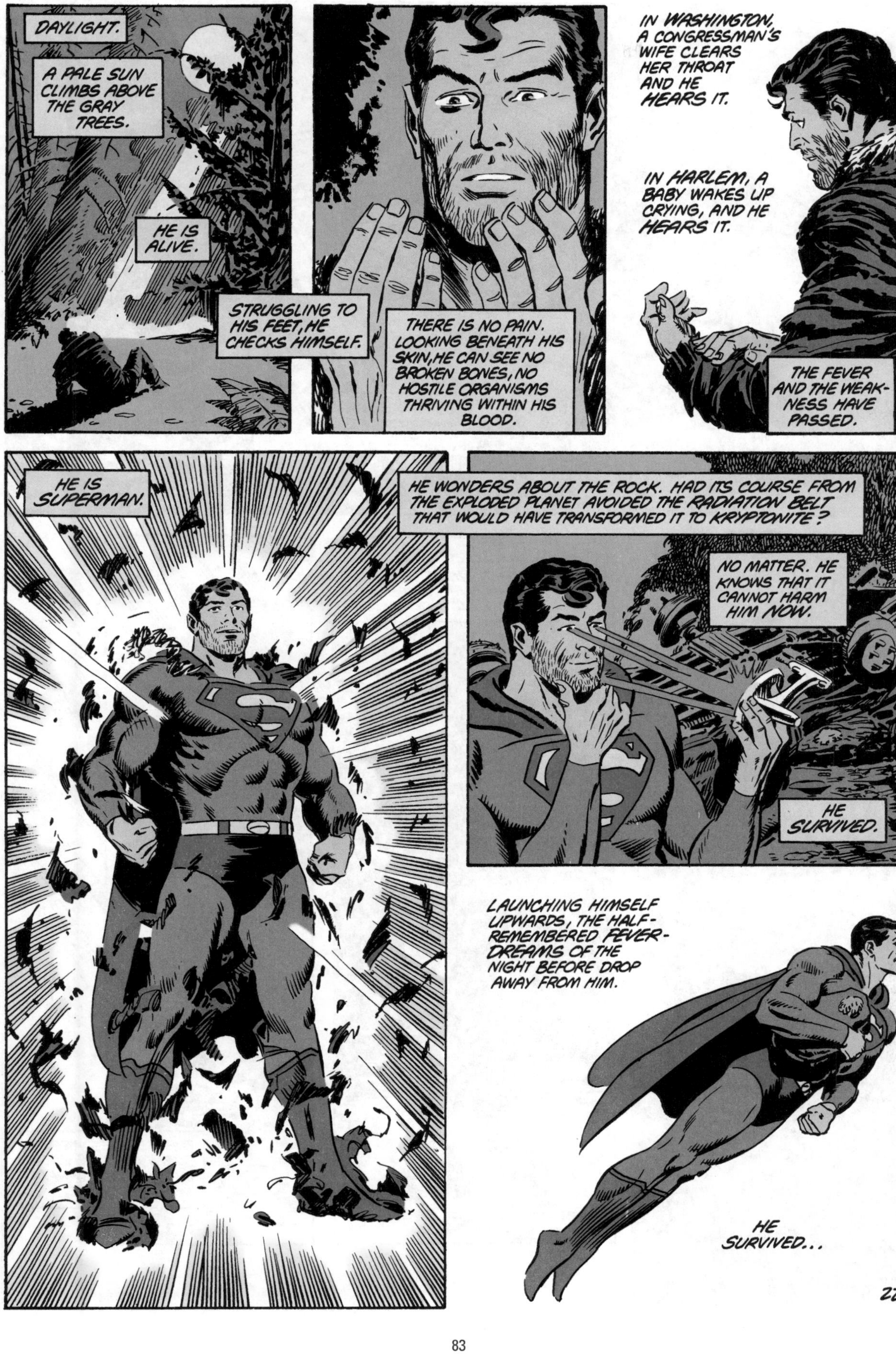
DAYLIGHT.
A PALE SUN CLIMBS ABOVE THE GRAY TREES.
HE IS ALIVE.
STRUGGLING TO HIS FEET, HE CHECKS HIMSELF.
THERE IS NO PAIN. LOOKING BENEATH HIS SKIN, HE CAN SEE NO BROKEN BONES, NO HOSTILE ORGANISMS THRIVING WITHIN HIS BLOOD.
IN WASHINGTON, A CONGRESSMAN'S WIFE CLEARS HER THROAT AND HE HEARS IT.
IN HARLEM, A BABY WAKES UP CRYING, AND HE HEARS IT.
THE FEVER AND THE WEAKNESS HAVE PASSED.
HE IS SUPERMAN.
HE WONDERS ABOUT THE ROCK. HAD ITS COURSE FROM THE EXPLODED PLANET AVOIDED THE RADIATION BELT THAT WOULD HAVE TRANSFORMED IT TO KRYPTONITE?
NO MATTER. HE KNOWS THAT IT CANNOT HARM HIM NOW.
HE SURVIVED.
LAUNCHING HIMSELF UPWARDS, THE HALF-REMEMBERED FEVER-DREAMS OF THE NIGHT BEFORE DROP AWAY FROM HIM.
HE SURVIVED...
22

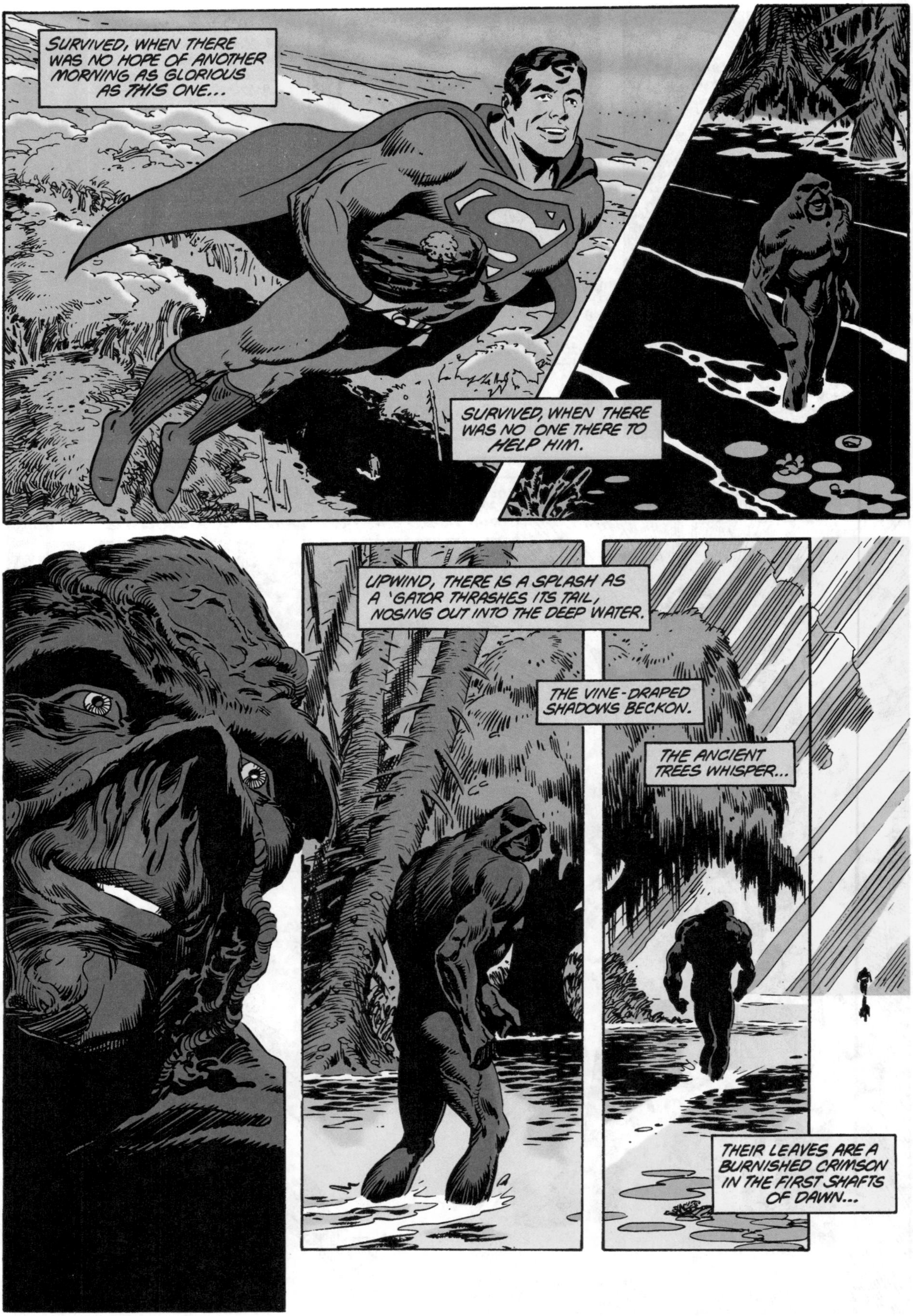
SURVIVED, WHEN THERE WAS NO HOPE OF ANOTHER MORNING AS GLORIOUS AS THIS ONE...
SURVIVED, WHEN THERE WAS NO ONE THERE TO HELP HIM.
UPWIND, THERE IS A SPLASH AS A 'GATOR THRASHES ITS TAIL, NOSING OUT INTO THE DEEP WATER.
THE VINE-DRAPED SHADOWS BECKON.
THE ANCIENT TREES WHISPER...
THEIR LEAVES ARE A BURNISHED CRIMSON IN THE FIRST SHAFTS OF DAWN...

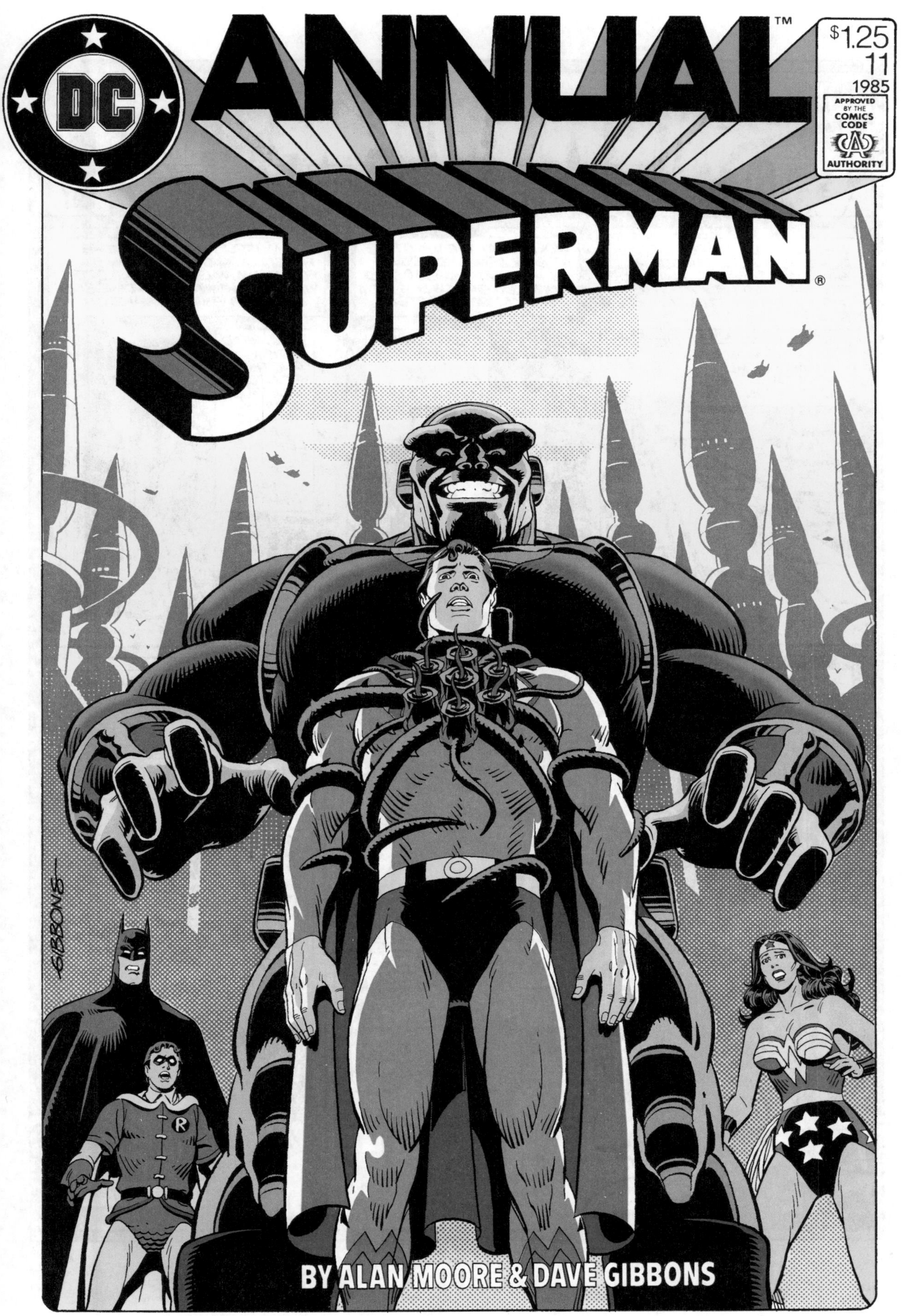
ANNUAL™
$1.25
11
1985
APPROVED BY THE COMICS CODE AUTHORITY
DC
SUPERMAN®
GIBBONS
BY ALAN MOORE & DAVE GIBBONS

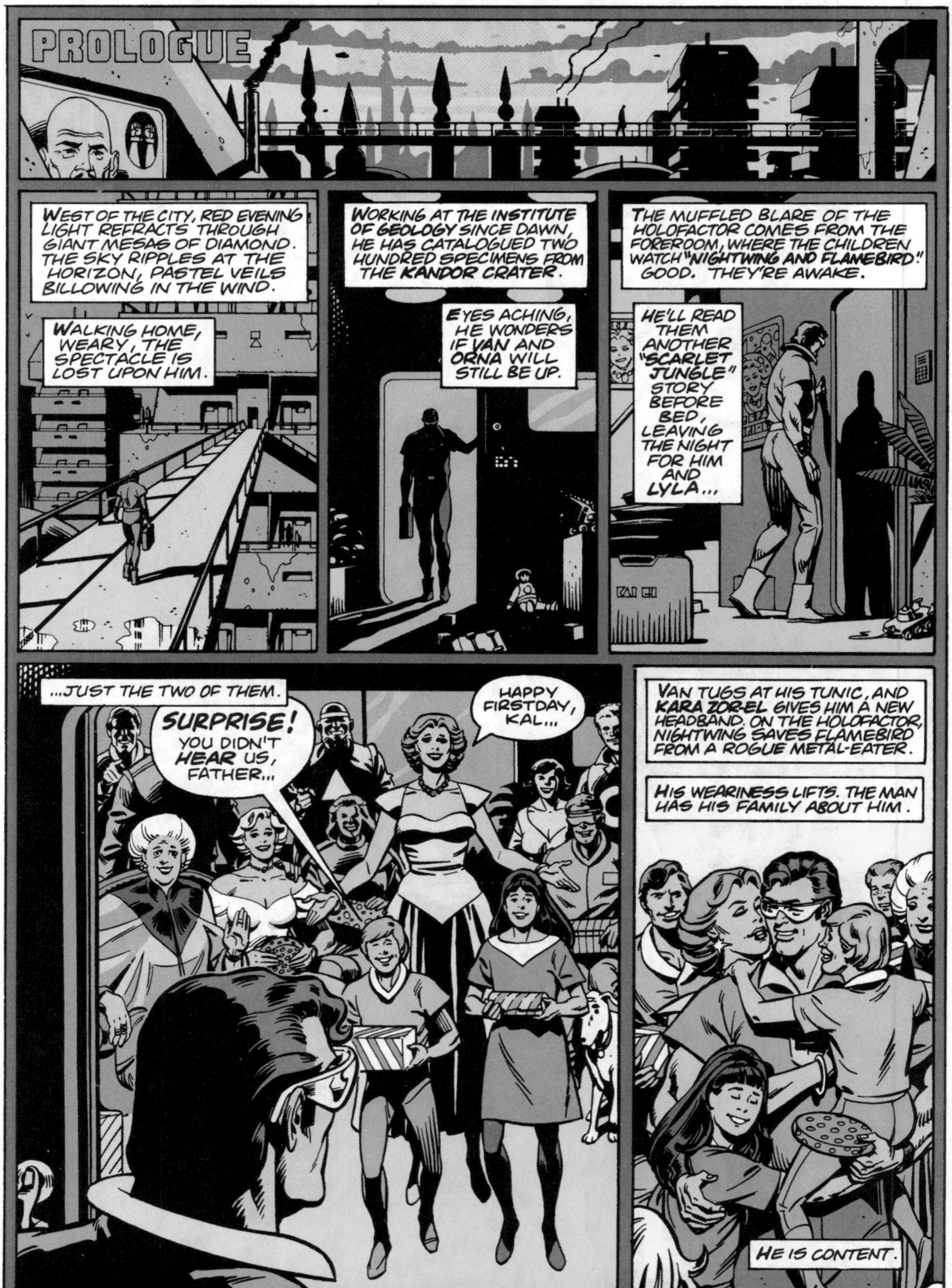
PROLOGUE
WEST OF THE CITY, RED EVENING LIGHT REFRACTS THROUGH GIANT MESAS OF DIAMOND. THE SKY RIPPLES AT THE HORIZON, PASTEL VEILS BILLOWING IN THE WIND.
WALKING HOME, WEARY, THE SPECTACLE IS LOST UPON HIM.
WORKING AT THE INSTITUTE OF GEOLOGY SINCE DAWN, HE HAS CATALOGUED TWO HUNDRED SPECIMENS FROM THE KANDOR CRATER.
EYES ACHING, HE WONDERS IF VAN AND ORNA WILL STILL BE UP.
THE MUFFLED BLARE OF THE HOLOFACTOR COMES FROM THE FOREROOM, WHERE THE CHILDREN WATCH "NIGHTWING AND FLAMEBIRD." GOOD. THEY'RE AWAKE.
HE'LL READ THEM ANOTHER "SCARLET JUNGLE" STORY BEFORE BED, LEAVING THE NIGHT FOR HIM AND LYLA...
...JUST THE TWO OF THEM.
SURPRISE! YOU DIDN'T HEAR US, FATHER...
HAPPY FIRSTDAY, KAL...
VAN TUGS AT HIS TUNIC, AND KARA ZOR-EL GIVES HIM A NEW HEADBAND. ON THE HOLOFACTOR, NIGHTWING SAVES FLAMEBIRD FROM A ROGUE METAL-EATER.
HIS WEARINESS LIFTS. THE MAN HAS HIS FAMILY ABOUT HIM.
HE IS CONTENT.
1

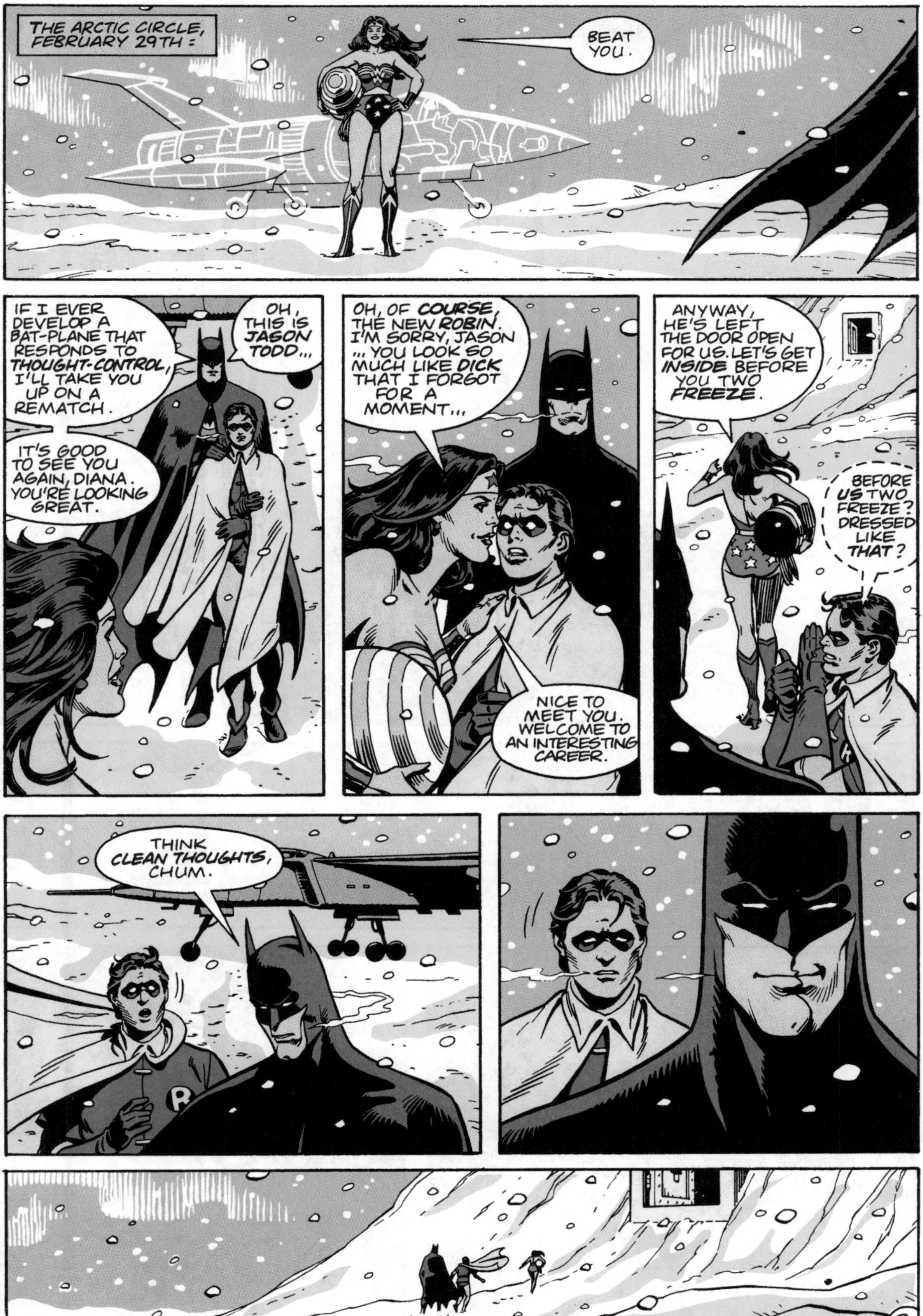
THE ARCTIC CIRCLE, FEBRUARY 29TH:
BEAT YOU.
IF I EVER DEVELOP A BAT-PLANE THAT RESPONDS TO THOUGHT-CONTROL, I'LL TAKE YOU UP ON A REMATCH.
IT'S GOOD TO SEE YOU AGAIN, DIANA. YOU'RE LOOKING GREAT.
OH, THIS IS JASON TODD...
OH, OF COURSE, THE NEW ROBIN. I'M SORRY, JASON ...YOU LOOK SO MUCH LIKE DICK THAT I FORGOT FOR A MOMENT...
NICE TO MEET YOU. WELCOME TO AN INTERESTING CAREER.
ANYWAY, HE'S LEFT THE DOOR OPEN FOR US. LET'S GET INSIDE BEFORE YOU TWO FREEZE.
BEFORE US TWO FREEZE? DRESSED LIKE THAT?
THINK CLEAN THOUGHTS, CHUM.
2

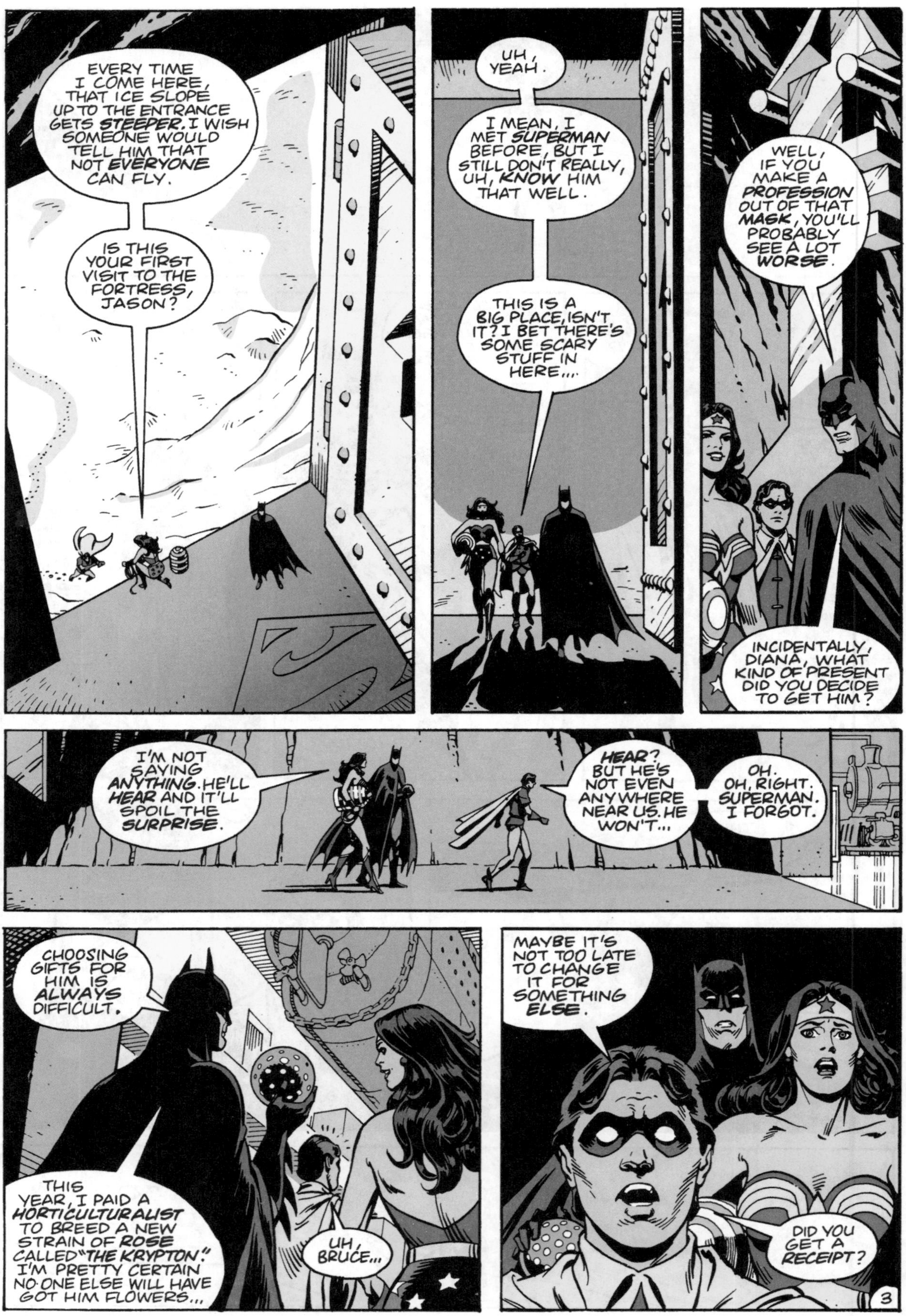
EVERY TIME I COME HERE, THAT ICE SLOPE UP TO THE ENTRANCE GETS STEEPER. I WISH SOMEONE WOULD TELL HIM THAT NOT EVERYONE CAN FLY.
IS THIS YOUR FIRST VISIT TO THE FORTRESS, JASON?
UH, YEAH.
I MEAN, I MET SUPERMAN BEFORE, BUT I STILL DON'T REALLY, UH, KNOW HIM THAT WELL.
THIS IS A BIG PLACE, ISN'T IT? I BET THERE'S SOME SCARY STUFF IN HERE....
WELL, IF YOU MAKE A PROFESSION OUT OF THAT MASK, YOU'LL PROBABLY SEE A LOT WORSE.
INCIDENTALLY, DIANA, WHAT KIND OF PRESENT DID YOU DECIDE TO GET HIM?
I'M NOT SAYING ANYTHING. HE'LL HEAR AND IT'LL SPOIL THE SURPRISE.
HEAR? BUT HE'S NOT EVEN ANYWHERE NEAR US. HE WON'T...
OH. OH, RIGHT. SUPERMAN. I FORGOT.
CHOOSING GIFTS FOR HIM IS ALWAYS DIFFICULT.
THIS YEAR, I PAID A HORTICULTURALIST TO BREED A NEW STRAIN OF ROSE CALLED "THE KRYPTON." I'M PRETTY CERTAIN NO ONE ELSE WILL HAVE GOT HIM FLOWERS...
UH, BRUCE...
MAYBE IT'S NOT TOO LATE TO CHANGE IT FOR SOMETHING ELSE.
DID YOU GET A RECEIPT?
3

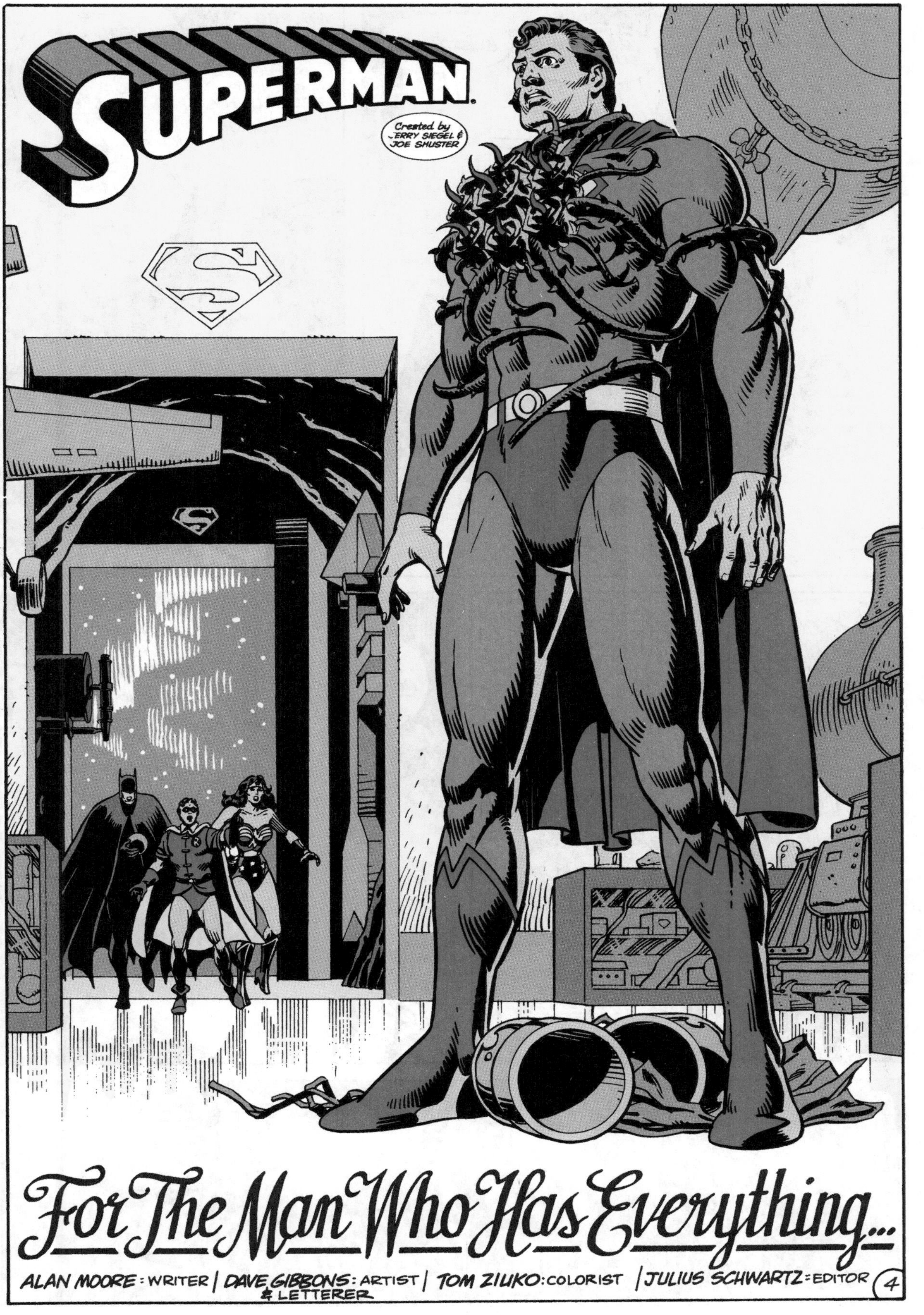
SUPERMAN
Created by JERRY SIEGEL & JOE SHUSTER
For The Man Who Has Everything...
ALAN MOORE: WRITER | DAVE GIBBONS: ARTIST & LETTERER | TOM ZIUKO: COLORIST | JULIUS SCHWARTZ: EDITOR
4

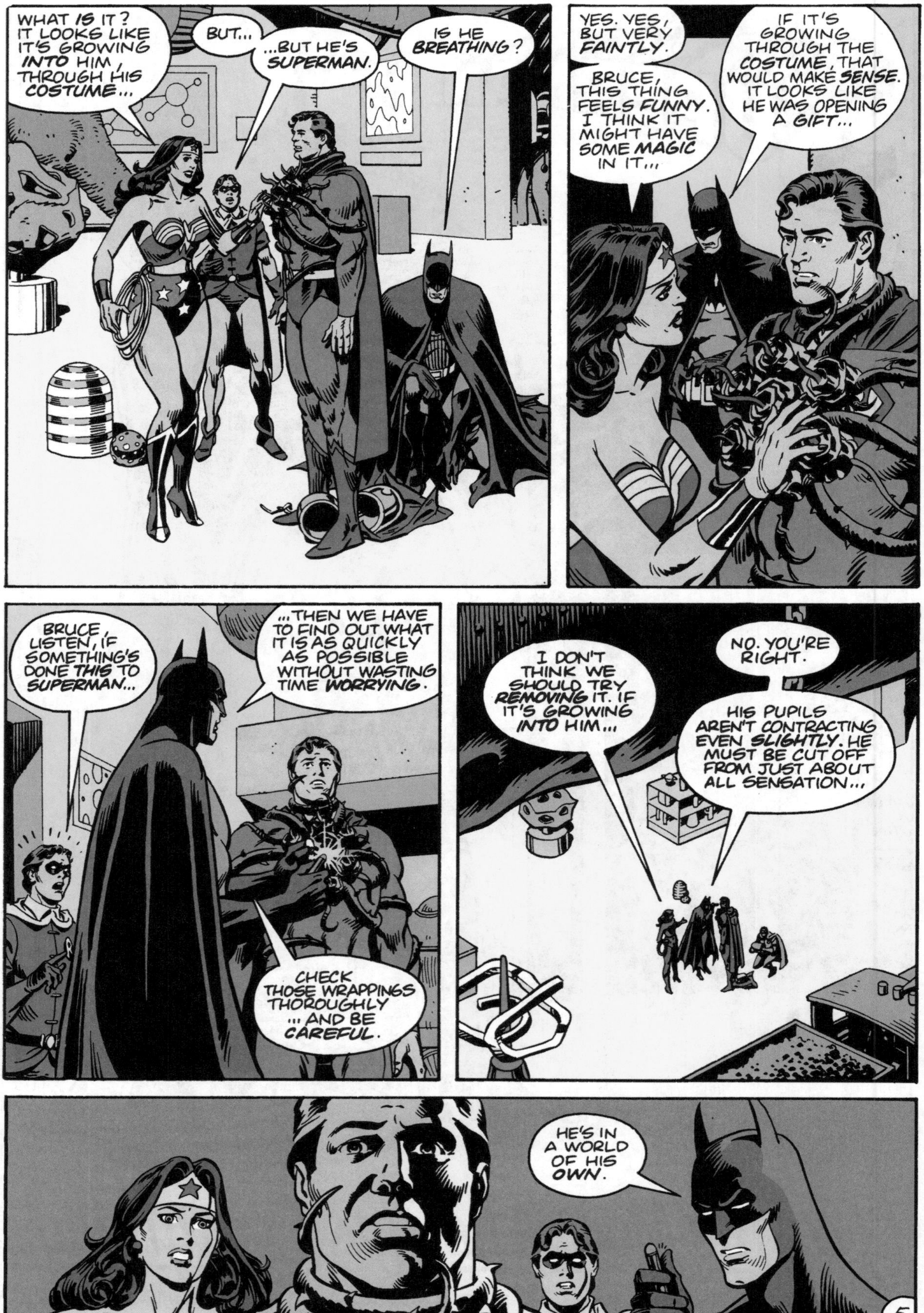
WHAT IS IT? IT LOOKS LIKE IT'S GROWING INTO HIM, THROUGH HIS COSTUME...
BUT...
...BUT HE'S SUPERMAN.
IS HE BREATHING?
YES. YES, BUT VERY FAINTLY.
BRUCE, THIS THING FEELS FUNNY. I THINK IT MIGHT HAVE SOME MAGIC IN IT...
IF IT'S GROWING THROUGH THE COSTUME, THAT WOULD MAKE SENSE. IT LOOKS LIKE HE WAS OPENING A GIFT...
BRUCE, LISTEN, IF SOMETHING'S DONE THIS TO SUPERMAN...
...THEN WE HAVE TO FIND OUT WHAT IT IS AS QUICKLY AS POSSIBLE WITHOUT WASTING TIME WORRYING.
CHECK THOSE WRAPPINGS THOROUGHLY ...AND BE CAREFUL.
I DON'T THINK WE SHOULD TRY REMOVING IT. IF IT'S GROWING INTO HIM...
NO. YOU'RE RIGHT.
HIS PUPILS AREN'T CONTRACTING EVEN SLIGHTLY. HE MUST BE CUT OFF FROM JUST ABOUT ALL SENSATION...
HE'S IN A WORLD OF HIS OWN.
5

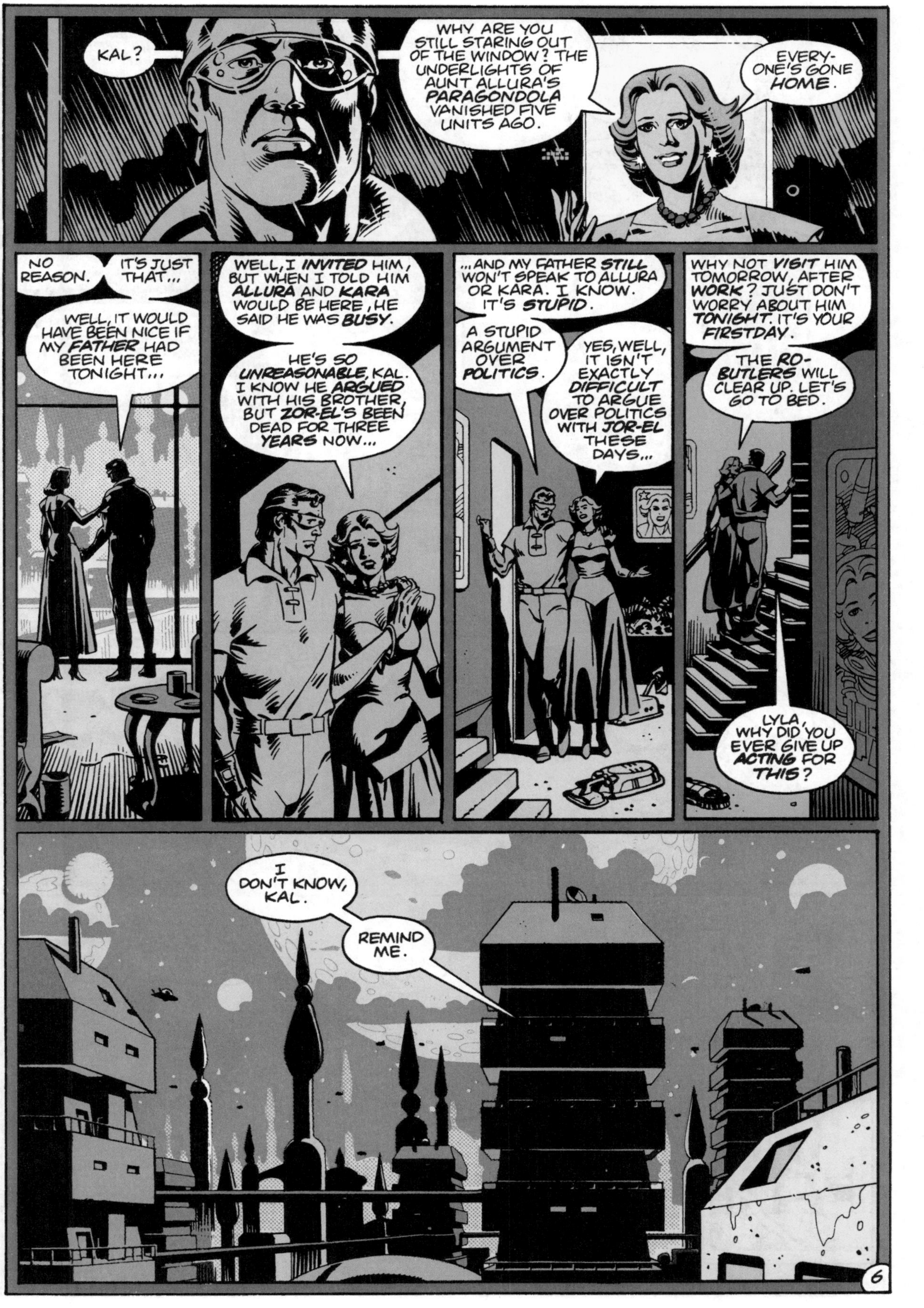
KAL?
WHY ARE YOU STILL STARING OUT OF THE WINDOW? THE UNDERLIGHTS OF AUNT ALLURA'S PARAGONDOLA VANISHED FIVE UNITS AGO.
EVERY-ONE'S GONE HOME.
NO REASON.
IT'S JUST THAT...
WELL, IT WOULD HAVE BEEN NICE IF MY FATHER HAD BEEN HERE TONIGHT...
WELL, I INVITED HIM, BUT WHEN I TOLD HIM ALLURA AND KARA WOULD BE HERE, HE SAID HE WAS BUSY.
HE'S SO UNREASONABLE, KAL. I KNOW HE ARGUED WITH HIS BROTHER, BUT ZOR-EL'S BEEN DEAD FOR THREE YEARS NOW...
...AND MY FATHER STILL WON'T SPEAK TO ALLURA OR KARA. I KNOW. IT'S STUPID.
A STUPID ARGUMENT OVER POLITICS.
YES, WELL, IT ISN'T EXACTLY DIFFICULT TO ARGUE OVER POLITICS WITH JOR-EL THESE DAYS...
WHY NOT VISIT HIM TOMORROW, AFTER WORK? JUST DON'T WORRY ABOUT HIM TONIGHT. IT'S YOUR FIRSTDAY.
THE RO-BUTLERS WILL CLEAR UP. LET'S GO TO BED.
LYLA, WHY DID YOU EVER GIVE UP ACTING FOR THIS?
I DON'T KNOW, KAL.
REMIND ME.
6

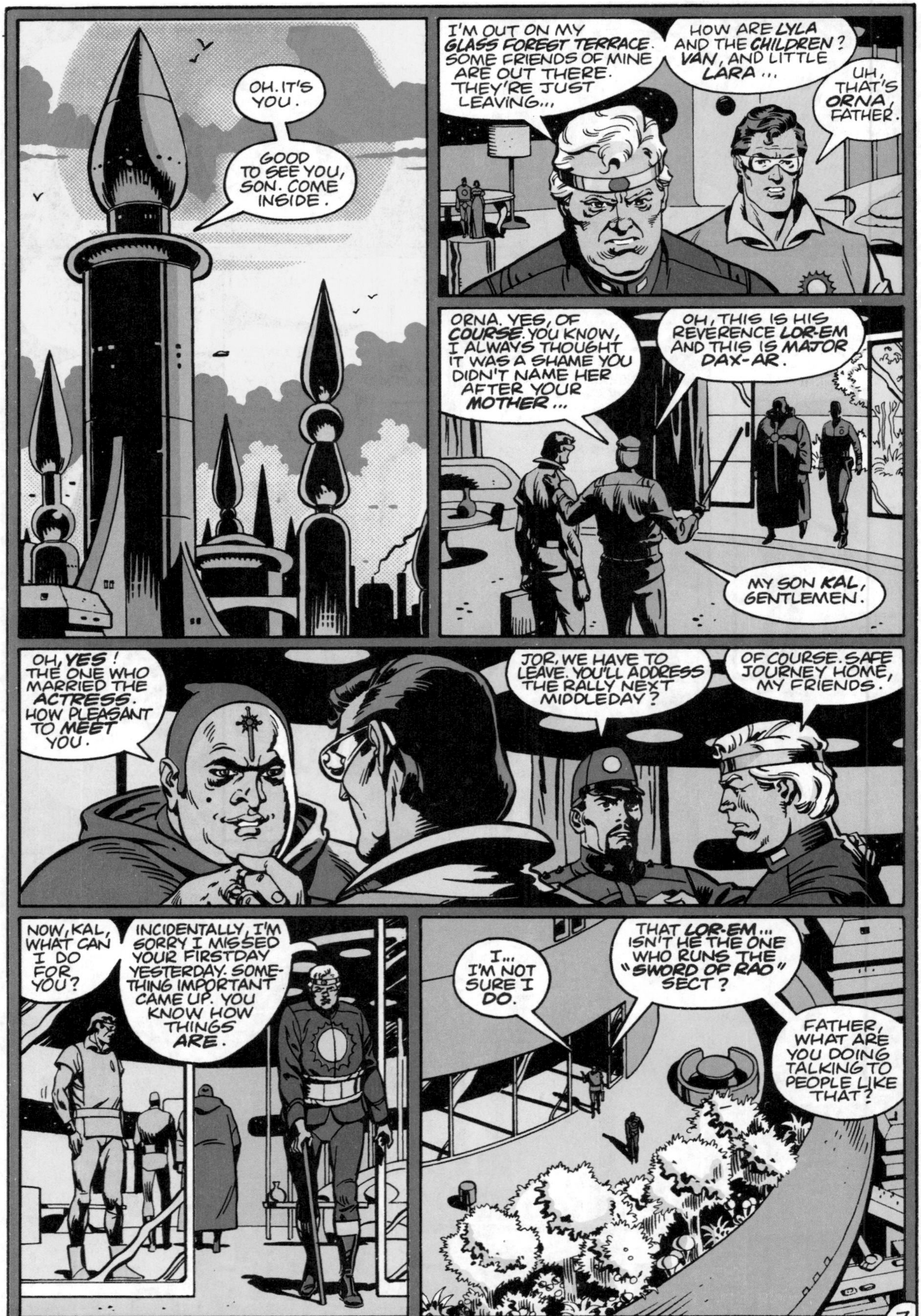
OH. IT'S YOU.
GOOD TO SEE YOU, SON. COME INSIDE.
I'M OUT ON MY GLASS FOREST TERRACE. SOME FRIENDS OF MINE ARE OUT THERE. THEY'RE JUST LEAVING...
HOW ARE LYLA AND THE CHILDREN? VAN, AND LITTLE LARA...
UH, THAT'S ORNA, FATHER.
ORNA. YES, OF COURSE. YOU KNOW, I ALWAYS THOUGHT IT WAS A SHAME YOU DIDN'T NAME HER AFTER YOUR MOTHER...
OH, THIS IS HIS REVERENCE LOR-EM AND THIS IS MAJOR DAX-AR.
MY SON KAL, GENTLEMEN.
OH, YES! THE ONE WHO MARRIED THE ACTRESS. HOW PLEASANT TO MEET YOU.
JOR, WE HAVE TO LEAVE. YOU'LL ADDRESS THE RALLY NEXT MIDDLEDAY?
OF COURSE. SAFE JOURNEY HOME, MY FRIENDS.
NOW, KAL, WHAT CAN I DO FOR YOU?
INCIDENTALLY, I'M SORRY I MISSED YOUR FIRSTDAY YESTERDAY. SOMETHING IMPORTANT CAME UP. YOU KNOW HOW THINGS ARE.
I... I'M NOT SURE I DO.
THAT LOR-EM... ISN'T HE THE ONE WHO RUNS THE "SWORD OF RAO" SECT?
FATHER, WHAT ARE YOU DOING TALKING TO PEOPLE LIKE THAT?
7

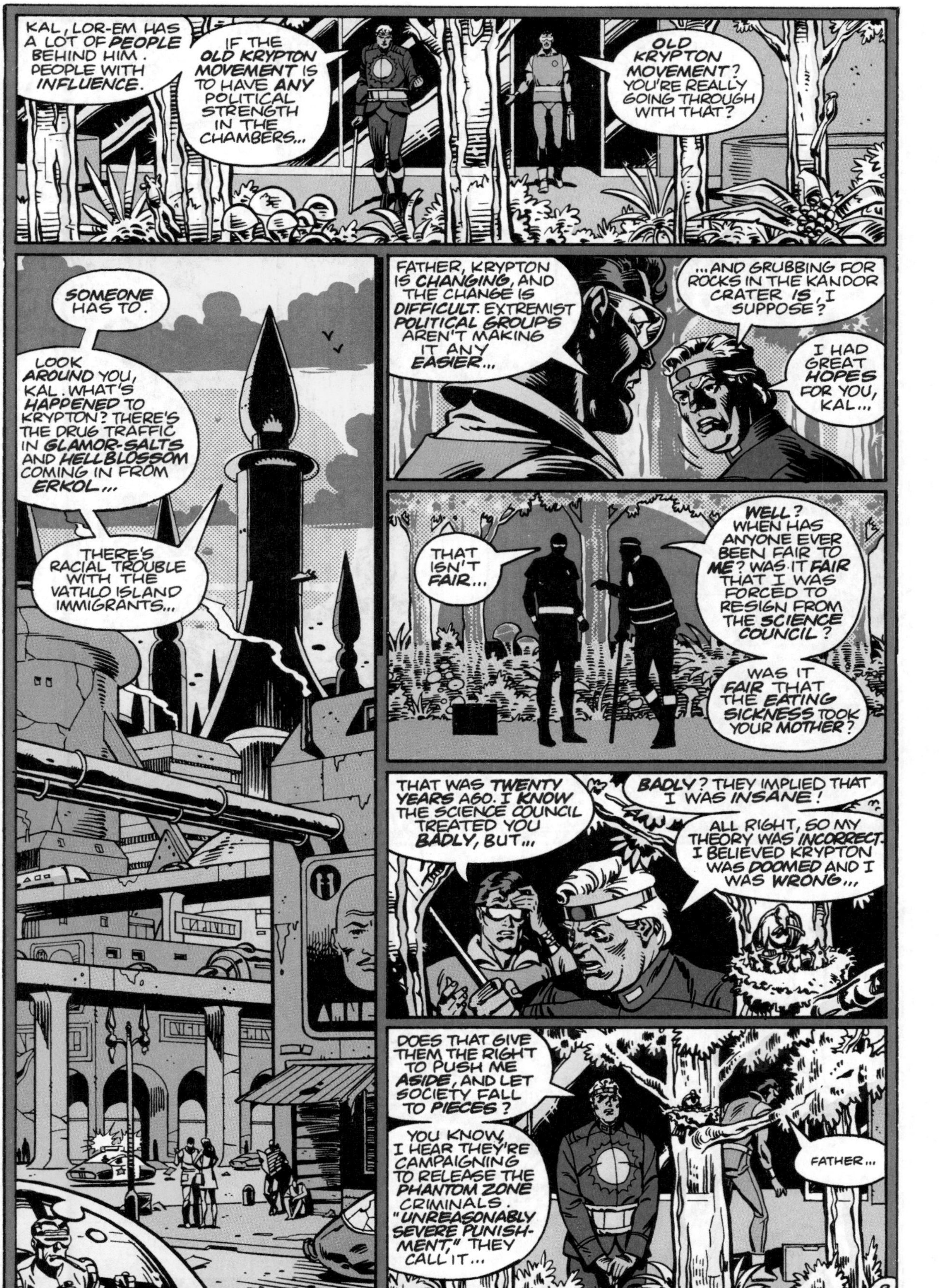
KAL, LOR-EM HAS A LOT OF PEOPLE BEHIND HIM. PEOPLE WITH INFLUENCE.
IF THE OLD KRYPTON MOVEMENT IS TO HAVE ANY POLITICAL STRENGTH IN THE CHAMBERS...
OLD KRYPTON MOVEMENT? YOU'RE REALLY GOING THROUGH WITH THAT?
SOMEONE HAS TO.
LOOK AROUND YOU, KAL. WHAT'S HAPPENED TO KRYPTON? THERE'S THE DRUG TRAFFIC IN GLAMOR-SALTS AND HELLBLOSSOM COMING IN FROM ERKOL...
THERE'S RACIAL TROUBLE WITH THE VATHLO ISLAND IMMIGRANTS...
FATHER, KRYPTON IS CHANGING, AND THE CHANGE IS DIFFICULT. EXTREMIST POLITICAL GROUPS AREN'T MAKING IT ANY EASIER...
...AND GRUBBING FOR ROCKS IN THE KANDOR CRATER IS, I SUPPOSE?
I HAD GREAT HOPES FOR YOU, KAL...
THAT ISN'T FAIR...
WELL? WHEN HAS ANYONE EVER BEEN FAIR TO ME? WAS IT FAIR THAT I WAS FORCED TO RESIGN FROM THE SCIENCE COUNCIL?
WAS IT FAIR THAT THE EATING SICKNESS TOOK YOUR MOTHER?
THAT WAS TWENTY YEARS AGO. I KNOW THE SCIENCE COUNCIL TREATED YOU BADLY, BUT...
BADLY? THEY IMPLIED THAT I WAS INSANE!
ALL RIGHT, SO MY THEORY WAS INCORRECT. I BELIEVED KRYPTON WAS DOOMED AND I WAS WRONG...
DOES THAT GIVE THEM THE RIGHT TO PUSH ME ASIDE, AND LET SOCIETY FALL TO PIECES?
YOU KNOW, I HEAR THEY'RE CAMPAIGNING TO RELEASE THE PHANTOM ZONE CRIMINALS. "UNREASONABLY SEVERE PUNISHMENT," THEY CALL IT...
FATHER...
8

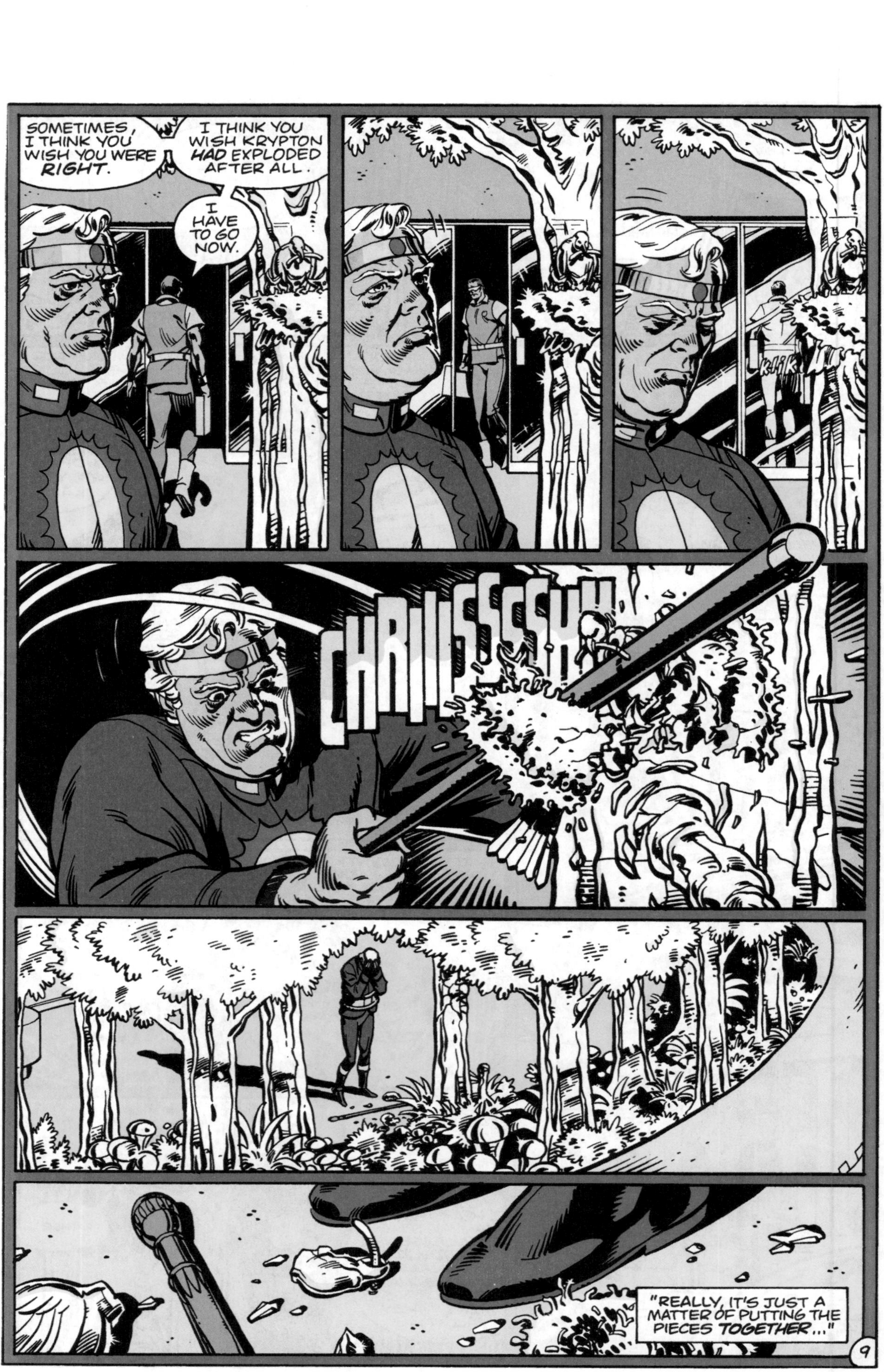
SOMETIMES, I THINK YOU WISH YOU WERE RIGHT.
I THINK YOU WISH KRYPTON HAD EXPLODED AFTER ALL.
I HAVE TO GO NOW.
CHRUUSSSSHH
"REALLY, IT'S JUST A MATTER OF PUTTING THE PIECES TOGETHER..."
9

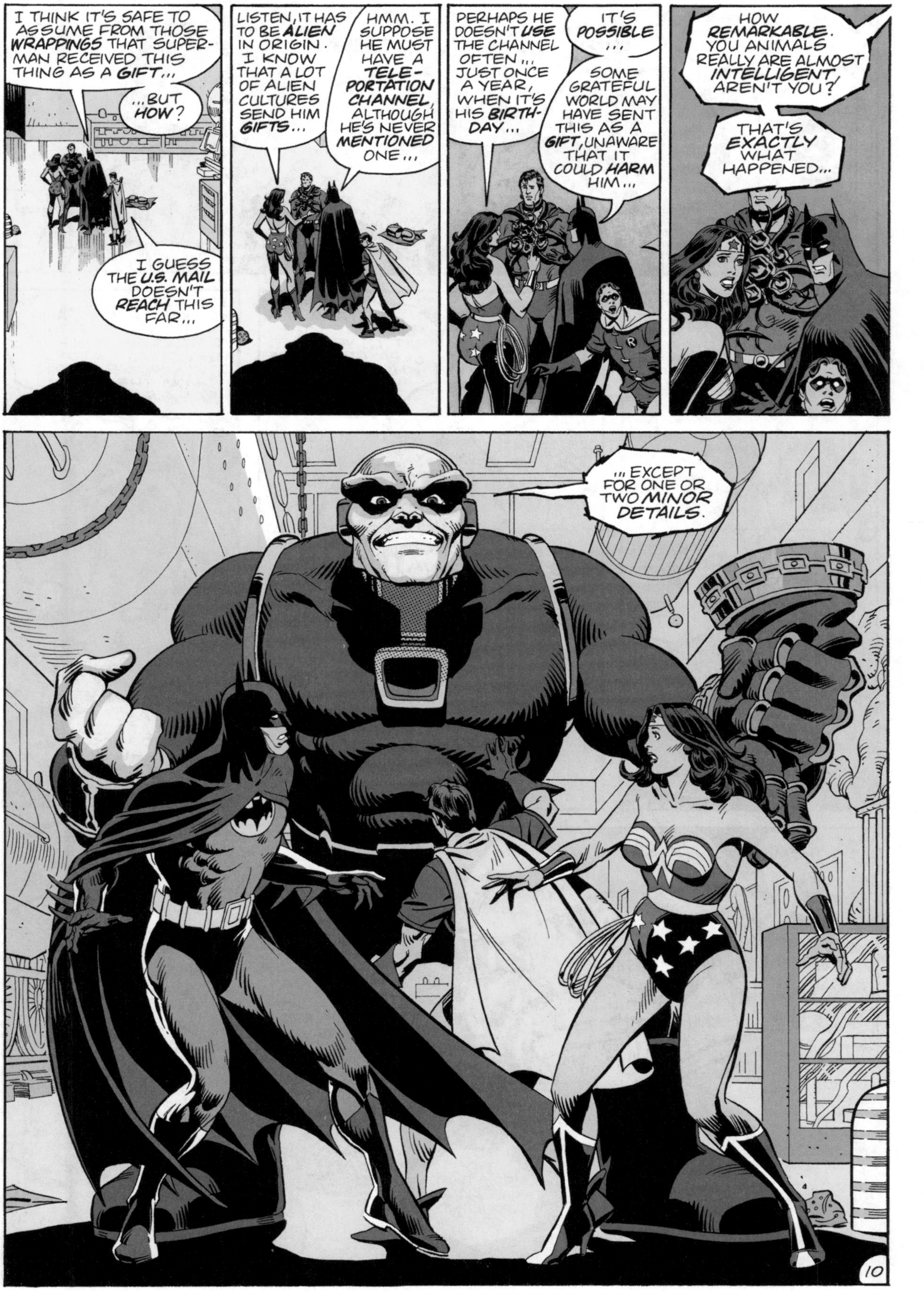
I THINK IT'S SAFE TO ASSUME FROM THOSE WRAPPINGS THAT SUPER-MAN RECEIVED THIS THING AS A GIFT...
...BUT HOW?
I GUESS THE U.S. MAIL DOESN'T REACH THIS FAR...
LISTEN, IT HAS TO BE ALIEN IN ORIGIN. I KNOW THAT A LOT OF ALIEN CULTURES SEND HIM GIFTS...
HMM. I SUPPOSE HE MUST HAVE A TELE-PORTATION CHANNEL, ALTHOUGH HE'S NEVER MENTIONED ONE...
PERHAPS HE DOESN'T USE THE CHANNEL OFTEN... JUST ONCE A YEAR, WHEN IT'S HIS BIRTH-DAY...
IT'S POSSIBLE...
SOME GRATEFUL WORLD MAY HAVE SENT THIS AS A GIFT, UNAWARE THAT IT COULD HARM HIM...
HOW REMARKABLE. YOU ANIMALS REALLY ARE ALMOST INTELLIGENT, AREN'T YOU?
THAT'S EXACTLY WHAT HAPPENED...
...EXCEPT FOR ONE OR TWO MINOR DETAILS.
10

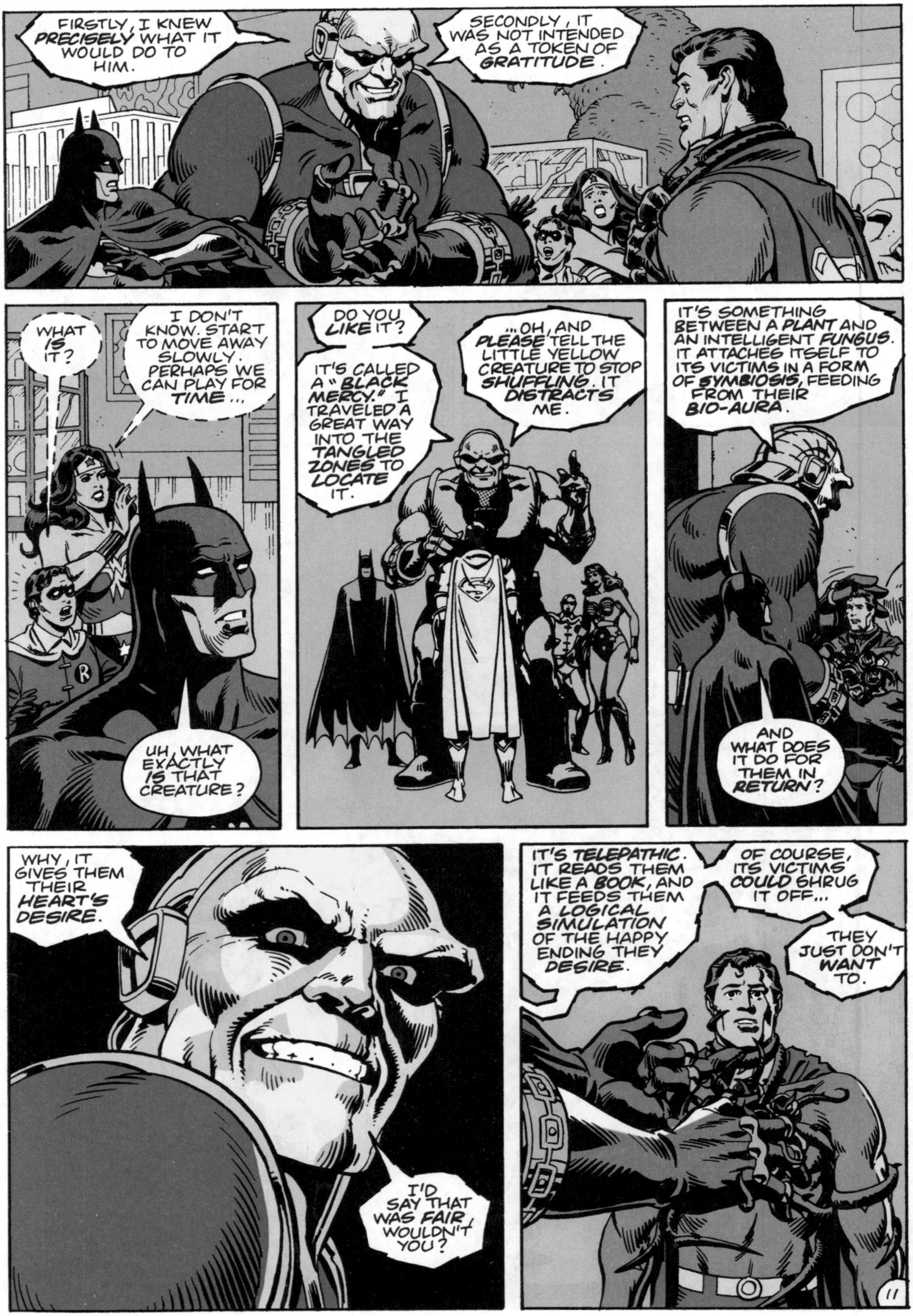
FIRSTLY, I KNEW PRECISELY WHAT IT WOULD DO TO HIM.
SECONDLY, IT WAS NOT INTENDED AS A TOKEN OF GRATITUDE.
WHAT IS IT?
I DON'T KNOW. START TO MOVE AWAY SLOWLY. PERHAPS WE CAN PLAY FOR TIME...
UH, WHAT EXACTLY IS THAT CREATURE?
DO YOU LIKE IT?
IT'S CALLED A "BLACK MERCY." I TRAVELED A GREAT WAY INTO THE TANGLED ZONES TO LOCATE IT.
...OH, AND PLEASE TELL THE LITTLE YELLOW CREATURE TO STOP SHUFFLING. IT DISTRACTS ME.
IT'S SOMETHING BETWEEN A PLANT AND AN INTELLIGENT FUNGUS. IT ATTACHES ITSELF TO ITS VICTIMS IN A FORM OF SYMBIOSIS, FEEDING FROM THEIR BIO-AURA.
AND WHAT DOES IT DO FOR THEM IN RETURN?
WHY, IT GIVES THEM THEIR HEART'S DESIRE.
I'D SAY THAT WAS FAIR, WOULDN'T YOU?
IT'S TELEPATHIC. IT READS THEM LIKE A BOOK, AND IT FEEDS THEM A LOGICAL SIMULATION OF THE HAPPY ENDING THEY DESIRE.
OF COURSE, ITS VICTIMS COULD SHRUG IT OFF...
THEY JUST DON'T WANT TO.
11

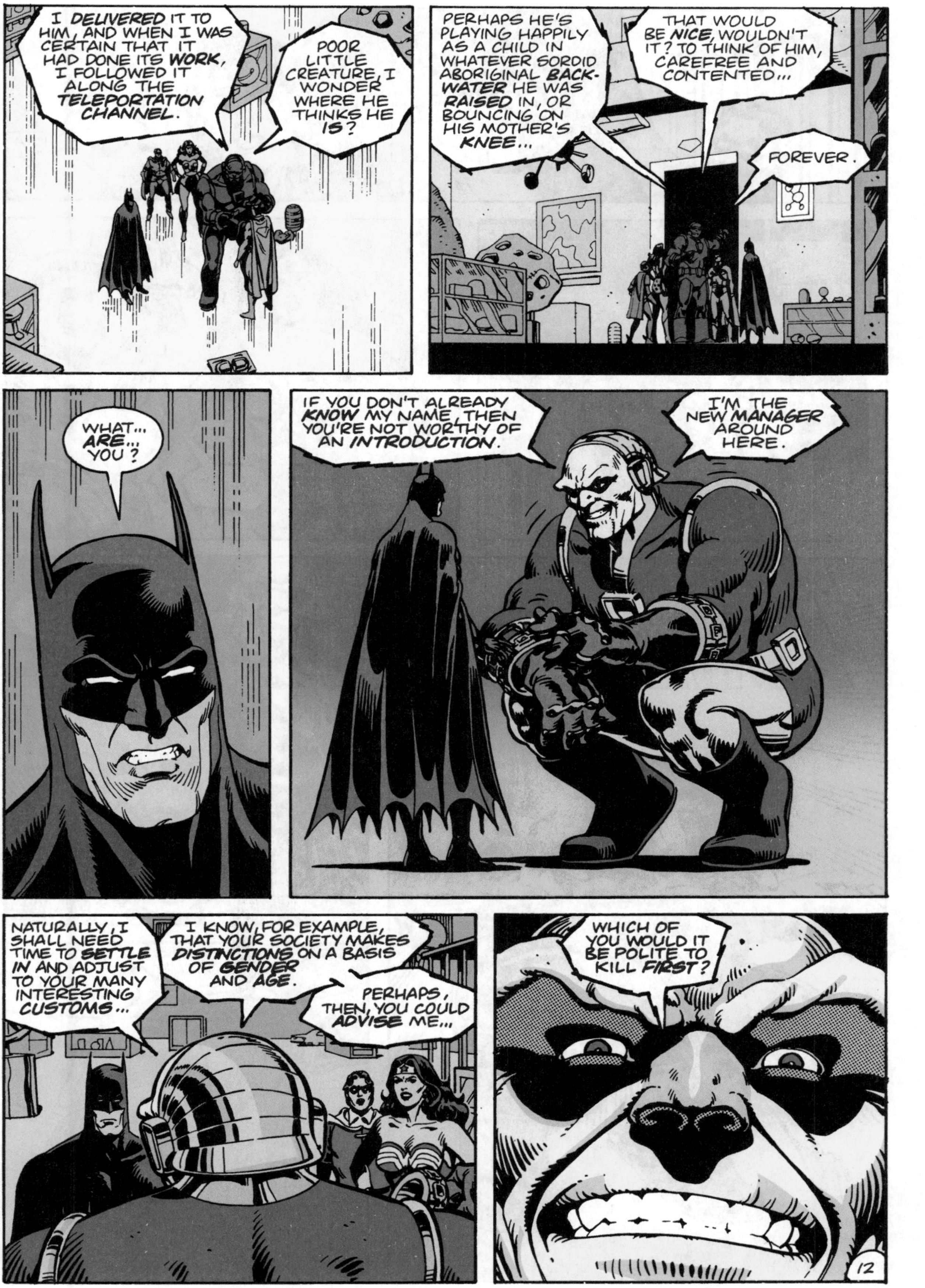
I DELIVERED IT TO HIM, AND WHEN I WAS CERTAIN THAT IT HAD DONE ITS WORK, I FOLLOWED IT ALONG THE TELEPORTATION CHANNEL.
POOR LITTLE CREATURE, I WONDER WHERE HE THINKS HE IS?
PERHAPS HE'S PLAYING HAPPILY AS A CHILD IN WHATEVER SORDID ABORIGINAL BACK-WATER HE WAS RAISED IN, OR BOUNCING ON HIS MOTHER'S KNEE...
THAT WOULD BE NICE, WOULDN'T IT? TO THINK OF HIM, CAREFREE AND CONTENTED...
FOREVER.
WHAT... ARE... YOU?
IF YOU DON'T ALREADY KNOW MY NAME, THEN YOU'RE NOT WORTHY OF AN INTRODUCTION.
I'M THE NEW MANAGER AROUND HERE.
NATURALLY, I SHALL NEED TIME TO SETTLE IN AND ADJUST TO YOUR MANY INTERESTING CUSTOMS...
I KNOW, FOR EXAMPLE, THAT YOUR SOCIETY MAKES DISTINCTIONS ON A BASIS OF GENDER AND AGE.
PERHAPS, THEN, YOU COULD ADVISE ME...
WHICH OF YOU WOULD IT BE POLITE TO KILL FIRST?
12

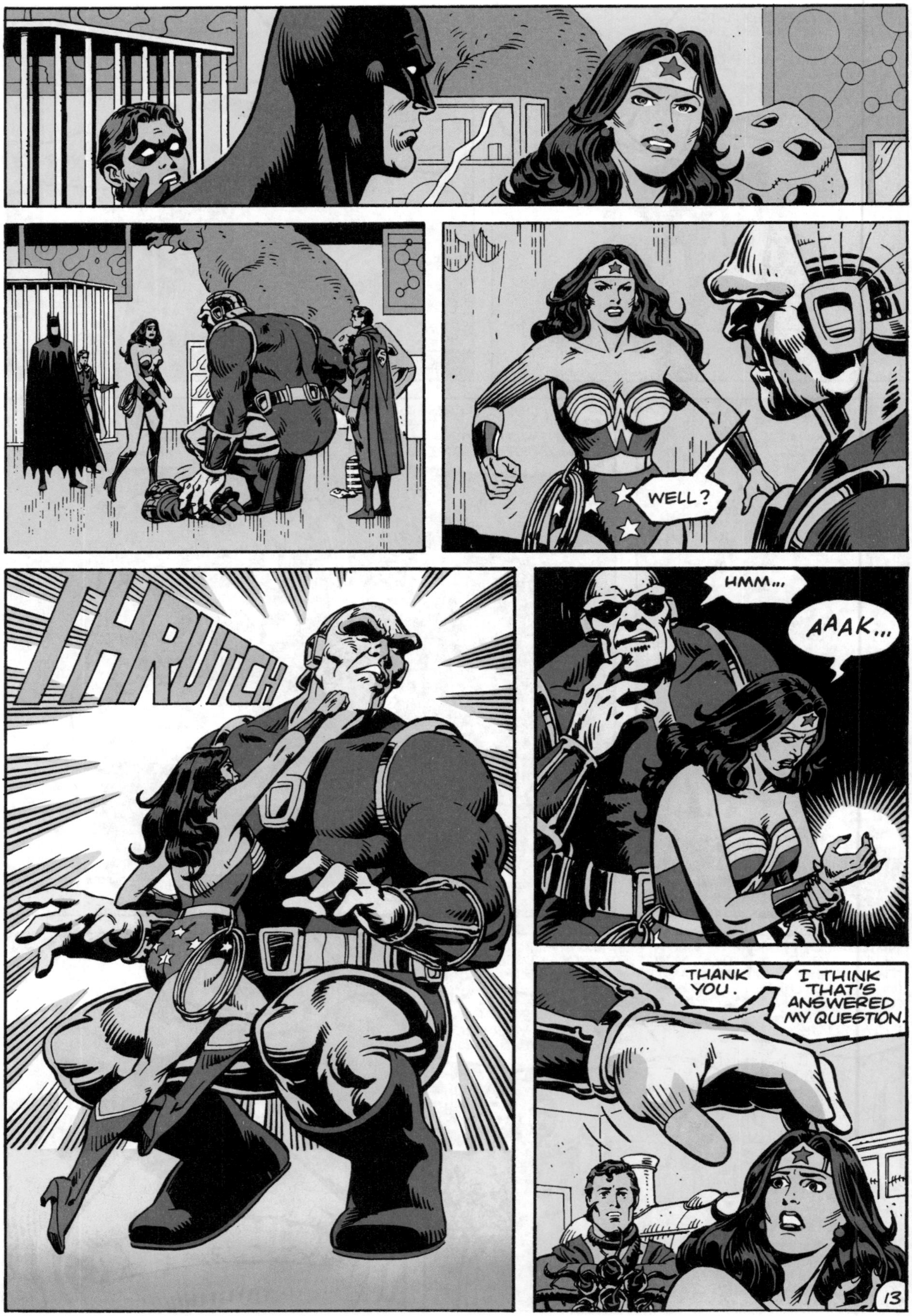
WELL?
THRUTCH
HMM...
AAAK...
THANK YOU.
I THINK THAT'S ANSWERED MY QUESTION.
13

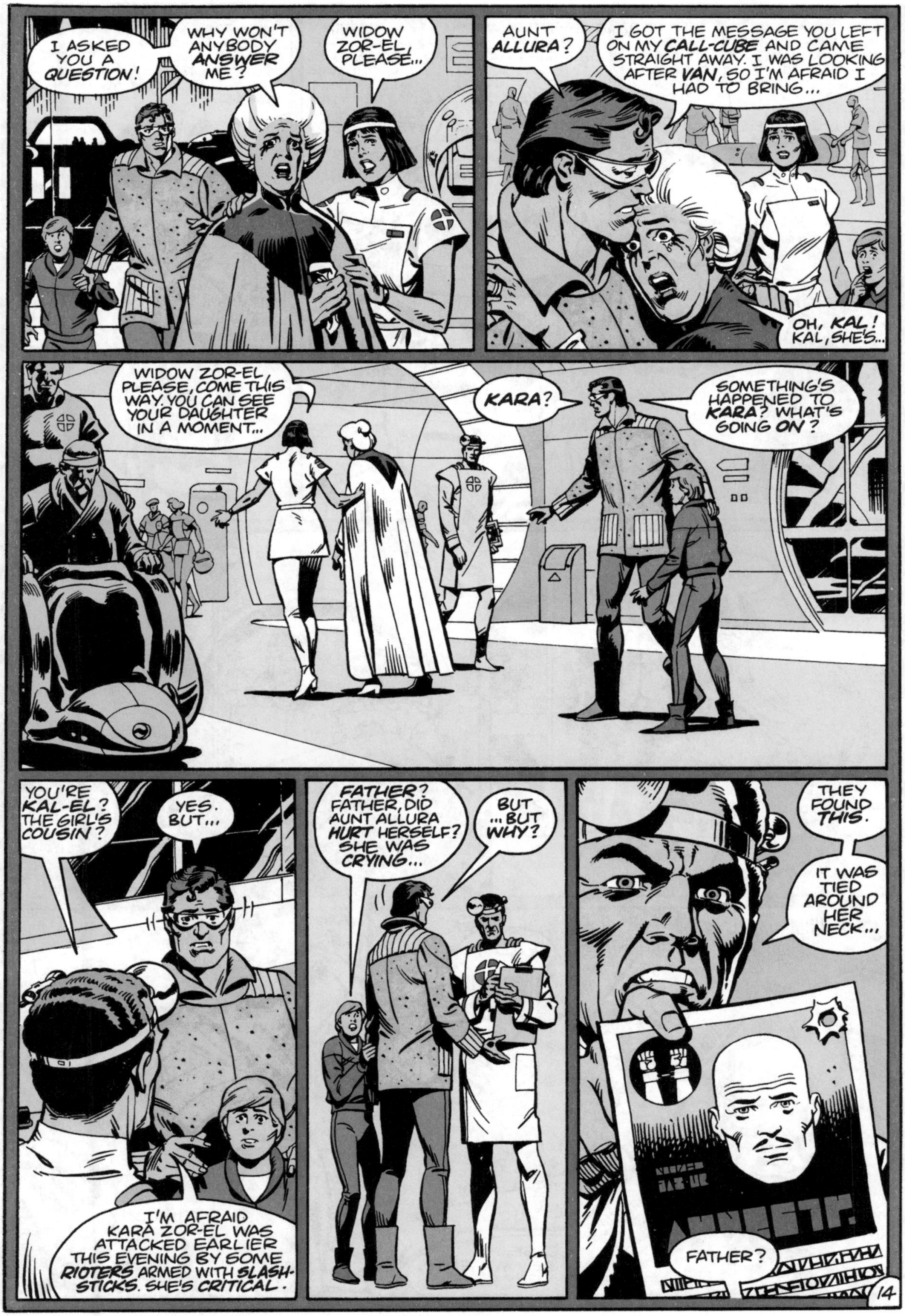
I ASKED YOU A QUESTION!
WHY WON'T ANYBODY ANSWER ME?
WIDOW ZOR-EL, PLEASE...
AUNT ALLURA?
I GOT THE MESSAGE YOU LEFT ON MY CALL-CUBE AND CAME STRAIGHT AWAY. I WAS LOOKING AFTER VAN, SO I'M AFRAID I HAD TO BRING...
OH, KAL! KAL, SHE'S...
WIDOW ZOR-EL PLEASE, COME THIS WAY. YOU CAN SEE YOUR DAUGHTER IN A MOMENT...
KARA?
SOMETHING'S HAPPENED TO KARA? WHAT'S GOING ON?
YOU'RE KAL-EL? THE GIRL'S COUSIN?
YES. BUT...
I'M AFRAID KARA ZOR-EL WAS ATTACKED EARLIER THIS EVENING BY SOME RIOTERS ARMED WITH SLASH-STICKS. SHE'S CRITICAL.
FATHER? FATHER, DID AUNT ALLURA HURT HERSELF? SHE WAS CRYING...
BUT ...BUT WHY?
THEY FOUND THIS.
IT WAS TIED AROUND HER NECK...
FATHER?
14

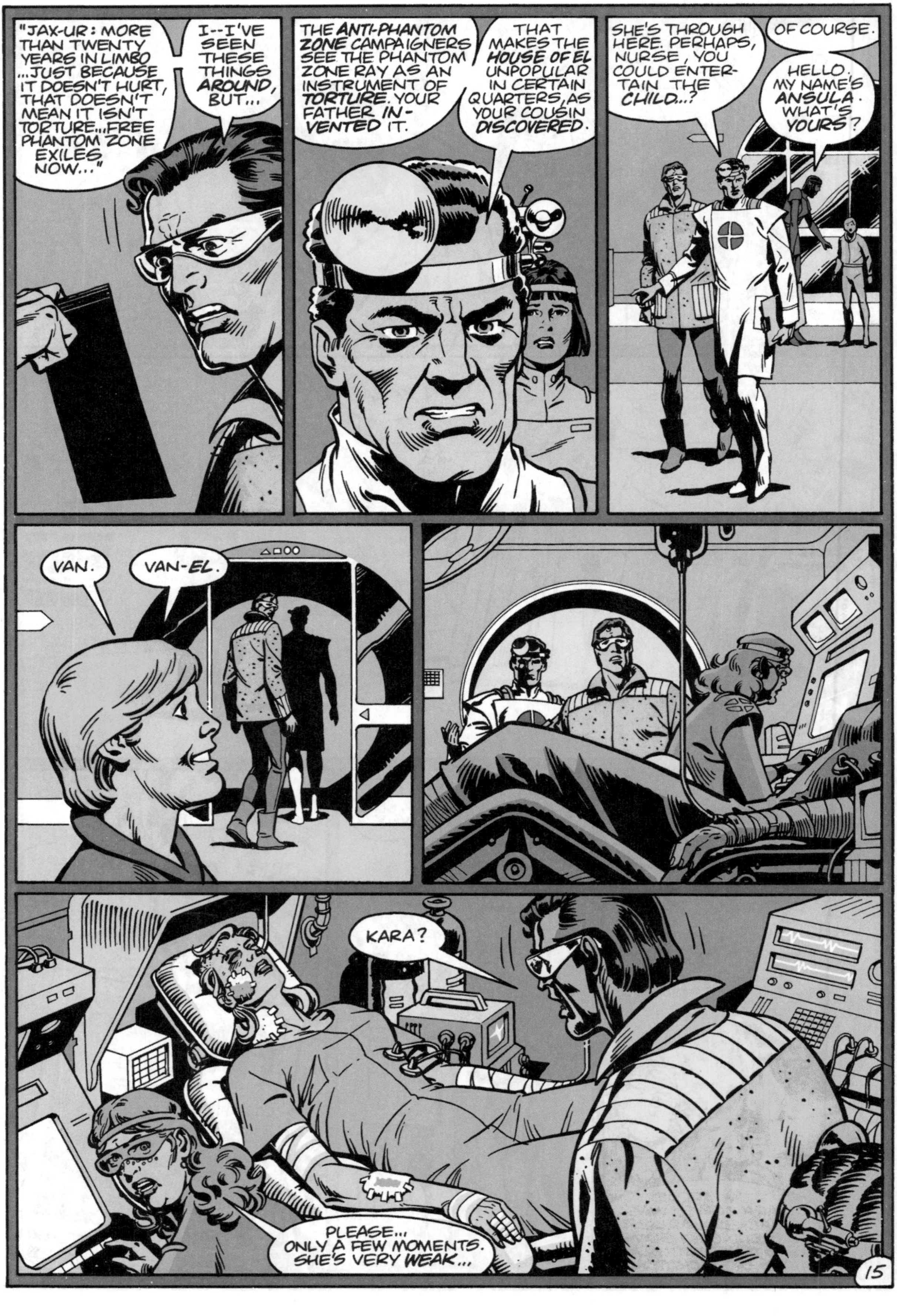
"JAX-UR: MORE THAN TWENTY YEARS IN LIMBO ...JUST BECAUSE IT DOESN'T HURT, THAT DOESN'T MEAN IT ISN'T TORTURE...FREE PHANTOM ZONE EXILES NOW..."
I--I'VE SEEN THESE THINGS AROUND, BUT...
THE ANTI-PHANTOM ZONE CAMPAIGNERS SEE THE PHANTOM ZONE RAY AS AN INSTRUMENT OF TORTURE. YOUR FATHER INVENTED IT.
THAT MAKES THE HOUSE OF EL UNPOPULAR IN CERTAIN QUARTERS, AS YOUR COUSIN DISCOVERED.
SHE'S THROUGH HERE. PERHAPS, NURSE, YOU COULD ENTERTAIN THE CHILD...?
OF COURSE.
HELLO. MY NAME'S ANSULA. WHAT'S YOURS?
VAN.
VAN-EL.
KARA?
PLEASE... ONLY A FEW MOMENTS. SHE'S VERY WEAK...
15

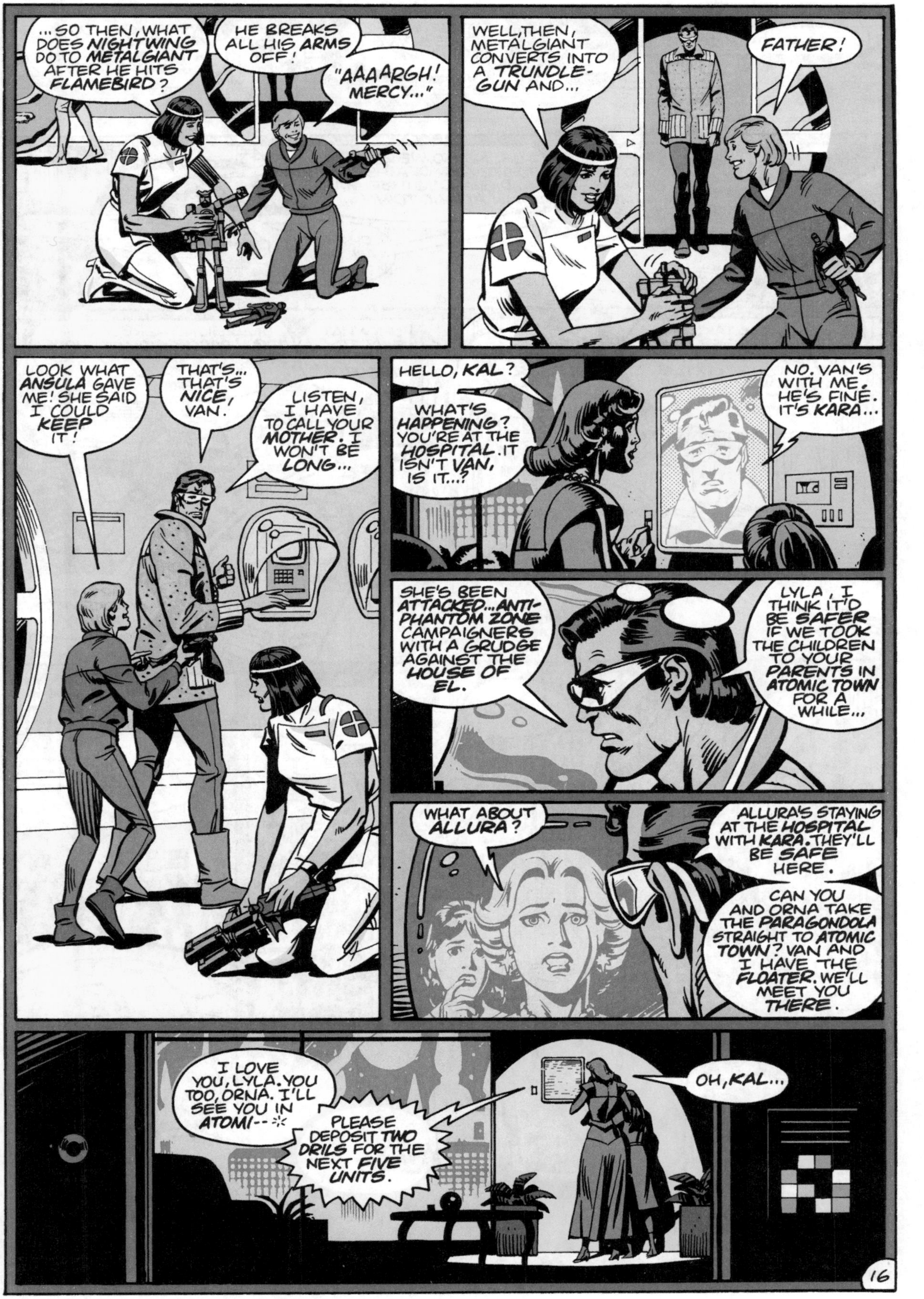
...SO THEN, WHAT DOES NIGHTWING DO TO METALGIANT AFTER HE HITS FLAMEBIRD?
HE BREAKS ALL HIS ARMS OFF!
"AAAARGH! MERCY..."
WELL, THEN, METALGIANT CONVERTS INTO A TRUNDLE-GUN AND...
FATHER!
LOOK WHAT ANSULA GAVE ME! SHE SAID I COULD KEEP IT!
THAT'S... THAT'S NICE, VAN.
LISTEN, I HAVE TO CALL YOUR MOTHER. I WON'T BE LONG...
HELLO, KAL?
WHAT'S HAPPENING? YOU'RE AT THE HOSPITAL. IT ISN'T VAN, IS IT...?
NO. VAN'S WITH ME. HE'S FINE. IT'S KARA...
SHE'S BEEN ATTACKED... ANTI-PHANTOM ZONE CAMPAIGNERS WITH A GRUDGE AGAINST THE HOUSE OF EL.
LYLA, I THINK IT'D BE SAFER IF WE TOOK THE CHILDREN TO YOUR PARENTS IN ATOMIC TOWN FOR A WHILE...
WHAT ABOUT ALLURA?
ALLURA'S STAYING AT THE HOSPITAL WITH KARA. THEY'LL BE SAFE HERE.
CAN YOU AND ORNA TAKE THE PARAGONDOLA STRAIGHT TO ATOMIC TOWN? VAN AND I HAVE THE FLOATER. WE'LL MEET YOU THERE.
I LOVE YOU, LYLA. YOU TOO, ORNA. I'LL SEE YOU IN ATOMI--
PLEASE DEPOSIT TWO DRILS FOR THE NEXT FIVE UNITS.
OH, KAL...
16

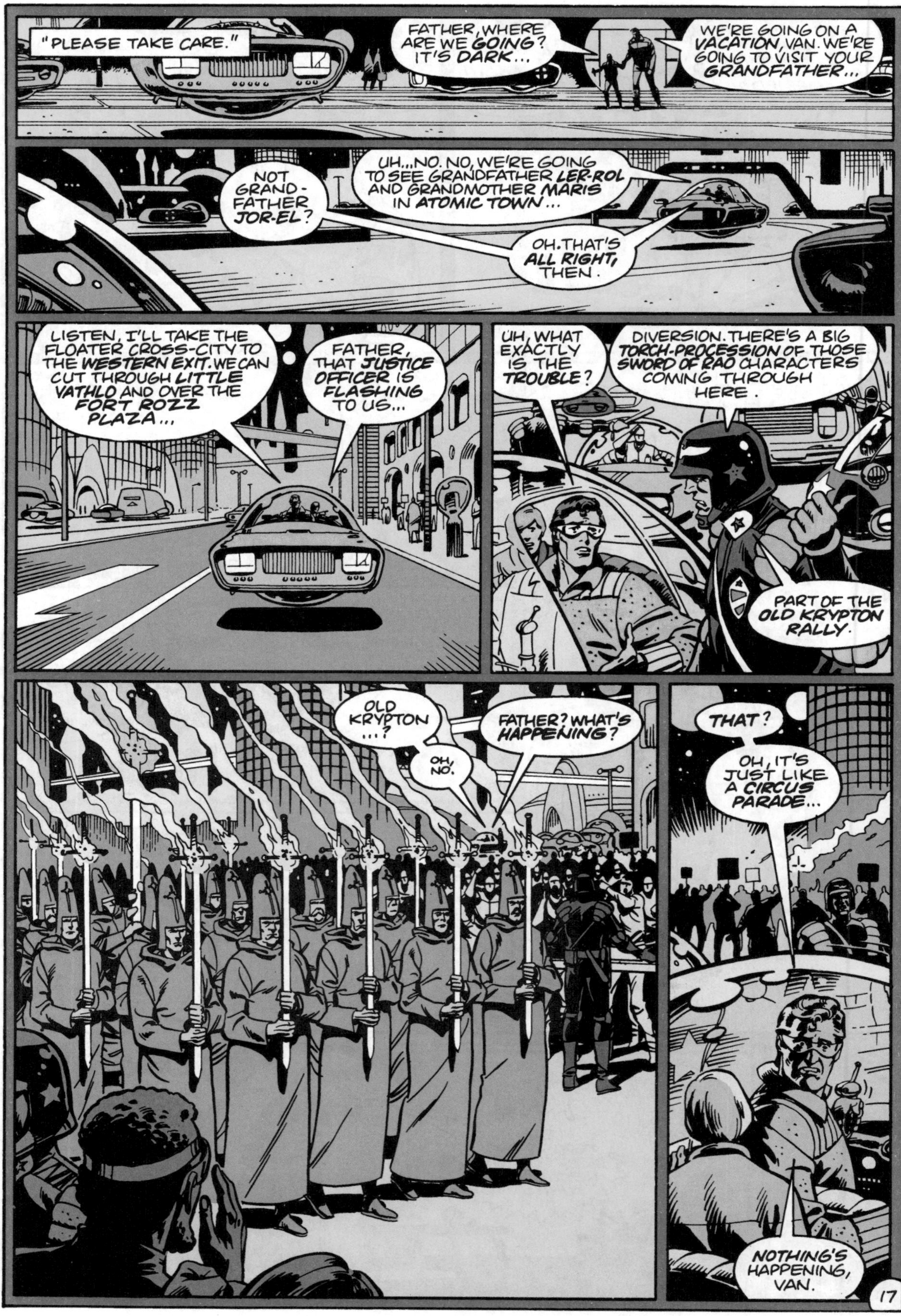
"PLEASE TAKE CARE."
FATHER, WHERE ARE WE GOING? IT'S DARK...
WE'RE GOING ON A VACATION, VAN. WE'RE GOING TO VISIT YOUR GRANDFATHER...
NOT GRAND-FATHER JOR-EL?
UH...NO. NO, WE'RE GOING TO SEE GRANDFATHER LER-ROL AND GRANDMOTHER MARIS IN ATOMIC TOWN...
OH. THAT'S ALL RIGHT, THEN.
LISTEN, I'LL TAKE THE FLOATER CROSS-CITY TO THE WESTERN EXIT. WE CAN CUT THROUGH LITTLE VATHLO AND OVER THE FORT ROZZ PLAZA...
FATHER, THAT JUSTICE OFFICER IS FLASHING TO US...
UH, WHAT EXACTLY IS THE TROUBLE?
DIVERSION. THERE'S A BIG TORCH-PROCESSION OF THOSE SWORD OF RAO CHARACTERS COMING THROUGH HERE.
PART OF THE OLD KRYPTON RALLY.
OLD KRYPTON...?
OH, NO.
FATHER? WHAT'S HAPPENING?
THAT?
OH, IT'S JUST LIKE A CIRCUS PARADE...
NOTHING'S HAPPENING, VAN.
17

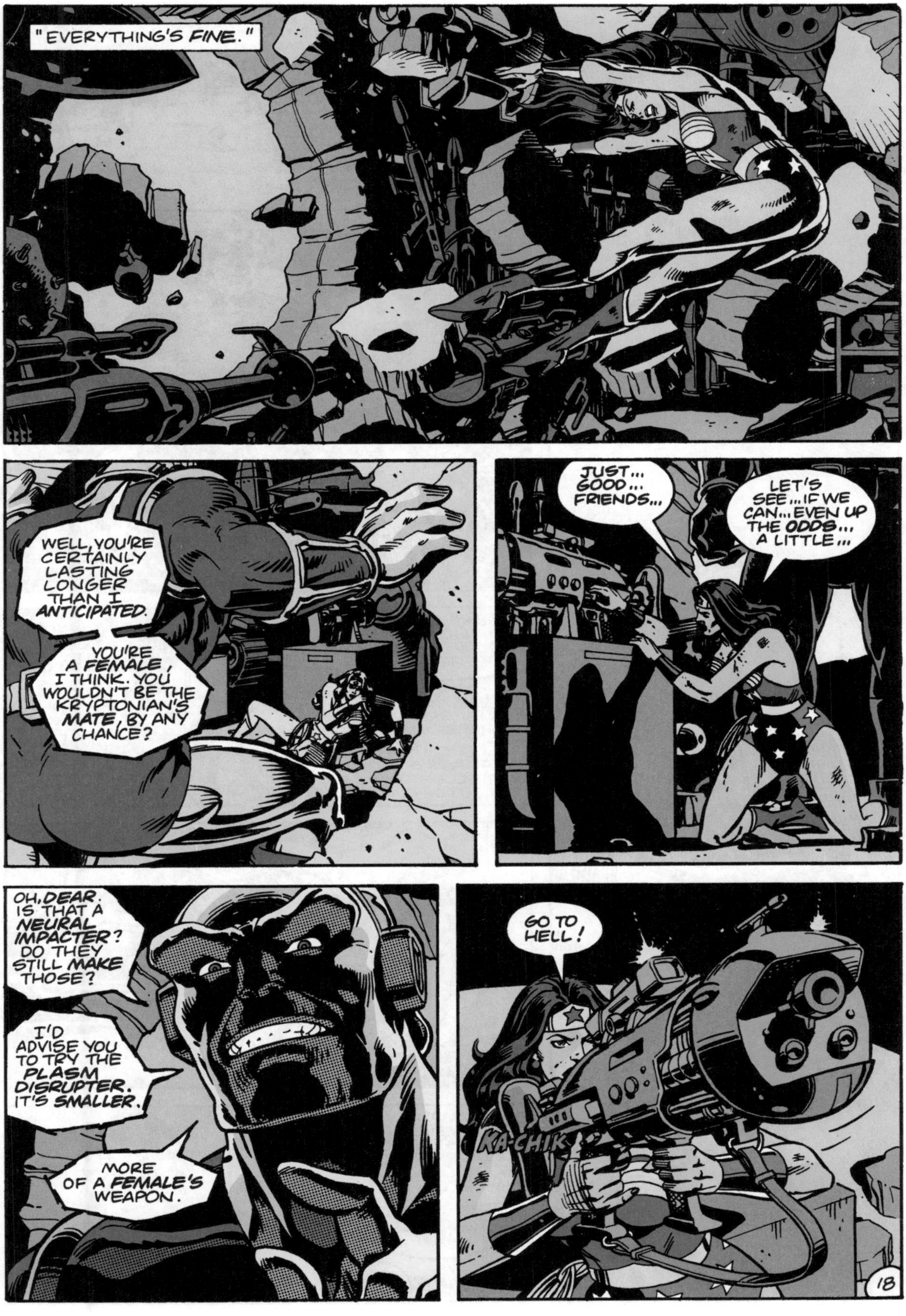
"EVERYTHING'S FINE."
WELL, YOU'RE CERTAINLY LASTING LONGER THAN I ANTICIPATED.
YOU'RE A FEMALE, I THINK. YOU WOULDN'T BE THE KRYPTONIAN'S MATE, BY ANY CHANCE?
JUST... GOOD... FRIENDS...
LET'S SEE... IF WE CAN... EVEN UP THE ODDS... A LITTLE...
OH, DEAR. IS THAT A NEURAL IMPACTER? DO THEY STILL MAKE THOSE?
I'D ADVISE YOU TO TRY THE PLASM DISRUPTER. IT'S SMALLER.
MORE OF A FEMALE'S WEAPON.
GO TO HELL!
KA-CHIK
18

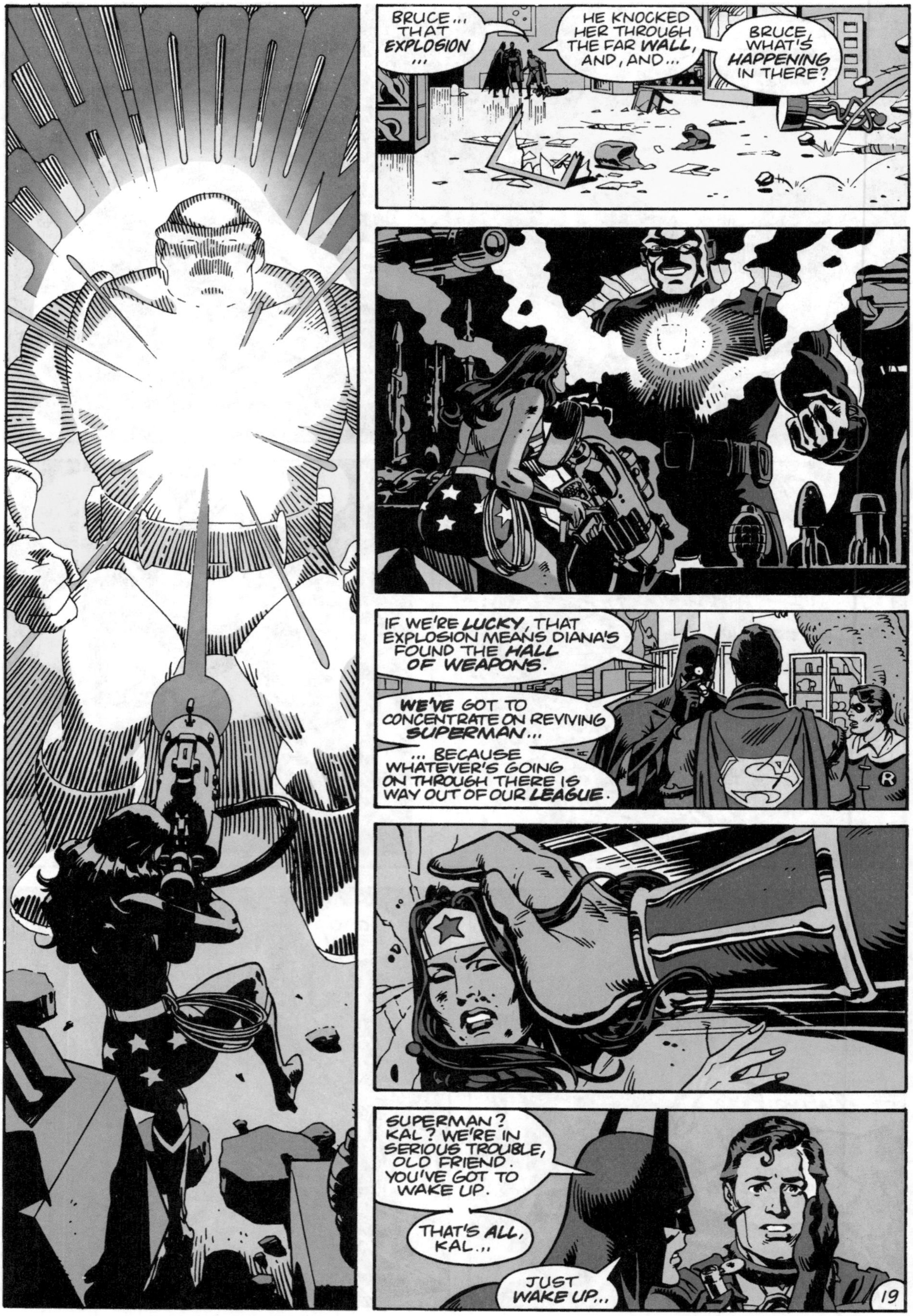
BRUCE... THAT EXPLOSION ...
HE KNOCKED HER THROUGH THE FAR WALL, AND, AND...
BRUCE, WHAT'S HAPPENING IN THERE?
IF WE'RE LUCKY, THAT EXPLOSION MEANS DIANA'S FOUND THE HALL OF WEAPONS.
WE'VE GOT TO CONCENTRATE ON REVIVING SUPERMAN...
... BECAUSE WHATEVER'S GOING ON THROUGH THERE IS WAY OUT OF OUR LEAGUE.
SUPERMAN? KAL? WE'RE IN SERIOUS TROUBLE, OLD FRIEND. YOU'VE GOT TO WAKE UP.
THAT'S ALL, KAL...
JUST WAKE UP...
19

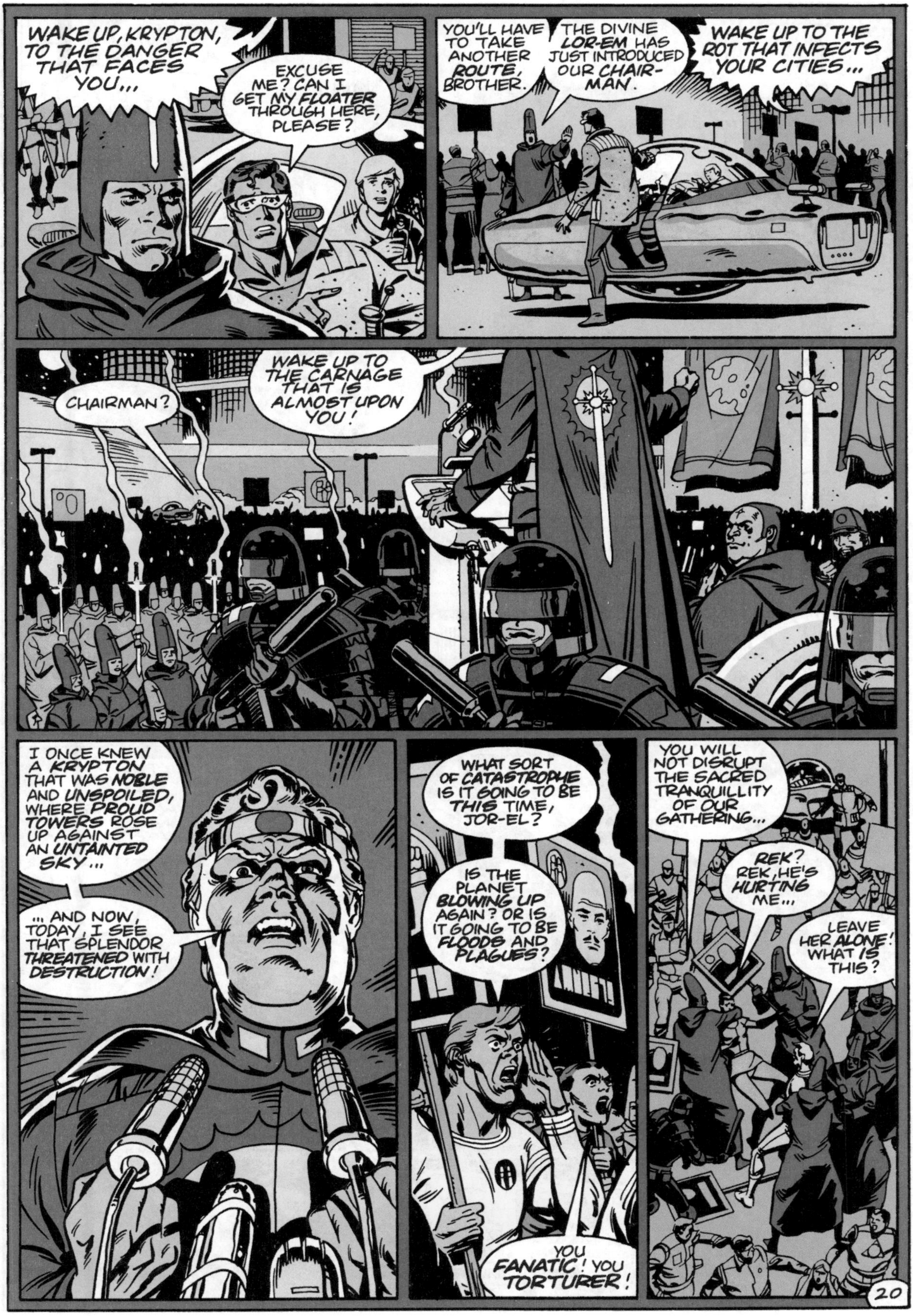
WAKE UP, KRYPTON, TO THE DANGER THAT FACES YOU...
EXCUSE ME? CAN I GET MY FLOATER THROUGH HERE, PLEASE?
YOU'LL HAVE TO TAKE ANOTHER ROUTE, BROTHER.
THE DIVINE LOR-EM HAS JUST INTRODUCED OUR CHAIRMAN.
WAKE UP TO THE ROT THAT INFECTS YOUR CITIES...
CHAIRMAN?
WAKE UP TO THE CARNAGE THAT IS ALMOST UPON YOU!
I ONCE KNEW A KRYPTON THAT WAS NOBLE AND UNSPOILED, WHERE PROUD TOWERS ROSE UP AGAINST AN UNTAINTED SKY...
... AND NOW, TODAY, I SEE THAT SPLENDOR THREATENED WITH DESTRUCTION!
WHAT SORT OF CATASTROPHE IS IT GOING TO BE THIS TIME, JOR-EL?
IS THE PLANET BLOWING UP AGAIN? OR IS IT GOING TO BE FLOODS AND PLAGUES?
YOU FANATIC! YOU TORTURER!
YOU WILL NOT DISRUPT THE SACRED TRANQUILLITY OF OUR GATHERING...
REK? REK, HE'S HURTING ME...
LEAVE HER ALONE! WHAT IS THIS?
20

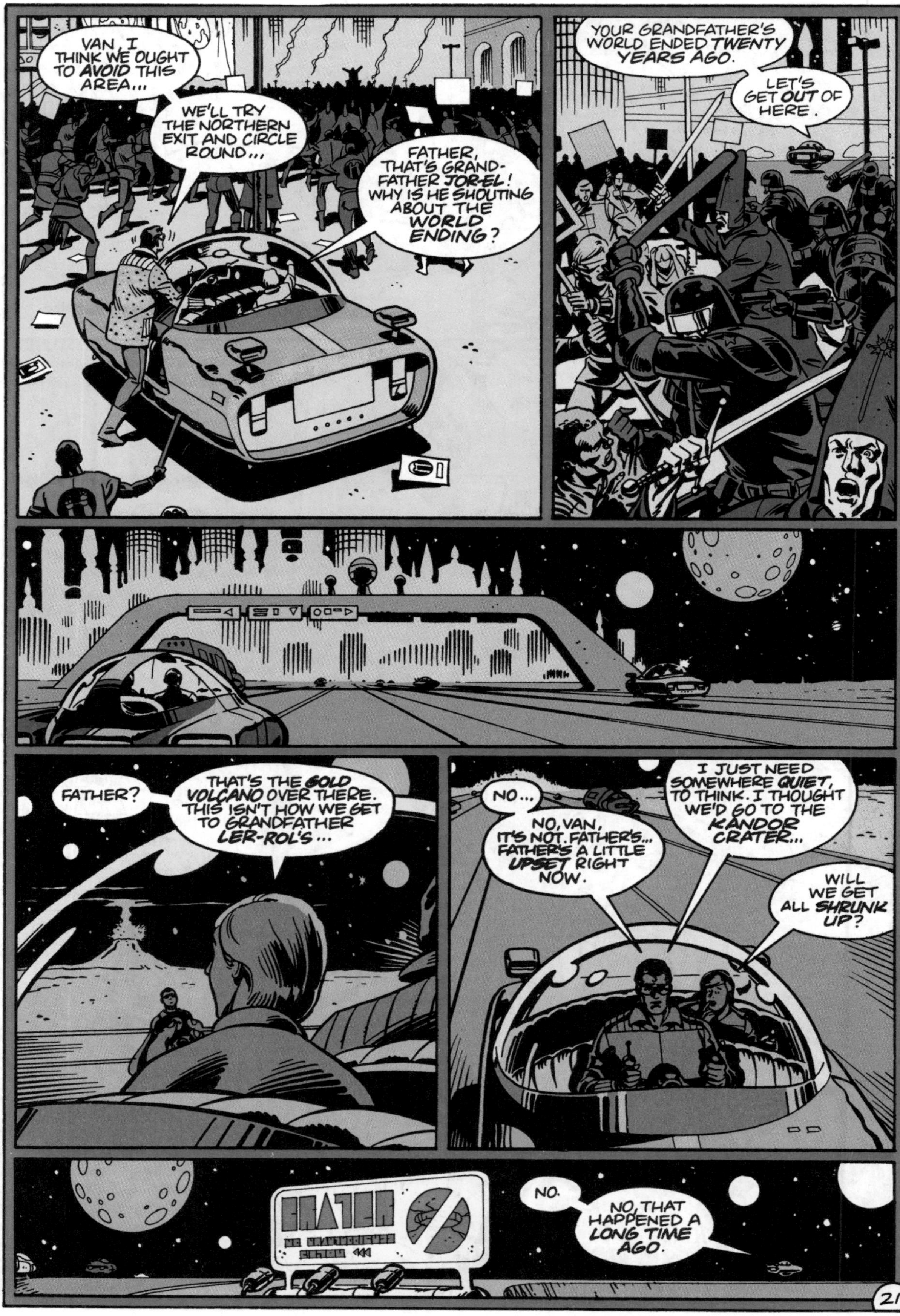
VAN, I THINK WE OUGHT TO AVOID THIS AREA...
WE'LL TRY THE NORTHERN EXIT AND CIRCLE ROUND...
FATHER, THAT'S GRAND-FATHER JOR-EL! WHY IS HE SHOUTING ABOUT THE WORLD ENDING?
YOUR GRANDFATHER'S WORLD ENDED TWENTY YEARS AGO.
LET'S GET OUT OF HERE.
FATHER?
THAT'S THE GOLD VOLCANO OVER THERE. THIS ISN'T HOW WE GET TO GRANDFATHER LER-ROL'S...
NO...
NO, VAN, IT'S NOT. FATHER'S... FATHER'S A LITTLE UPSET RIGHT NOW.
I JUST NEED SOMEWHERE QUIET, TO THINK. I THOUGHT WE'D GO TO THE KANDOR CRATER...
WILL WE GET ALL SHRUNK UP?
NO.
NO, THAT HAPPENED A LONG TIME AGO.
21

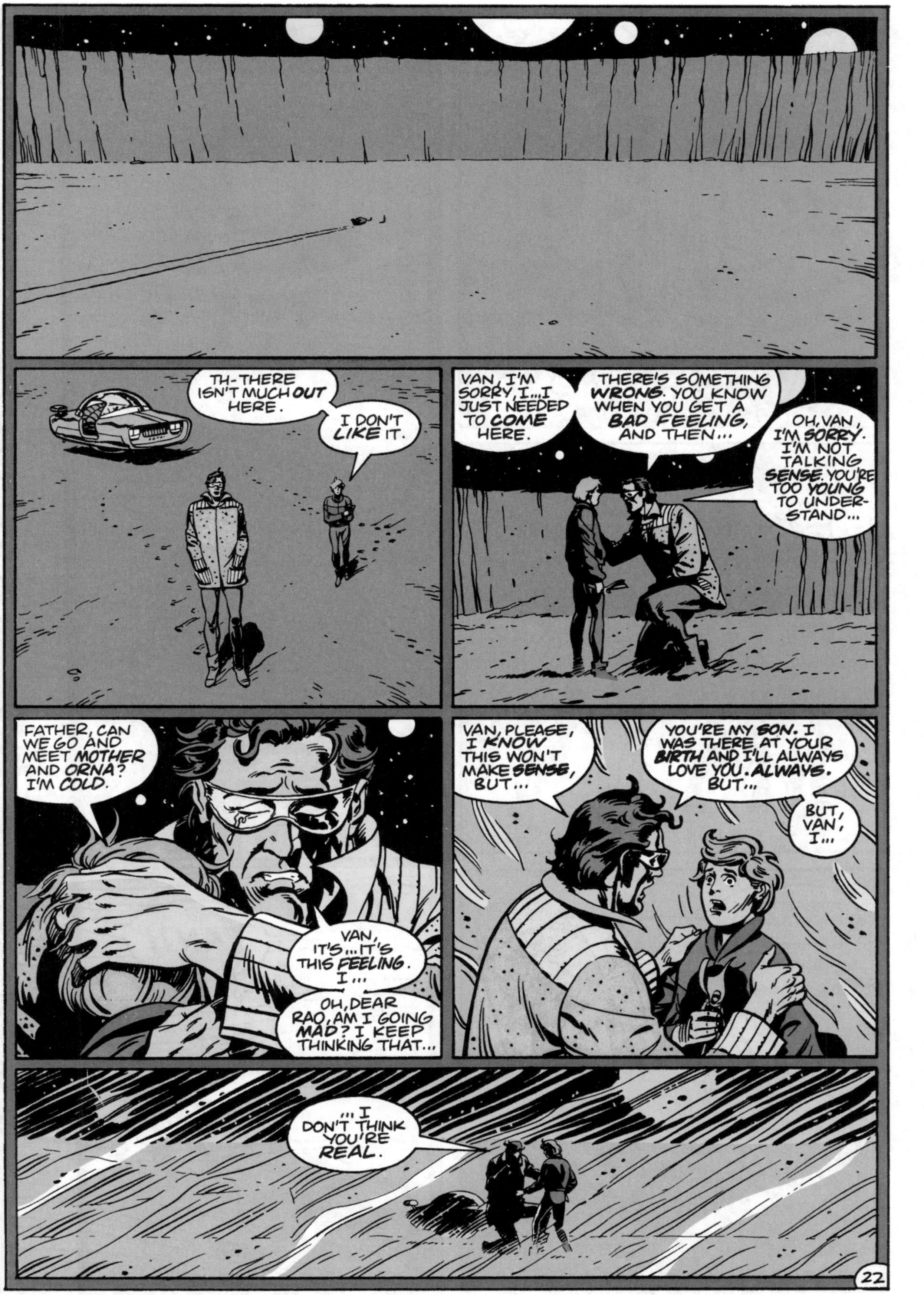
TH-THERE ISN'T MUCH OUT HERE.
I DON'T LIKE IT.
VAN, I'M SORRY, I...I JUST NEEDED TO COME HERE.
THERE'S SOMETHING WRONG. YOU KNOW WHEN YOU GET A BAD FEELING, AND THEN...
OH, VAN, I'M SORRY. I'M NOT TALKING SENSE. YOU'RE TOO YOUNG TO UNDER-STAND...
FATHER, CAN WE GO AND MEET MOTHER AND ORNA? I'M COLD.
VAN, IT'S...IT'S THIS FEELING. I...
OH, DEAR RAO, AM I GOING MAD? I KEEP THINKING THAT...
VAN, PLEASE, I KNOW THIS WON'T MAKE SENSE, BUT...
YOU'RE MY SON. I WAS THERE AT YOUR BIRTH AND I'LL ALWAYS LOVE YOU. ALWAYS. BUT...
BUT, VAN, I...
...I DON'T THINK YOU'RE REAL.
22

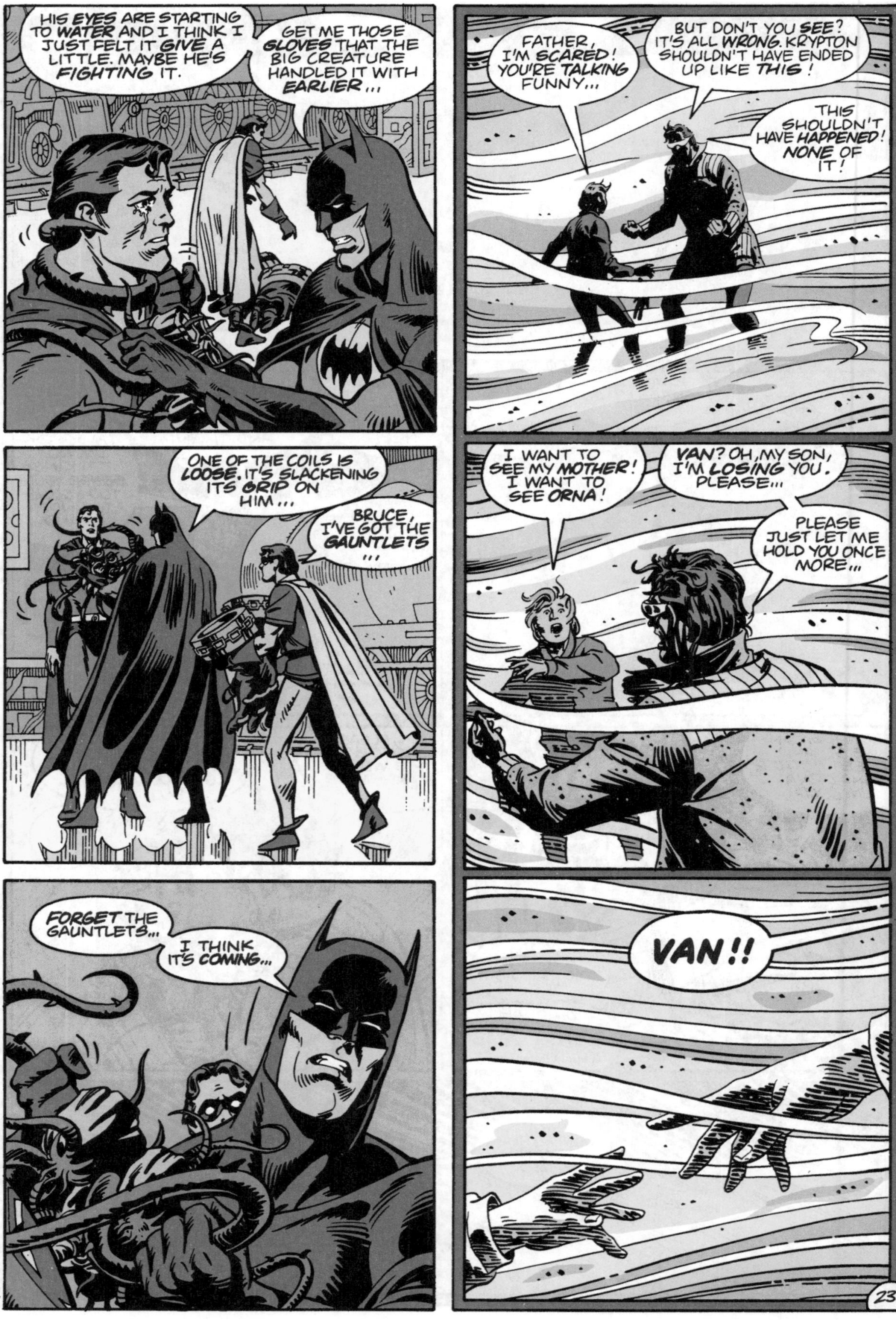
HIS EYES ARE STARTING TO WATER AND I THINK I JUST FELT IT GIVE A LITTLE. MAYBE HE'S FIGHTING IT.
GET ME THOSE GLOVES THAT THE BIG CREATURE HANDLED IT WITH EARLIER...
FATHER, I'M SCARED! YOU'RE TALKING FUNNY...
BUT DON'T YOU SEE? IT'S ALL WRONG. KRYPTON SHOULDN'T HAVE ENDED UP LIKE THIS!
THIS SHOULDN'T HAVE HAPPENED! NONE OF IT!
ONE OF THE COILS IS LOOSE. IT'S SLACKENING ITS GRIP ON HIM...
BRUCE, I'VE GOT THE GAUNTLETS...
I WANT TO SEE MY MOTHER! I WANT TO SEE ORNA!
VAN? OH, MY SON, I'M LOSING YOU. PLEASE...
PLEASE JUST LET ME HOLD YOU ONCE MORE...
FORGET THE GAUNTLETS...
I THINK IT'S COMING...
VAN!!
23

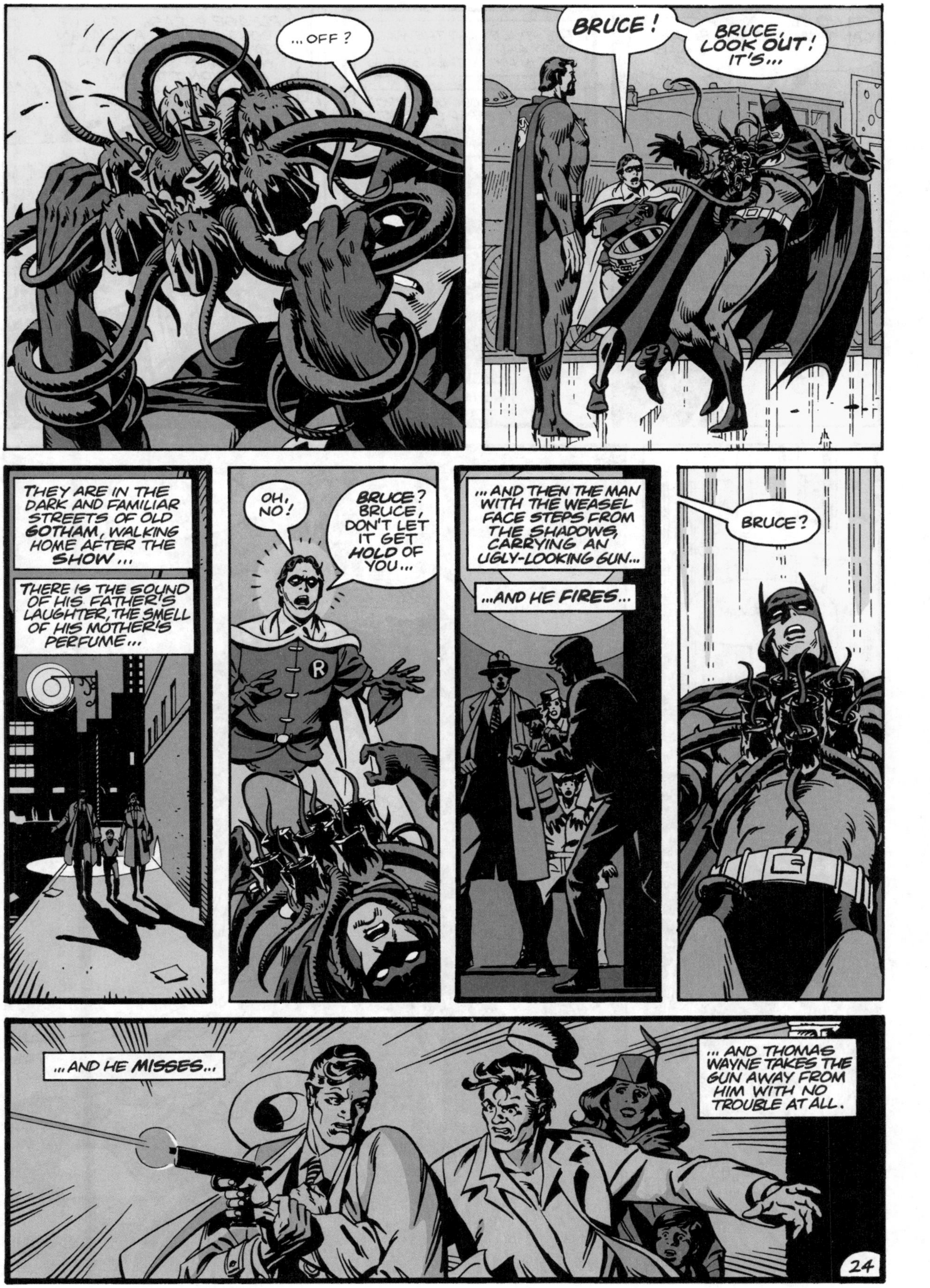
...OFF ?
BRUCE !
BRUCE, LOOK OUT ! IT'S...
THEY ARE IN THE DARK AND FAMILIAR STREETS OF OLD GOTHAM, WALKING HOME AFTER THE SHOW...
THERE IS THE SOUND OF HIS FATHER'S LAUGHTER, THE SMELL OF HIS MOTHER'S PERFUME...
OH, NO !
BRUCE? BRUCE, DON'T LET IT GET HOLD OF YOU...
...AND THEN THE MAN WITH THE WEASEL FACE STEPS FROM THE SHADOWS, CARRYING AN UGLY-LOOKING GUN...
...AND HE FIRES...
BRUCE?
...AND HE MISSES...
... AND THOMAS WAYNE TAKES THE GUN AWAY FROM HIM WITH NO TROUBLE AT ALL.
24

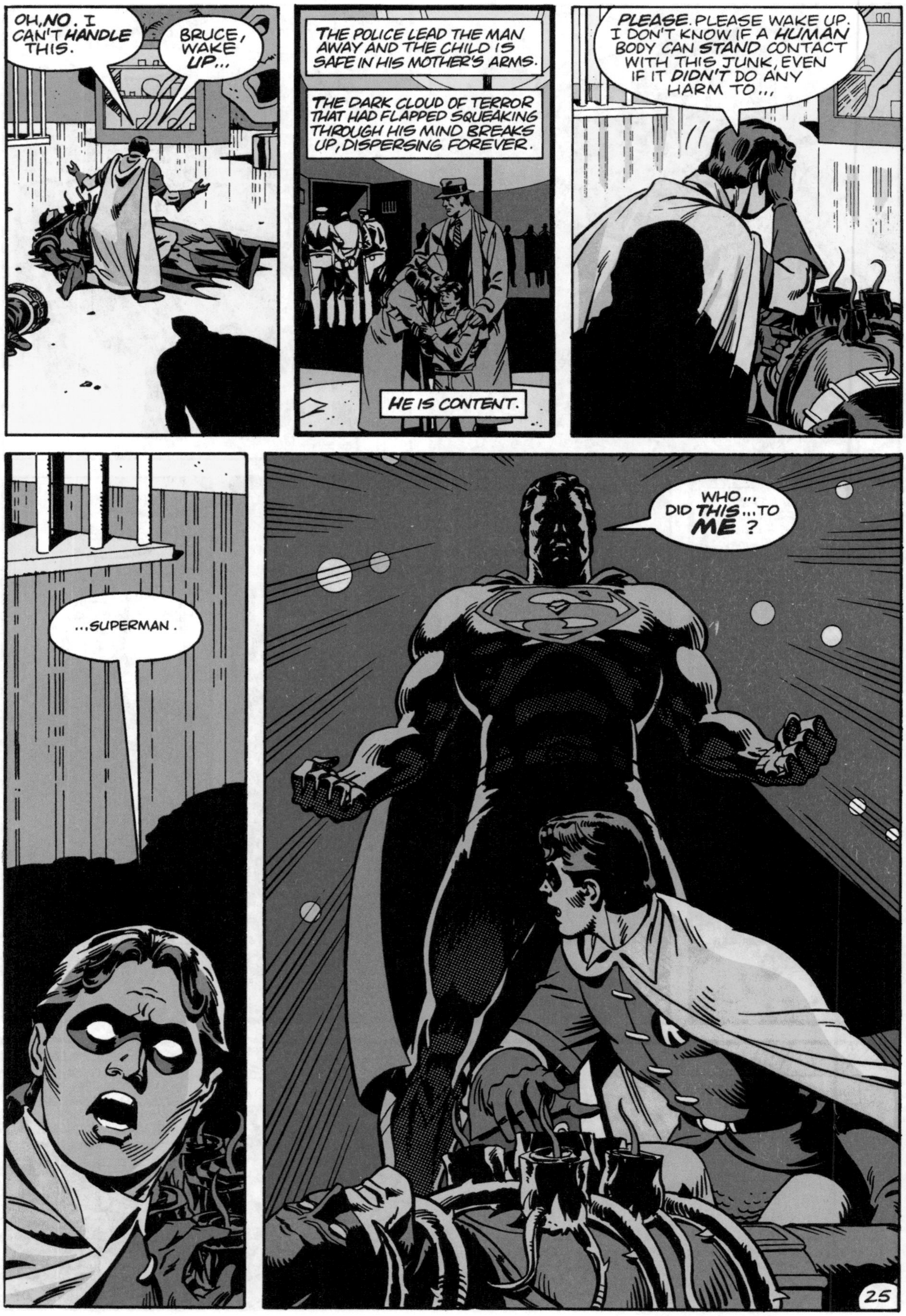

OH, NO. I CAN'T HANDLE THIS.
BRUCE, WAKE UP...
THE POLICE LEAD THE MAN AWAY AND THE CHILD IS SAFE IN HIS MOTHER'S ARMS.
THE DARK CLOUD OF TERROR THAT HAD FLAPPED SQUEAKING THROUGH HIS MIND BREAKS UP, DISPERSING FOREVER.
HE IS CONTENT.
PLEASE. PLEASE WAKE UP. I DON'T KNOW IF A HUMAN BODY CAN STAND CONTACT WITH THIS JUNK, EVEN IF IT DIDN'T DO ANY HARM TO...
...SUPERMAN.
WHO... DID THIS... TO ME?
25

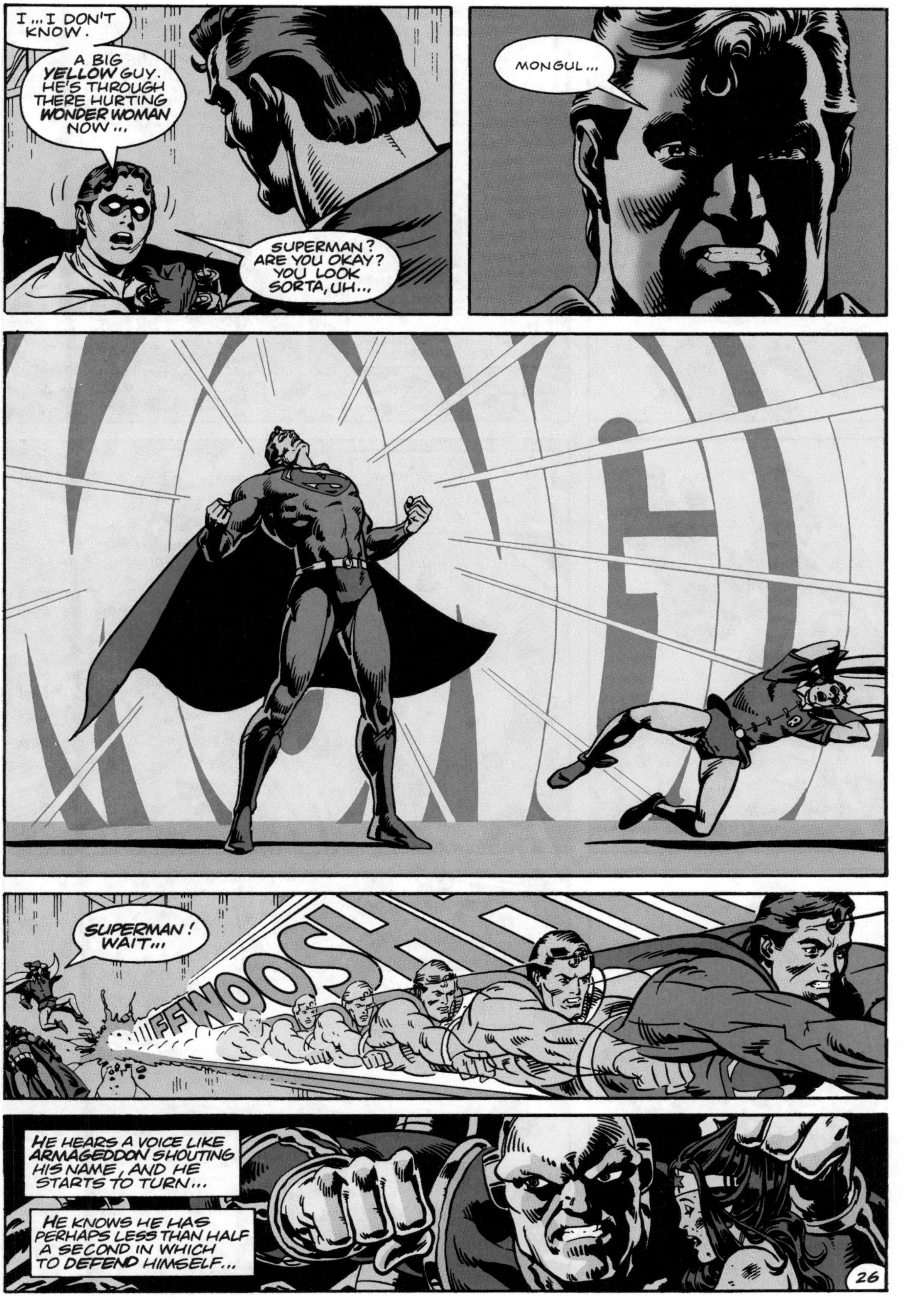
I... I DON'T KNOW.
A BIG YELLOW GUY. HE'S THROUGH THERE HURTING WONDER WOMAN NOW...
SUPERMAN? ARE YOU OKAY? YOU LOOK SORTA, UH...
MONGUL...
SUPERMAN! WAIT...
FFWOOSH
HE HEARS A VOICE LIKE ARMAGEDDON SHOUTING HIS NAME, AND HE STARTS TO TURN...
HE KNOWS HE HAS PERHAPS LESS THAN HALF A SECOND IN WHICH TO DEFEND HIMSELF...
26

WHAT AM I GOING TO DO ABOUT *BRUCE?* I CAN'T...

UH...

HE STARTS TO REACH TOWARDS HIS ARMOR'S WEAPON SYSTEMS, LETTING THE UNCONSCIOUS WOMAN CRUMPLE TO THE FLOOR...

...BUT THE ROCK OF THE FAR WALL SEEMS TO RIPPLE OUTWARDS IN A SUDDEN CASCADE OF POWDER...

...AND A FOUR-HUNDRED-MILE-AN-HOUR WIND SLAMS INTO HIM LIKE A STEAM HAMMER AS BIG AS THE WORLD...

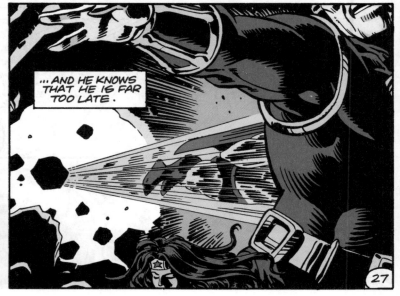

...AND HE KNOWS THAT HE IS FAR TOO LATE.

27

112

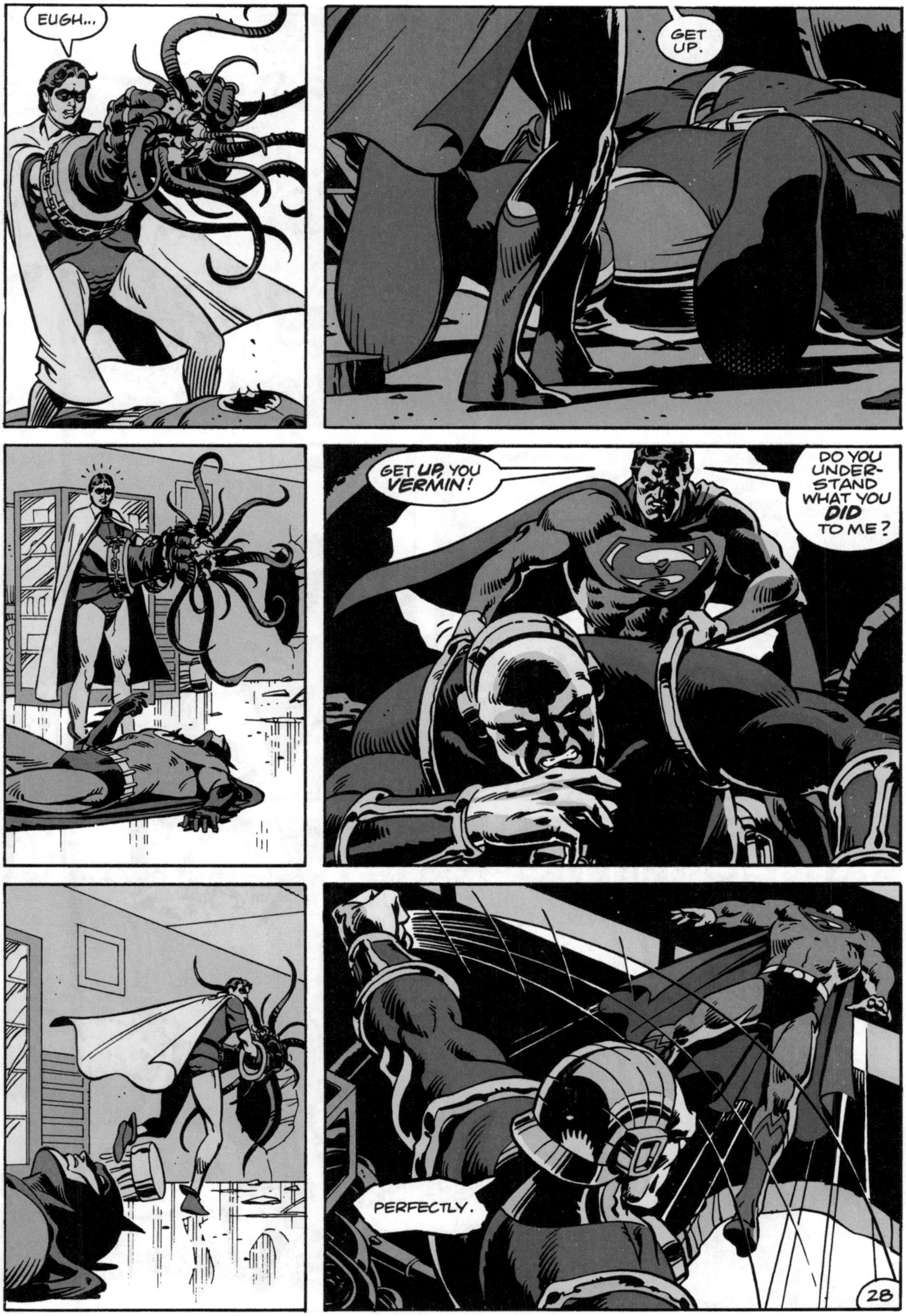
EUGH...
GET UP.
GET UP, YOU VERMIN!
DO YOU UNDER-STAND WHAT YOU DID TO ME?
PERFECTLY.
28

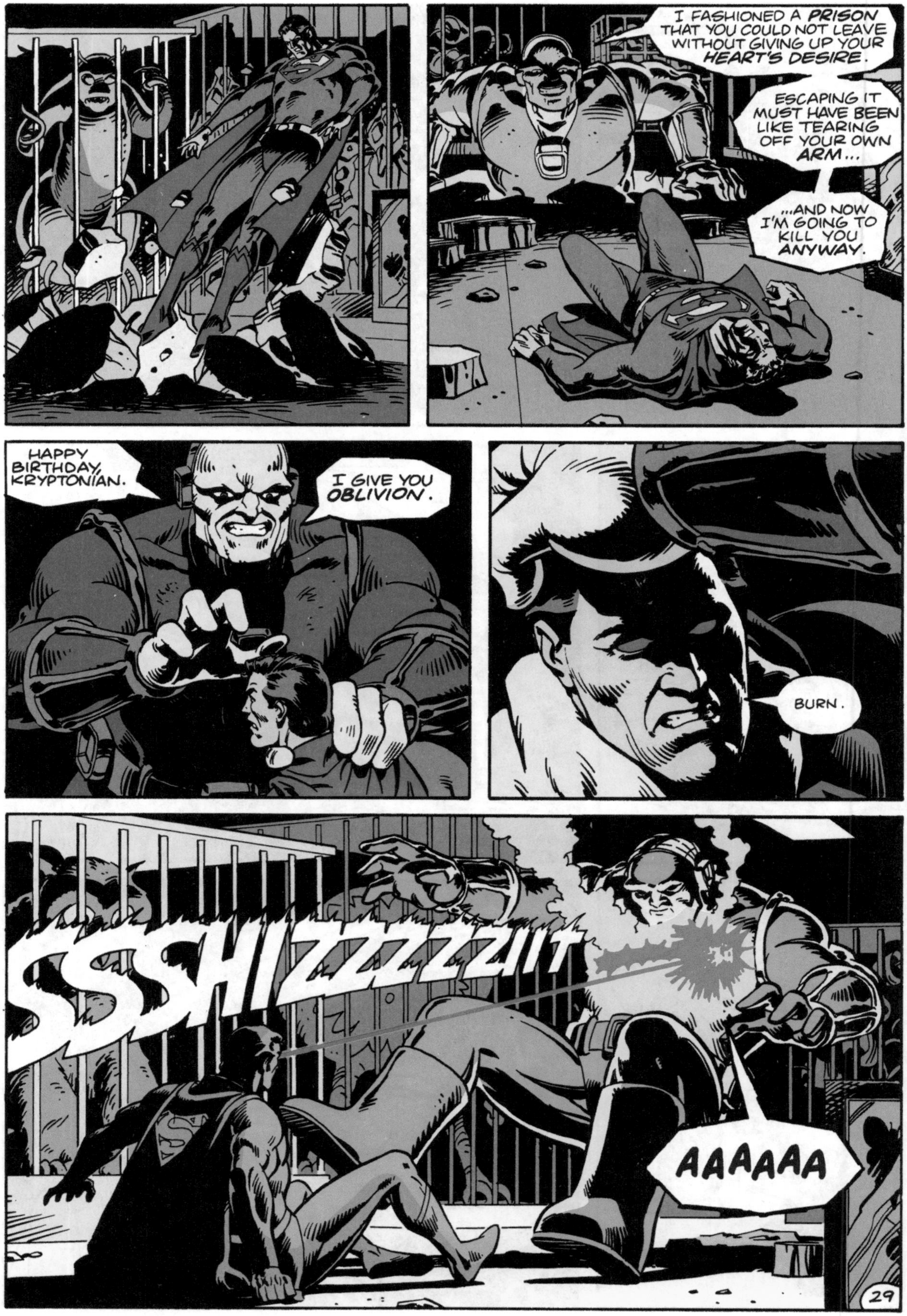
I FASHIONED A PRISON THAT YOU COULD NOT LEAVE WITHOUT GIVING UP YOUR HEART'S DESIRE.
ESCAPING IT MUST HAVE BEEN LIKE TEARING OFF YOUR OWN ARM...
...AND NOW I'M GOING TO KILL YOU ANYWAY.
HAPPY BIRTHDAY, KRYPTONIAN.
I GIVE YOU OBLIVION.
BURN.
SSHIZZZZZIIT
AAAAAA
29

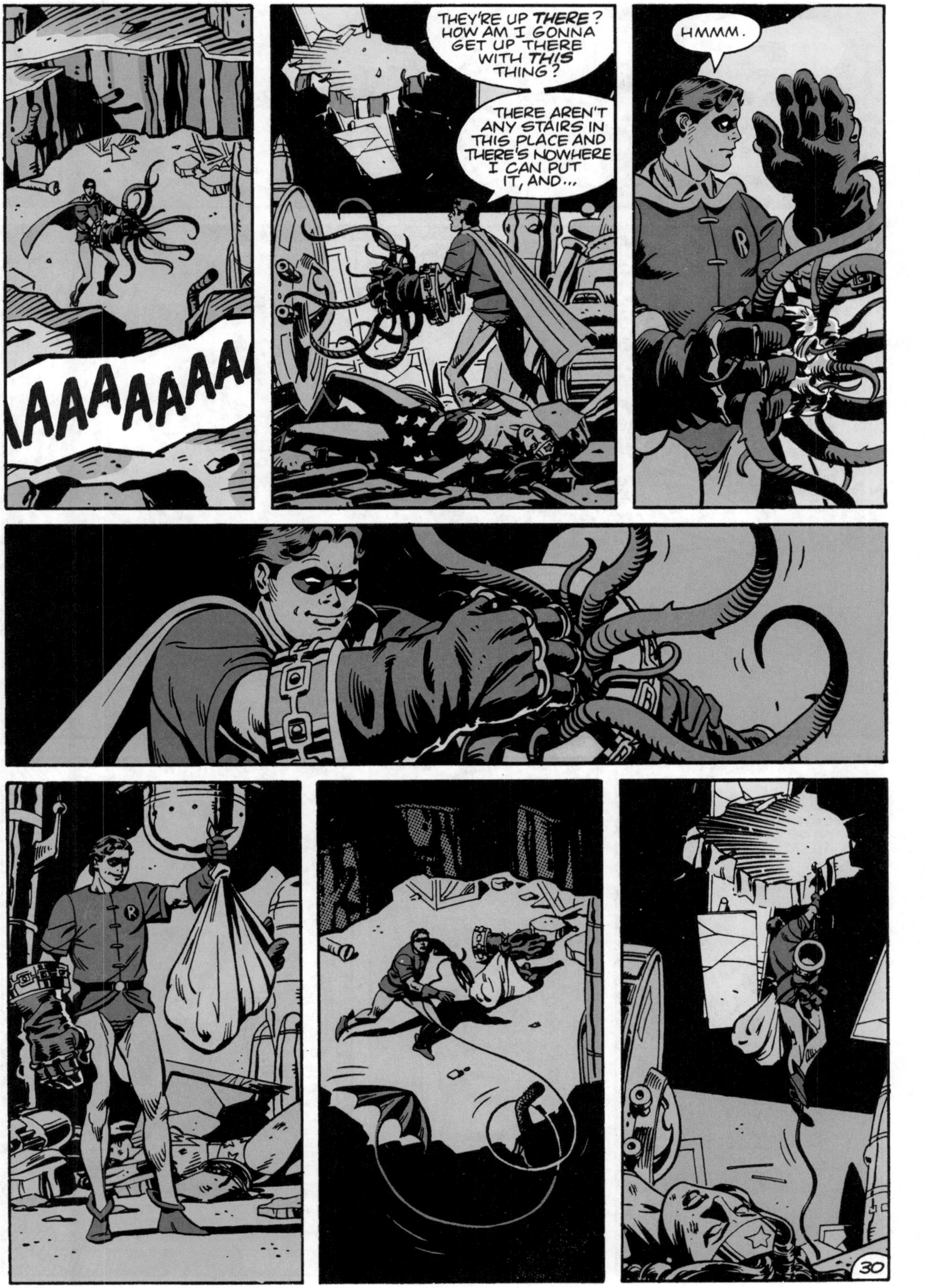
AAAAAAAA
THEY'RE UP THERE? HOW AM I GONNA GET UP THERE WITH THIS THING?
THERE AREN'T ANY STAIRS IN THIS PLACE AND THERE'S NOWHERE I CAN PUT IT, AND...
HMMM.
30

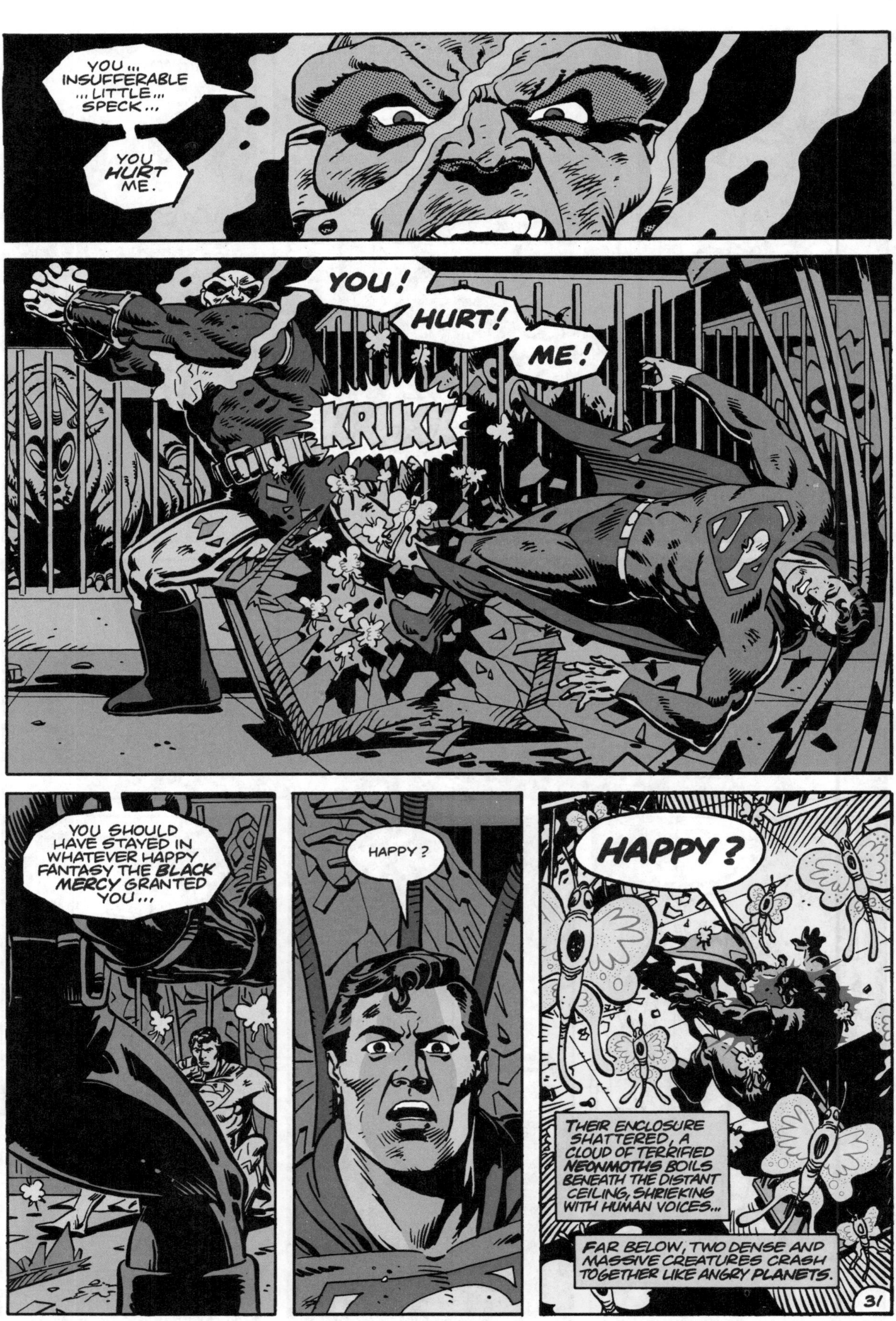
YOU... INSUFFERABLE ...LITTLE... SPECK...
YOU HURT ME.
YOU!
HURT!
ME!
KRUKK
YOU SHOULD HAVE STAYED IN WHATEVER HAPPY FANTASY THE BLACK MERCY GRANTED YOU...
HAPPY?
HAPPY?
THEIR ENCLOSURE SHATTERED, A CLOUD OF TERRIFIED NEONMOTHS BOILS BENEATH THE DISTANT CEILING, SHRIEKING WITH HUMAN VOICES...
FAR BELOW, TWO DENSE AND MASSIVE CREATURES CRASH TOGETHER LIKE ANGRY PLANETS.
31

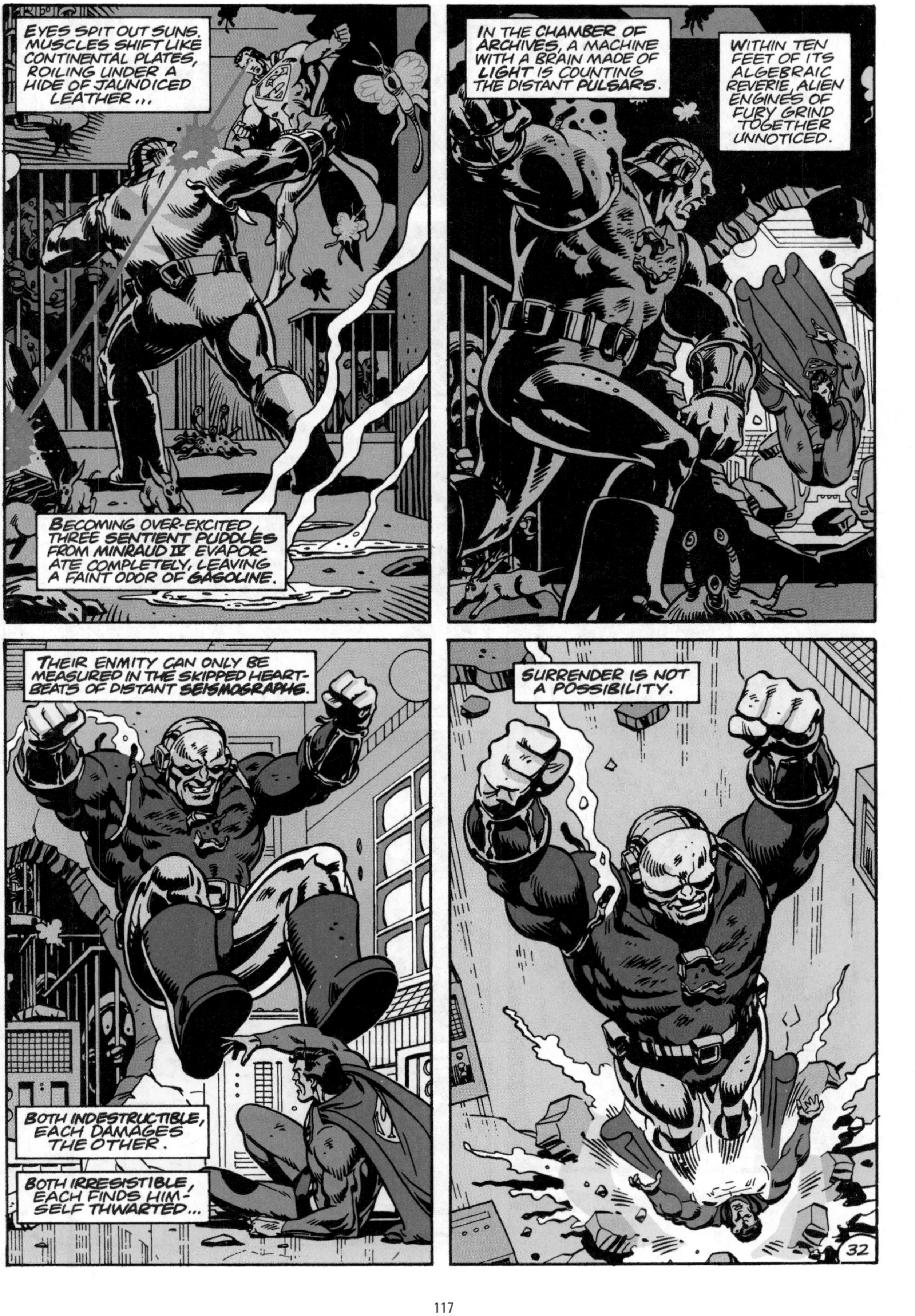
EYES SPIT OUT SUNS. MUSCLES SHIFT LIKE CONTINENTAL PLATES, ROILING UNDER A HIDE OF JAUNDICED LEATHER...
BECOMING OVER-EXCITED, THREE SENTIENT PUDDLES FROM MINRAUD IV EVAPORATE COMPLETELY, LEAVING A FAINT ODOR OF GASOLINE.
IN THE CHAMBER OF ARCHIVES, A MACHINE WITH A BRAIN MADE OF LIGHT IS COUNTING THE DISTANT PULSARS.
WITHIN TEN FEET OF ITS ALGEBRAIC REVERIE, ALIEN ENGINES OF FURY GRIND TOGETHER UNNOTICED.
THEIR ENMITY CAN ONLY BE MEASURED IN THE SKIPPED HEARTBEATS OF DISTANT SEISMOGRAPHS.
BOTH INDESTRUCTIBLE, EACH DAMAGES THE OTHER.
BOTH IRRESISTIBLE, EACH FINDS HIMSELF THWARTED...
SURRENDER IS NOT A POSSIBILITY.
32

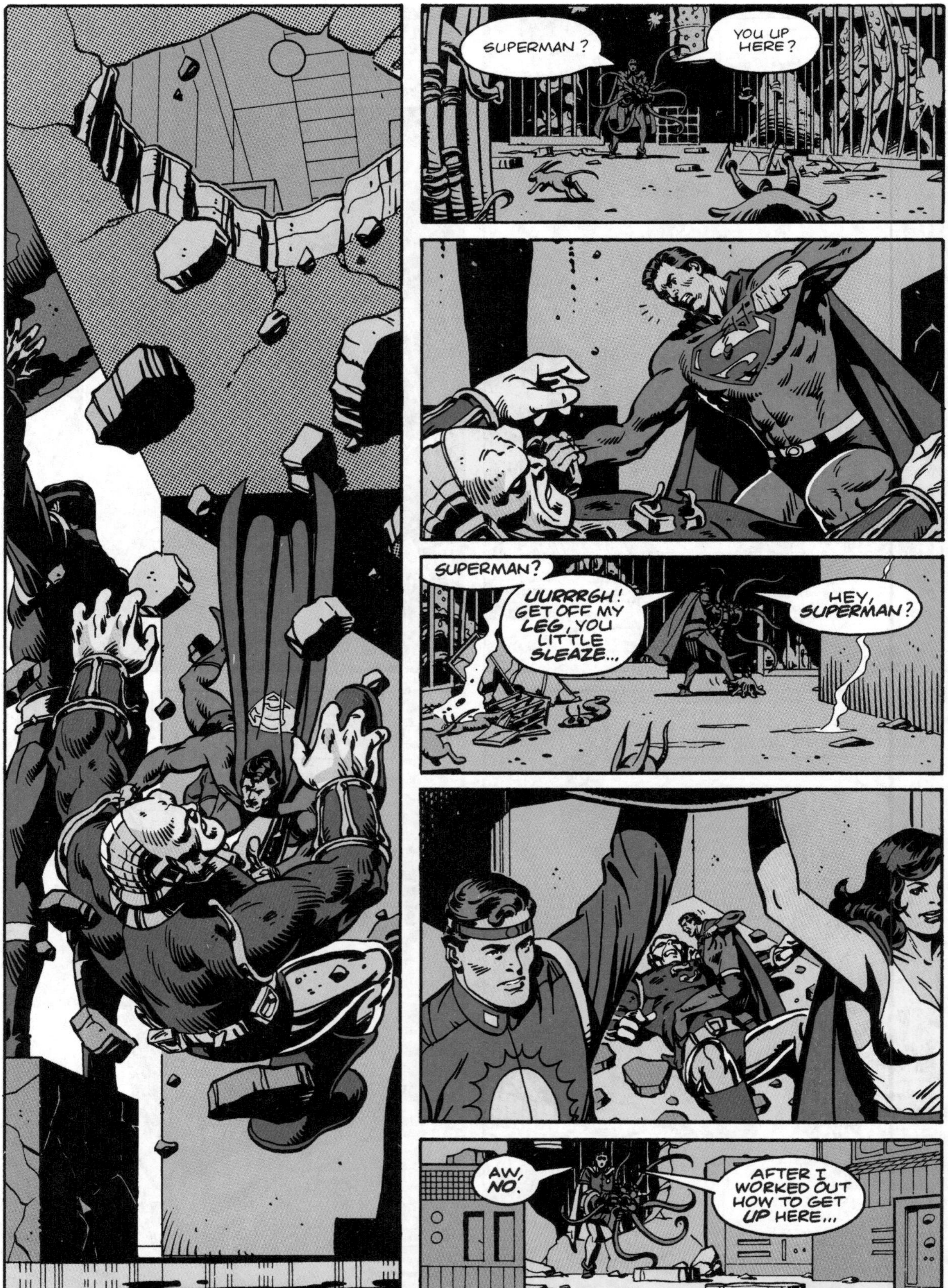
SUPERMAN?
YOU UP HERE?
SUPERMAN?
UURRRGH! GET OFF MY LEG, YOU LITTLE SLEAZE...
HEY, SUPERMAN?
AW, NO.
AFTER I WORKED OUT HOW TO GET UP HERE...
33

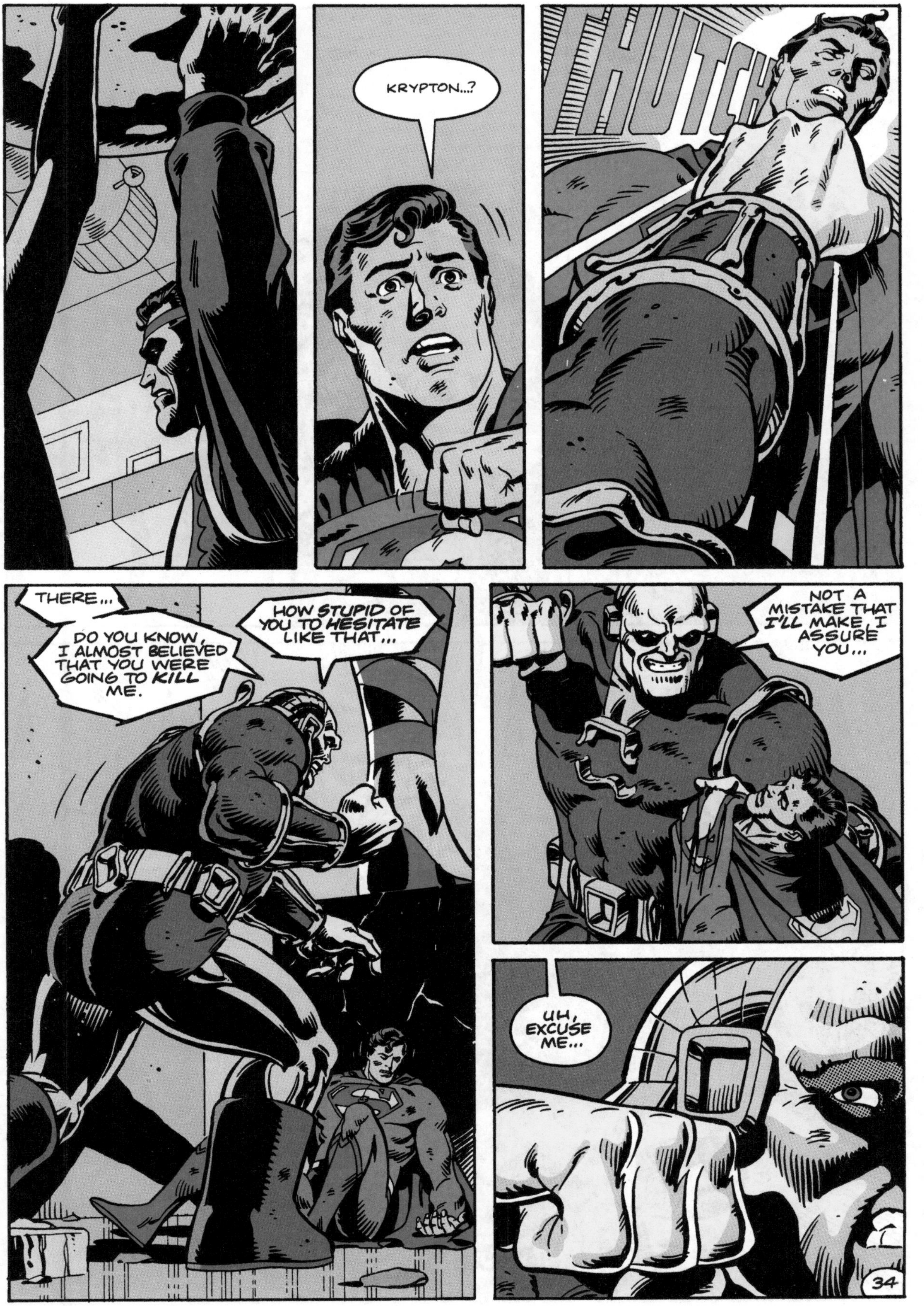
KRYPTON...?
CHUTCH
THERE...
DO YOU KNOW, I ALMOST BELIEVED THAT YOU WERE GOING TO KILL ME.
HOW STUPID OF YOU TO HESITATE LIKE THAT...
NOT A MISTAKE THAT I'LL MAKE, I ASSURE YOU...
UH, EXCUSE ME...
34

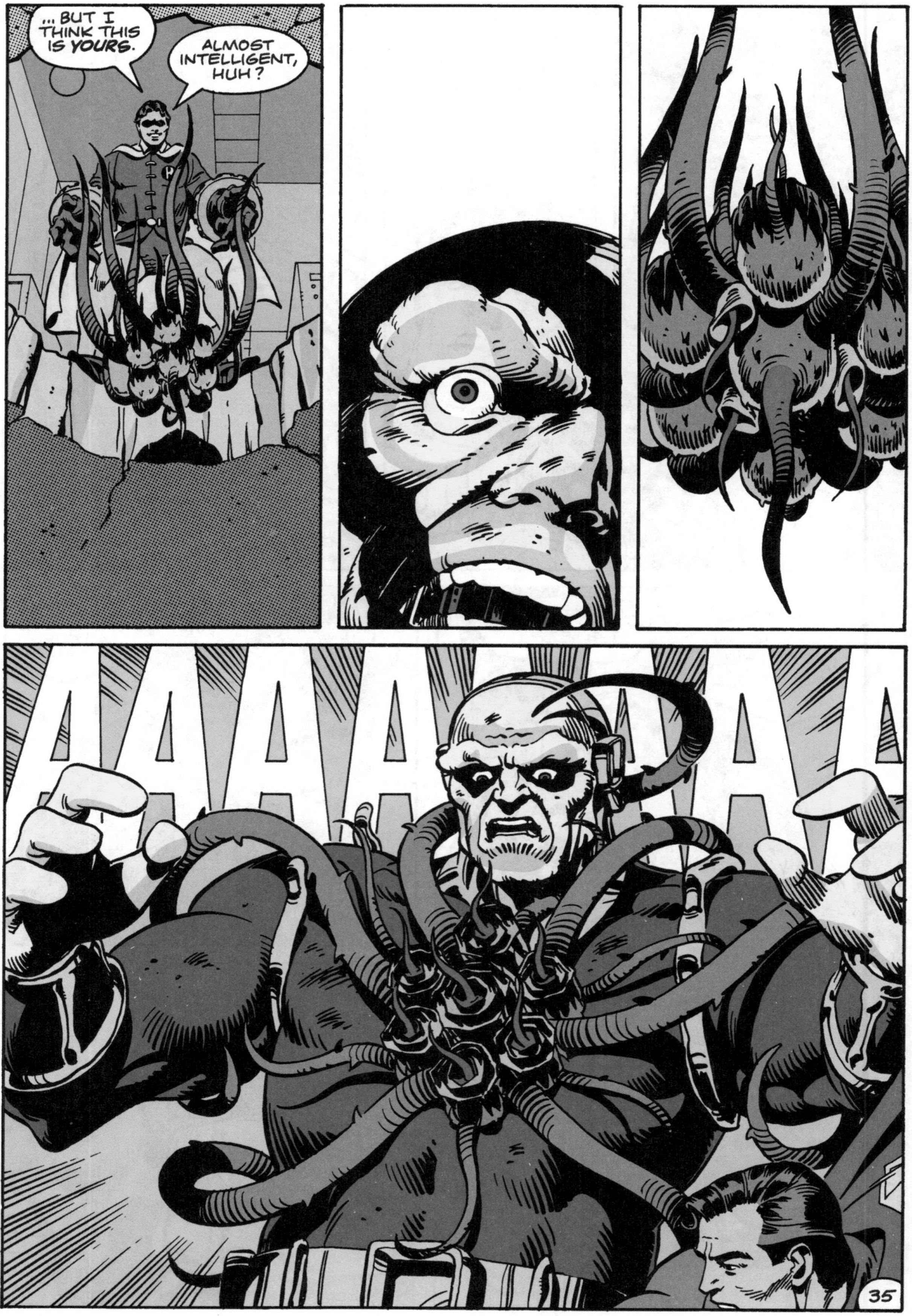
...BUT I THINK THIS IS YOURS.
ALMOST INTELLIGENT, HUH?

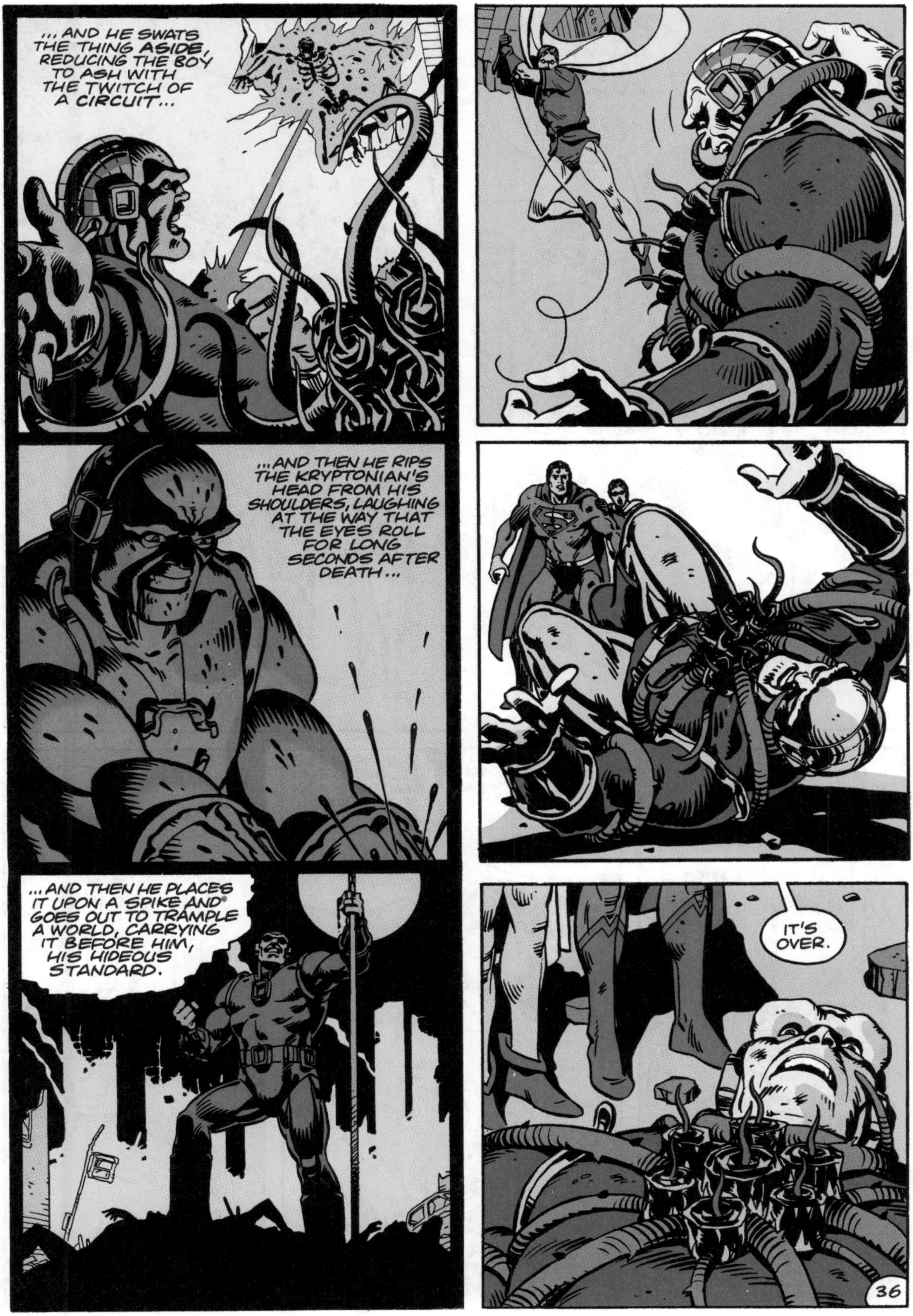
...AND HE SWATS THE THING ASIDE, REDUCING THE BOY TO ASH WITH THE TWITCH OF A CIRCUIT...
...AND THEN HE RIPS THE KRYPTONIAN'S HEAD FROM HIS SHOULDERS, LAUGHING AT THE WAY THAT THE EYES ROLL FOR LONG SECONDS AFTER DEATH...
...AND THEN HE PLACES IT UPON A SPIKE AND GOES OUT TO TRAMPLE A WORLD, CARRYING IT BEFORE HIM, HIS HIDEOUS STANDARD.
IT'S OVER.
36

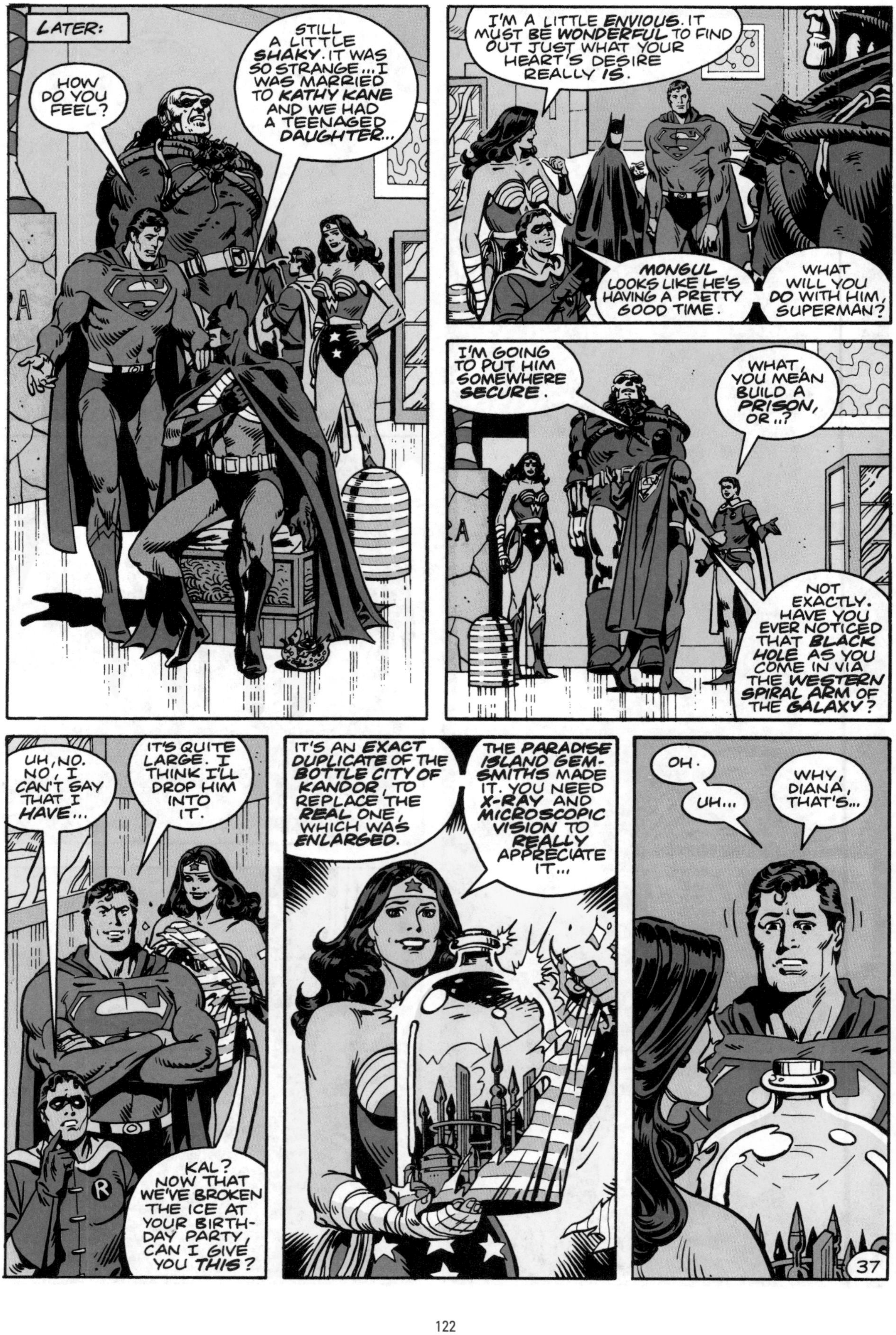
LATER:
HOW DO YOU FEEL?
STILL A LITTLE SHAKY. IT WAS SO STRANGE... I WAS MARRIED TO KATHY KANE AND WE HAD A TEENAGED DAUGHTER...
I'M A LITTLE ENVIOUS. IT MUST BE WONDERFUL TO FIND OUT JUST WHAT YOUR HEART'S DESIRE REALLY IS.
MONGUL LOOKS LIKE HE'S HAVING A PRETTY GOOD TIME.
WHAT WILL YOU DO WITH HIM, SUPERMAN?
I'M GOING TO PUT HIM SOMEWHERE SECURE.
WHAT, YOU MEAN BUILD A PRISON, OR..?
NOT EXACTLY. HAVE YOU EVER NOTICED THAT BLACK HOLE AS YOU COME IN VIA THE WESTERN SPIRAL ARM OF THE GALAXY?
UH, NO. NO, I CAN'T SAY THAT I HAVE...
IT'S QUITE LARGE. I THINK I'LL DROP HIM INTO IT.
KAL? NOW THAT WE'VE BROKEN THE ICE AT YOUR BIRTHDAY PARTY, CAN I GIVE YOU THIS?
IT'S AN EXACT DUPLICATE OF THE BOTTLE CITY OF KANDOR, TO REPLACE THE REAL ONE, WHICH WAS ENLARGED.
THE PARADISE ISLAND GEM-SMITHS MADE IT. YOU NEED X-RAY AND MICROSCOPIC VISION TO REALLY APPRECIATE IT...
OH.
UH...
WHY, DIANA, THAT'S...
37

...JUST...

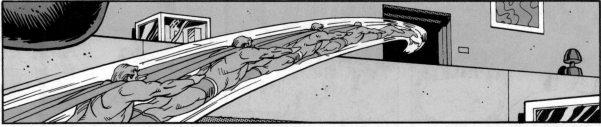

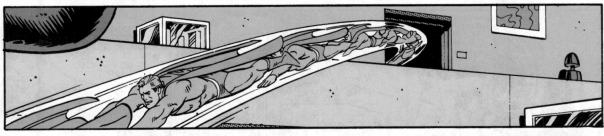

...JUST...

38

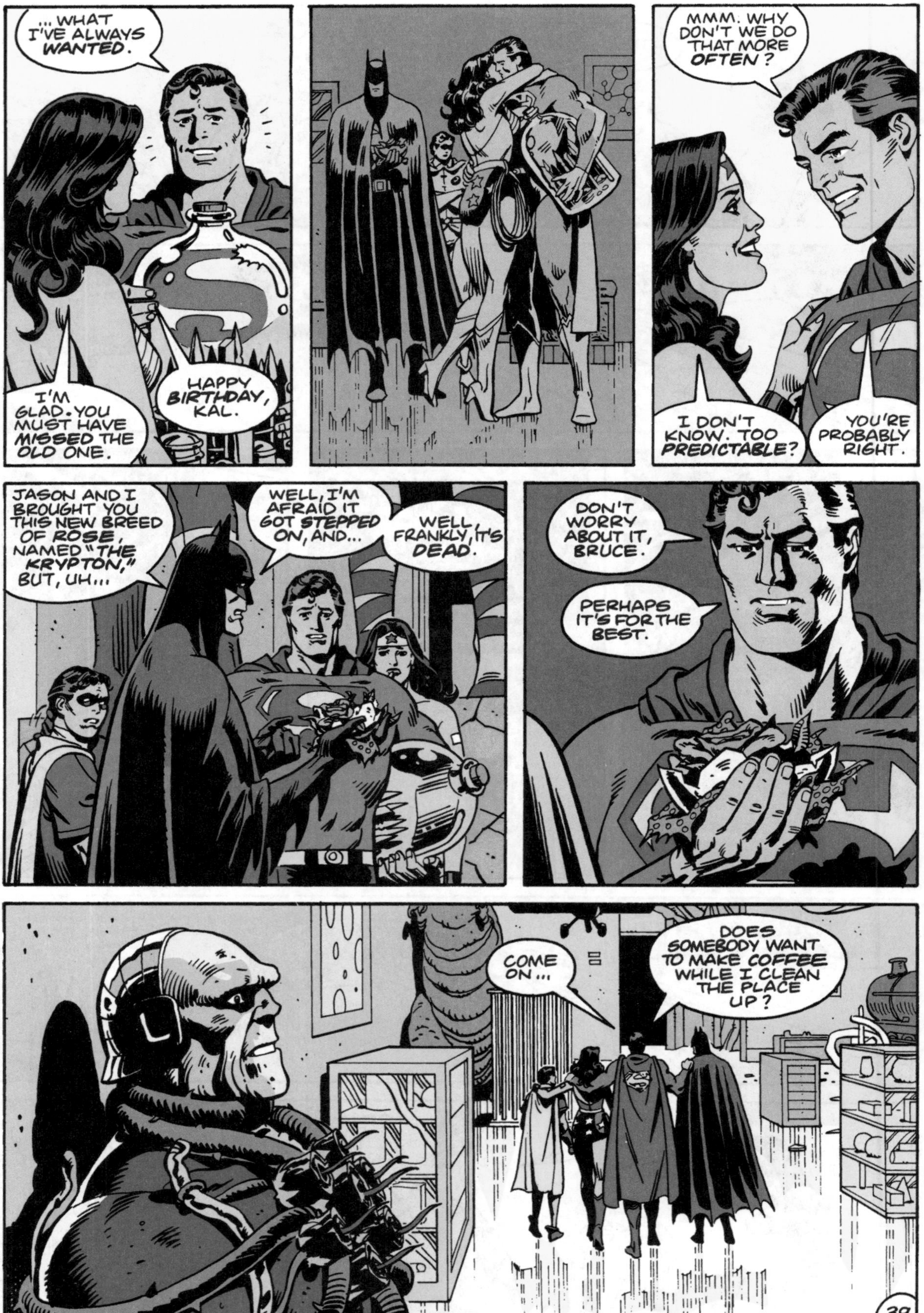
...WHAT I'VE ALWAYS WANTED.
I'M GLAD. YOU MUST HAVE MISSED THE OLD ONE.
HAPPY BIRTHDAY, KAL.
MMM. WHY DON'T WE DO THAT MORE OFTEN?
I DON'T KNOW. TOO PREDICTABLE?
YOU'RE PROBABLY RIGHT.
JASON AND I BROUGHT YOU THIS NEW BREED OF ROSE, NAMED "THE KRYPTON," BUT, UH...
WELL, I'M AFRAID IT GOT STEPPED ON, AND...
WELL, FRANKLY, IT'S DEAD.
DON'T WORRY ABOUT IT, BRUCE.
PERHAPS IT'S FOR THE BEST.
COME ON...
DOES SOMEBODY WANT TO MAKE COFFEE WHILE I CLEAN THE PLACE UP?
39

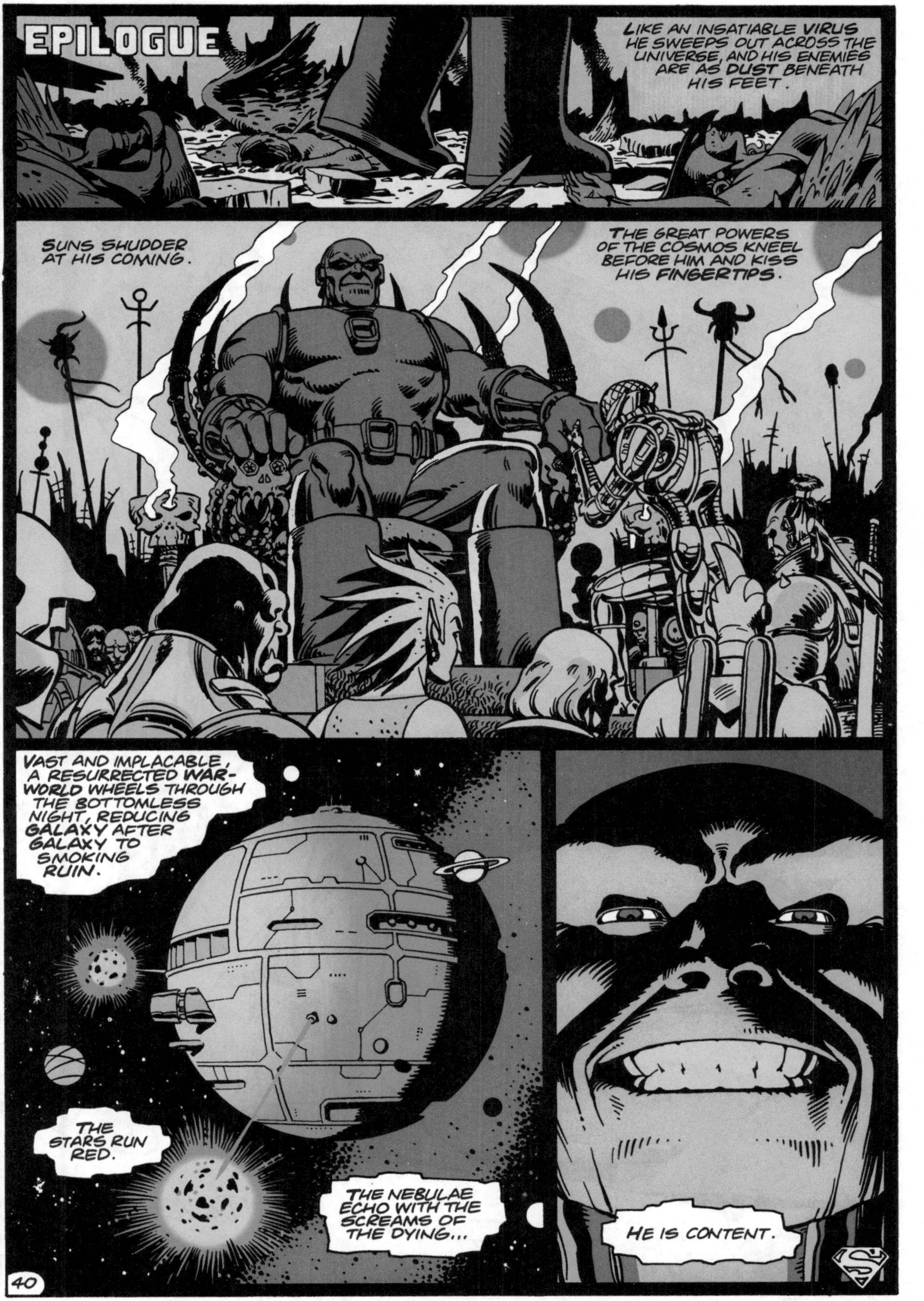
EPILOGUE
LIKE AN INSATIABLE VIRUS HE SWEEPS OUT ACROSS THE UNIVERSE, AND HIS ENEMIES ARE AS DUST BENEATH HIS FEET.
SUNS SHUDDER AT HIS COMING.
THE GREAT POWERS OF THE COSMOS KNEEL BEFORE HIM AND KISS HIS FINGERTIPS.
VAST AND IMPLACABLE, A RESURRECTED WAR-WORLD WHEELS THROUGH THE BOTTOMLESS NIGHT, REDUCING GALAXY AFTER GALAXY TO SMOKING RUIN.
THE STARS RUN RED.
THE NEBULAE ECHO WITH THE SCREAMS OF THE DYING...
HE IS CONTENT.
40

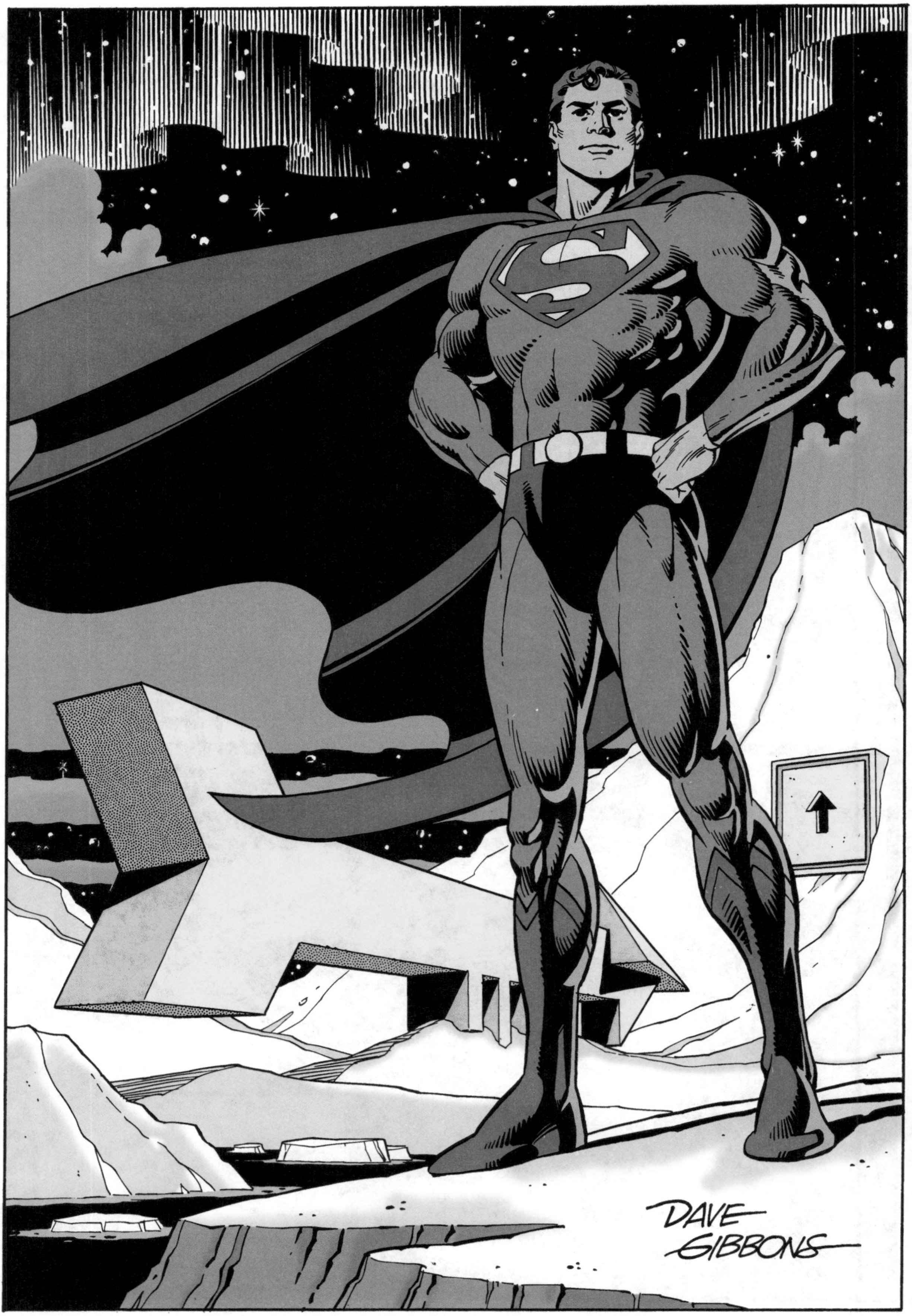
DAVE
GIBBONS

ALAN MOORE is perhaps the most acclaimed writer in the graphic story medium, having garnered countless awards for works such as WATCHMEN, V FOR VENDETTA, *From Hell, Miracleman* and SWAMP THING. He is also the mastermind behind the America's Best Comics line, through which he has created (along with many talented illustrators) THE LEAGUE OF EXTRAORDINARY GENTLEMEN, PROMETHEA, TOM STRONG, TOMORROW STORIES and TOP 10. As one of the medium's most important innovators since the early 1980s, Moore has influenced an entire generation of comics creators, and his work continues to inspire an ever-growing audience. Moore resides in central England.

CURT SWAN entered the art field intending to become not a cartoonist but a "slick" magazine illustrator like Norman Rockwell or Joseph Leyendecker. While serving during World War II illustrating the Army newspaper *Stars and Stripes,* Swan worked with DC writer France E. Herron. On Herron's suggestion, Swan found work at DC after the war. Swan's versatile pencils, which he remembers applying first to BOY COMMANDOS, soon appeared on various DC features, including Superman, Batman, the Newsboy Legion, Big Town, Mr. District Attorney, Tommy Tomorrow, and Swan's longest assignment up to that time, Superboy. His familiarity with both Superman and Batman specially suited him to draw the original Superman-Batman team-up in 1952. Swan served various stints, regular and semi-regular, on almost all the Superman titles of the 1950s and 1960s, and remained the near-exclusive Superman penciller throughout the 1970s and much of the 1980s. Although he "retired" in 1986, Swan continued to work for DC until his death in 1996. To generations of professionals and fans, Curt Swan's Superman will always be the definitive version.

DAVE GIBBONS has worked in comics since 1973. Cutting his teeth on underground comics and fanzines, he became a frequent contributor to the UK anthology magazine *2000 AD,* illustrating such features as Harlem Heroes, Dan Dare and Rogue Trooper (which he co-created), as well as providing work to *Doctor Who Magazine.* In 1982 he landed an assignment on GREEN LANTERN, beginning his long association with DC Comics. Since then he has both drawn and written many of their major characters, including Superman and Batman. In 1986 Gibbons and writer Alan Moore co-created the landmark series WATCHMEN, which is widely acknowledged to be one of the greatest graphic narratives ever published. Since then, he has collaborated with a wide variety of writers and artists, including Frank Miller (*Give Me Liberty, Martha Washington Goes to War*), Garth Ennis (WAR STORY: SCREAMING EAGLES) and Geoff Johns (GREEN LANTERN CORPS: RECHARGE), and in 2005 his Vertigo graphic novel THE ORIGINALS won the Eisner Award for Best New Graphic Album.

RICK VEITCH worked in the underground comics scene before attending the Joe Kubert School of Cartoon and Graphic Art. After graduating, he worked with Stephen Bissette on *Bizarre Adventures* before creating and illustrating *The One,* the innovative Epic Comics miniseries. In addition to writing and drawing an acclaimed run on SWAMP THING, he is the creator/cartoonist of *Brat Pack, Maximortal* and the dream-based *Rare Bit Fiends,* and a contributing artist on *1963.* He is also the writer and artist of the miniseries *Greyshirt: Indigo Sunset* from America's Best Comics, and the creator of the critically acclaimed graphic novel CAN'T GET NO and the spectacularly satirical series ARMY@LOVE from Vertigo.

GEORGE PÉREZ started drawing at the age of five and hasn't stopped since. Born on June 9, 1954, Pérez began his professional comics career as an assistant to Rich Buckler in 1973. After establishing himself as a penciller at Marvel Comics, Pérez came to DC in 1980, bringing his highly detailed art style to such titles as JUSTICE LEAGUE OF AMERICA and FIRESTORM. After co-creating THE NEW TEEN TITANS in 1980, Pérez and writer Marv Wolfman reunited for the landmark miniseries CRISIS ON INFINITE EARTHS in 1985. In the aftermath of that universe-smashing event, Pérez revitalized WONDER WOMAN as the series' writer and artist, reestablishing her as one of DC's most preeminent characters and bringing in some of the best sales the title has ever experienced. He has since gone on to illustrate celebrated runs on Marvel's *The Avengers*, CrossGen's *Solus* and DC's THE BRAVE AND THE BOLD.

KURT SCHAFFENBERGER began his comics career in 1941 as a member of the Binder brothers shop, illustrating a number of different features for numerous publishers. His best-loved work, however, was for Fawcett Comics — the home of the original Captain Marvel and the Marvel Family. Besides the Big Red Cheese, Schaffenberger also drew the adventures of Bulletman, Ibis, Spy Smasher, Mr. Scarlet and Golden Arrow for Fawcett until the company's demise in 1953. In demand for romance comics because of his ultra-smooth line, Schaffenberger was actually proficient in a number of styles, including horror stories for ACG and early Marvel Comics, crime stories for *Premier*, and war illustration for *Soldier of Fortune* magazine. In 1959 he began work at DC (then National Periodical Publications), becoming the primary artist on SUPERMAN'S GIRLFRIEND, LOIS LANE and illustrating dozens of Superman-related stories. He became so identified with Lois Lane (and Lana Lang), that he would often be called upon to redraw their heads on other

artists' stories of the period. Schaffenberger had a long run on the Supergirl feature and also worked on WONDER WOMAN and WORLD'S FINEST COMICS before returning to Captain Marvel and the Marvel family when DC revived the characters in 1973.

One of the industry's most acclaimed and prolific artists, **AL WILLIAMSON** began his comics career in 1948 assisting Burne Hogarth on the Sunday *Tarzan* newspaper strip. After honing his skills at publishers like Eastern, ACG, Avon and Toby Press, Williamson became one of the youngest regular artists for E.C.'s classic line of horror and science fiction titles in the mid-1950s. Since then he has worked for nearly every major comic book publisher in America, including DC, Marvel, Dell, Harvey, Fawcett, Charlton, Warren, Western and Dark Horse. He is also a veteran of the syndicated comic strip world, providing art for such classic features as *Rip Kirby, Flash Gordon* and *Star Wars* and enjoying lengthy runs on *Big Ben Bolt* and *Secret Agent Corrigan*. Williamson has won two Eisner Awards and an astonishing five Harvey Awards for Best Inker, and he was named Best Comic Book Artist (Story) by the National Cartoonists Society in 1966.

Heavily influenced by artists Lou Fine and Will Eisner, **MURPHY ANDERSON** entered the comics arena in 1944 as an artist for Fiction House. He took over the *Buck Rogers* comic strip for three years beginning in 1947, and in 1950 he began his lifelong association with DC Comics, pulling double duty as both a full illustrator (the Atomic Knights, Hawkman) and as an inker over other artists' pencil work (Adam Strange, Batman, Superman). Later in his career, Anderson ran Murphy Anderson Visual Concepts, a publishers' support service company. He now enjoys a well-deserved retirement.